Progress™
Mathematics

3

S® **Sadlier School**

Cover: *Series Design:* Studio Montage; *Title design:* Quarasan, Inc. **Photo Credits:** Cover: Getty Images/Jill Fromer: *right;* P Gadomski Michael: *right;* tioloco: *top left;* ULTRA.F: *bottom left.* Used under license from Shutterstock.com: RoboLab: *background.* Interior: Alamy/Novastock: 140 *top.* Blend Images/Marc Romanelli: 78 *top.* Dreamstime.com/Yuri Arcurs: 254 *top;* Steve Allen: vi *bottom left;* Lowlihjeng: 255; Njnightsky: vi *top right.* Getty Images/Digital Vision: 79; Jupiter Images: 8 *top;* Tony Metaxas: 216 *top;* tioloco: vi *center.* Masterfile/Royalty Free: 9. Used under license from Shutterstock.com/Ilya Akinshin: vi *bottom right;* april70: 141 *background;* Jana Guothova: 8 *bottom,* 78 *bottom,* 140 *bottom,* 216 *bottom,* 254 *bottom;* koosen: vi *top left;* Dan Kosmayer: 141; RoboLab: 1, vi *background;* Ivan Ryabokon: vi *top left.* SuperStock/Exactostock/ Andy Sotiriou: 217. **Text Credit:** Common Core State Standards Copyright © 2010. National Governors Association Center for Best Practices and Council of Chief State School Officers. All rights reserved. **Illustrator Credit:** Dave Titus

For additional online resources, go to sadlierconnect.com.

William H. Sadlier, Inc.
9 Pine Street
New York, NY 10005-4700

Printed in the United States of America.
ISBN: 978-1-4217-3153-7
1 2 3 4 5 6 7 8 9 WEBC 18 17 16 15 14

Contents

Unit 5 Focus on Measurement and Data/Geometry

Welcome

You have an exciting year ahead of you. You will be learning more about mathematics and the tools you will need to solve everyday problems.

Did you know that you solve problems and use math all the time? Think about your day. When you play sports after school, shop at your favorite store, cook delicious food, build something awesome like a tree house, or travel in a car, bus or train, you are using math and applying that understanding to make sense of the world around you.

Progress Mathematics will help you improve problem-solving skills while becoming more confident in mathematics. That's why it's called *progress*.

Have a great year!

Progress Check

UNIT 1

Look at how the math concepts and skills you have learned and will learn connect.

It is very important for you to understand the math concepts and skills from the prior grade level so that you will be able to develop an understanding of operations and algebraic thinking in this unit and be prepared for next year. To practice your skills, go to sadlierconnect.com.

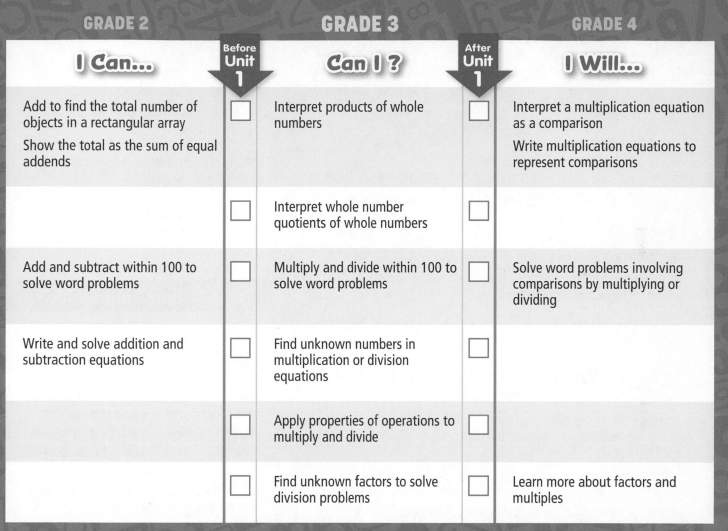

GRADE 2 — I Can...	Before Unit 1	GRADE 3 — Can I ?	After Unit 1	GRADE 4 — I Will...
Add to find the total number of objects in a rectangular array Show the total as the sum of equal addends	☐	Interpret products of whole numbers	☐	Interpret a multiplication equation as a comparison Write multiplication equations to represent comparisons
	☐	Interpret whole number quotients of whole numbers	☐	
Add and subtract within 100 to solve word problems	☐	Multiply and divide within 100 to solve word problems	☐	Solve word problems involving comparisons by multiplying or dividing
Write and solve addition and subtraction equations	☐	Find unknown numbers in multiplication or division equations	☐	
	☐	Apply properties of operations to multiply and divide	☐	
	☐	Find unknown factors to solve division problems	☐	Learn more about factors and multiples

HOME ◆ CONNECT...

In this unit your child will:

- Interpret products of whole numbers.

- Interpret quotients of whole numbers.

- Multiply and divide within 100 to solve problems.

- Find unknown numbers in multiplication or division equations.

- Apply properties of operations to multiply and divide.

- Find unknown factors to solve division problems.

Multiplying and dividing numbers are important skills for your child to master. Memorization of facts plays a crucial role in applying problem-solving skills, multiplying and dividing multi-digit numbers, and other Math concepts to come. Support your child by using the following Math vocabulary:

- The terms **factor** and **product** relate to multiplication. Factors are numbers you multiply to get a product.

$$5 \quad \times \quad 4 \quad = \quad 20$$
factor   factor   product

- The terms **divide** and **quotient** relate to division. You divide numbers to get a quotient.

$$20 \quad \div \quad 5 \quad = \quad 4$$
quotient

- Every multiplication fact has a related division fact. A **fact family** has related multiplication and division facts.

$4 \times 7 = 28 \quad 28 \div 7 = 4 \quad 7 \times 4 = 28 \quad 28 \div 4 = 7$

Ways to Help Your Child

Flash cards (both print and digital) are a fun way for your child to practice related multiplication and division facts. Your child can create a set of flash cards using index cards, or you can download a flash card app that you can customize. Encourage your child to review the flash cards daily. Challenge your child to create a game using the flash cards.

Activity: Create a book of fact families to show related multiplication and division facts. For example, a page for the fact family for 4, 5, and 20:

$4 \times \underline{\quad} = 20 \quad \underline{\quad} \times 5 = 20 \quad 20 \div 5 = \underline{\quad} \quad 20 \div 4 = \underline{\quad}$

Help your child complete the pages of the fact family book. Point out the factors, products, and quotients.

ONLINE

For more Home Connect activities, continue online at sadlierconnect.com

Focus on Operations and Algebraic Thinking

Essential Question:
How are multiplication and division related?

Interpret Products of Whole Numbers

Guided Instruction

In this lesson you will learn when you can multiply and what happens when you multiply.

Understand: What multiplication means

> Bella buys 5 packages of juice boxes.
> Each package has 3 juice boxes.
> How many juice boxes does Bella buy?

One way to find how many juice boxes in all is to add.

There are 5 groups of 3 boxes each.

| 3 | + | 3 | + | 3 | + | 3 | + | 3 | = 15 |

The sum of 5 threes is 15.

Each package has the same number of boxes, so the 5 groups are equal in size. When the groups are equal in size, you can multiply to find the number in all.

number of equal groups times number in each group is equal to number in all

| 5 equal groups | × | 3 in each group | = | 15 |

5 × 3 = 15 ← Read: 5 times 3 is equal to 15.

Each of the numbers you multiply is a factor.
The number in all is the product.

| factor | × | factor | = | product |
| 5 | × | 3 | = | 15 |

Multiplying 5 × 3 is the same as adding 5 threes.

➡ Bella buys 15 juice boxes.

✏ Why do you think the product and the sum are the same?

Guided Instruction

Understand: What a product means

Max uses stickers to make a picture.
He has 4 cards of dot stickers.
Each card has 5 stickers.
How many stickers are there in all?

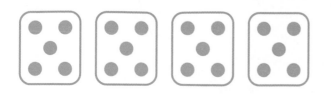

4 cards
5 stickers on each card
4 fives equals 20.

factor $\longrightarrow$ 4 $\times$ 5 $=$ 20 $\longleftarrow$ product

the number   the number   the number
of cards   of stickers on a card   of stickers in all

➡ There are 20 stickers in all.

A product is the result of multiplication. The product tells how many objects in all are in a number of equal groups of objects.

✏ Describe another example. Think of a number of groups of equal things. Draw or tell what they are and write the factors and the product.

Guided Instruction

Connect: Using factors and products to describe problem situations

Describe a situation for which 3 × 4 shows the total number of objects. Then ask and answer a question about the total number of objects.

To do this, you need to describe a number of equal groups of objects.

Step 1

Think: How many equal groups are there? ____ groups

What could the groups be? The groups could be 3 nests.

Step 2

Think: How many objects are in each group? ____ objects

What objects could be in each nest? Each nest could hold 4 eggs.

Step 3

Think: In what situation could there be 3 nests with 4 eggs?

My friends were in the park. They saw _____ in the trees.

In each nest, there were _____.

Step 4

Think: What is a question about this situation? What is its answer?

➡ How many _____ in all are in the 3 nests?

There are _____ in the 3 nests.

✏ Explain why you can multiply to answer your question. Tell what the factors and product are.

Guided Practice

Are all the groups equal? Write *yes* or *no*. Can you multiply to find the total number of stars? Write *yes* or *no*.

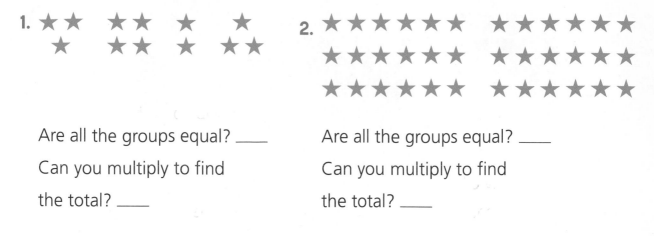

1. Are all the groups equal? _____

   Can you multiply to find

   the total? _____

2. Are all the groups equal? _____

   Can you multiply to find

   the total? _____

Find the number of groups. Tell how many are in each group. Then find how many there are in all.

3.

_____ groups

_____ in each group

_____ in all

$4 \times 2 =$ _____

4.

_____ groups

_____ in each group

_____ in all

$4 \times 5 =$ _____

5.

_____ groups

_____ in each group

_____ in all

$3 \times 6 =$ _____

Look at this multiplication: $6 \times 7 = 42$.

6. Name the factors. _____ _____

7. Name the product. _____

♥♥ Think•Pair•Share

MP7 8. Draw 3 groups with the same number of things in each group. Explain how you can find the total number of things.

Independent Practice

Find the total number of objects and complete the multiplication. You can use the drawing.

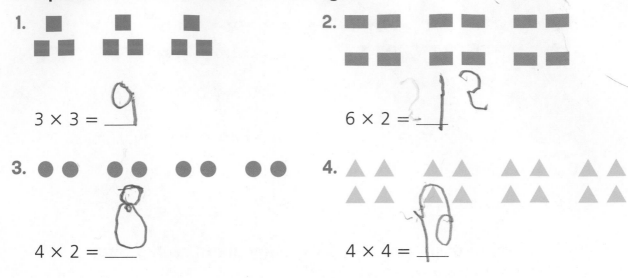

1. $3 \times 3 = \underline{9}$

2. $6 \times 2 = \underline{12}$

3. $4 \times 2 = \underline{8}$

4. $4 \times 4 = \underline{10}$

For exercises 5–8, find each product. Use a drawing to justify your answer.

MP4   5. $3 \times 4 = \underline{12}$

6. $2 \times 5 = \underline{}$

7. $5 \times 6 = \underline{}$

8. $7 \times 3 = \underline{}$

9. There are 6 boxes of 3 erasers each. Which choice shows how many erasers in all?

   a. 3

   b. 6 + 3

   c. 6 × 3 ✓

   d. 6

10. For which situation is the total number of marbles shown by 7 × 4?

    a. Joe has 7 marbles and gives Mike 4 marbles.

    b. Joe gives 4 marbles to each of 7 friends. ✓

    c. Joe wins 4 marbles from Mike and 7 marbles from Sam.

    d. Joe has 4 friends and 7 marbles.

11. Make a drawing that shows the product of 3 × 8. Then find the product.

    3 × 8 = _____

12. Show that 20 is the same as 4 fives. Explain how you know.

Independent Practice

13. In multiplication, what does the product show?

    a. how many factors there are

    b. how many things are in a group

    c. how many groups there are

    d. how many things in all

MP6 **14.** Describe a situation where the total number of soccer balls is shown as 4×6. Include the total number of soccer balls in your answer.

Answer _____

_____

Solve the problem.

MP6 **15.** There are 5 rows of desks in Jake's classroom. Each row has 5 desks. How many desks are in the classroom?

    ✏ **Show your work.**

Answer _____

MP4 **16.** Mia has 6 pairs of white socks. How many white socks does Mia have?

    ✏ **Use a drawing to justify your answer.**

Answer _____

Independent Practice

MP3 **17.** The class library has 6 bookshelves. Each shelf has 5 books. Ann says that there are 11 books in all. Is she correct?

Answer _____

✏️ **Justify your answer using words, drawings, or numbers.**

MP2 **18.** The team needs 16 baseballs. There are 3 baseballs in each package. If Mr. Tam buys 6 packages of baseballs for the team, will there be enough baseballs?

Answer _____

✏️ **Justify your answer using words, drawings, or numbers.**

MP5 **19.** The table shows totals for multiplying the number of groups by the number in each group. Complete the table.

<table>
<tr><td></td><th colspan="9">Number in Each Group</th></tr>
<tr><th>×</th><th>1</th><th>2</th><th>3</th><th>4</th><th>5</th><th>6</th><th>7</th><th>8</th><th>9</th></tr>
<tr><th>2</th><td>2</td><td>4</td><td>6</td><td></td><td></td><td></td><td></td><td></td><td></td></tr>
<tr><th>3</th><td></td><td></td><td></td><td>12</td><td></td><td></td><td>21</td><td></td><td></td></tr>
<tr><th>4</th><td></td><td></td><td></td><td></td><td></td><td></td><td></td><td></td><td></td></tr>
<tr><th>5</th><td>5</td><td>10</td><td>15</td><td>20</td><td></td><td></td><td></td><td></td><td></td></tr>
</table>

Number of Groups

Interpret Quotients of Whole Numbers

Essential Question:
What does it mean to divide?

Words to Know:
   division
   partition
   divide
   dividend
   divisor
   quotient

Guided Instruction

In this lesson you will learn how to use division to find the number of objects in an equal share or to find the number of equal shares.

Understand: Using division to find how many in an equal share

> Three friends have 12 marbles for a game.
> They will share the marbles equally.
> How many marbles will each friend get?

To find how many marbles each friend will get, partition, or share, the marbles equally.

One way to share the marbles is to use a diagram. Draw 3 circles for the 3 friends. Next draw marbles in each circle, 1 at a time, until you have drawn all 12 marbles. Then count to see that there are 4 marbles in each circle.

Another way to share the marbles is to divide.

total number divided by number of groups is equal to number in each group
   12 in all   ÷   3 groups   =   number in each group
        $12 \div 3 = 4$ ◄——— Read: 12 divided by 3 is equal to 4.

➡ Each friend will get 4 marbles.

Guided Instruction

Understand: Using division to separate

Payten has 18 heart stickers. She can put 6 stickers on each page of her sticker book. How many pages will Payten fill?

To find the number of pages, separate the total number of stickers into equal groups of 6.

One way to find the number of pages is to draw a diagram. Draw 18 dots to represent the 18 stickers.

Circle groups of 6 dots.

There are no stickers left over. Count to see that there are 3 groups.

Another way to find the number of pages is to divide.

total number *divided by* number in each group *is equal to* number of groups

$$18 \div 6 = 3$$

dividend   divisor   quotient

The dividend is the total number.

The divisor is the number by which the dividend is divided.

The quotient is the result of the division.

> Each part of a division has a name.

➡ Payten fills 3 pages of her sticker book.

✏ Describe another example. Think of a number of things you can partition into equal shares. Draw or tell what they are and write the division.

Guided Instruction

Connect: Using equal shares to describe problem situations

> Describe a situation for which 35 ÷ 5 shows the number in an equal share. Then ask and answer a question about the situation.

To do this, you need to describe a number of objects and the number of equal shares.

Step 1

Think: How many objects are there? ____ objects

What could the objects be?
The objects could be 35 oranges.

Step 2

Think: What does the 5 represent?

Five represents the _____ of shares.

What could be used to make the shares?
The shares could be 5 bags.

You can draw circles to represent the bags.

Step 3

Think: What situation tells about 35 oranges shared into 5 bags?

The Greenes pick _____ in an orange grove. They divide them equally

among _____.

Step 4

Think: What is a question about this situation? What is its answer?

How many _____ are in one bag?

There are _____ in one bag.

✏️ Explain how you answered the question. Tell why the number of oranges in one bag is the number in an equal share.

Guided Practice

Solve each problem. You can use the picture to the right of the problem.

1. The zookeeper has 15 bananas. If he shares the bananas equally among 3 monkeys, how many bananas will each monkey get?

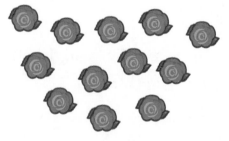

   15 bananas
   3 monkeys

   There are _____ bananas in each equal share.

   $15 \div 3 =$ _____

   Each monkey will get _____ bananas.

2. There are 12 flowers. If you put 6 flowers in each vase, how many vases will you need?

   12 flowers
   6 flowers in each vase

   You make _____ equal groups of flowers.

   $12 \div 6 =$ _____

   You will need _____ vases.

3. Make a drawing to show $40 \div 5$. Then find the quotient.

   $40 \div 5 =$ _____

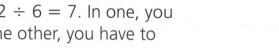 Think•Pair•Share

MP1 4. Write two word problems for the division $42 \div 6 = 7$. In one, you have to find the number in each share. In the other, you have to find the number of equal shares.

Independent Practice

For exercises 1 and 2, use the drawing to find the quotient.

1.
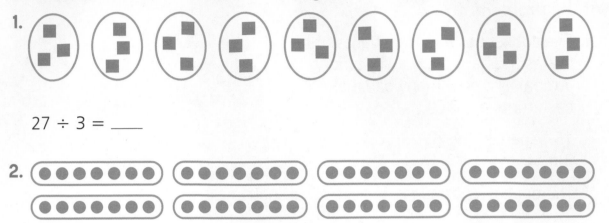

$27 \div 3 =$ _____

2.

$56 \div 8 =$ _____

3. For which situation is the number in a share expressed as $36 \div 9$?

   a. Betty shares 36 tickets for the softball game among 4 friends.

   b. Mrs. Baker makes 9 big batches of 36 muffins each for the school picnic.

   c. Lizzie has 36 guppies and 9 goldfish in her aquarium.

   d. Ms. Juarez shares 36 boxes of copy paper among the 9 classrooms in her school.

MP6 4. Describe a situation where the number of apples in a basket is expressed as $42 \div 6$. Then ask a question about the situation.

MP2 **5.** Explain how to share 36 things equally among 4 groups. Then find the quotient.

Find each quotient. Make a drawing to justify your answer.

MP4 **6.** $25 \div 5 = $ _____

7. $14 \div 2 = $ _____

Find each quotient. Describe a situation that can be represented by the division.

MP6 **8.** $6 \div 3 = $ _____

MP6 **9.** $32 \div 8 = $ _____

MP6 **10.** $20 \div 4 = $ _____

Independent Practice

11. There are 24 boxes of cereal at the food pantry. Each family will receive 3 boxes. Which choice shows how many families will receive boxes of cereal?

a. 3

b. 24 × 3

c. 24 ÷ 3

d. 24

12. Ms. Tucker has a package of 12 small notebooks. She makes a list to show how many she can give to different numbers of friends if she shares them equally. Complete the list.

2 friends   Each friend will get ____ notebooks.

3 friends   Each friend will get ____ notebooks.

4 friends   Each friend will get ____ notebooks.

6 friends   Each friend will get ____ notebooks.

Solve the problems.

MP6 **13.** Dan has 40 grapes. He wants to share the grapes equally among 5 fruit salads. How many grapes will Dan put in each fruit salad?

✏️ **Show your work.**

Answer _____

MP7 **14.** A toy store has 56 plush animals. The store clerk puts the plush animals on 7 shelves. Each shelf has the same number of plush animals. How many plush animals are on each shelf?

✏️ **Show your work.**

Answer _____

Independent Practice

MP4 **15.** The 24 students in Mr. Lee's class will rent vans to go on a field trip. Six students and 1 adult will ride in each van. How many vans are needed?

Answer _____

✏️ **Justify your answer using words, drawings, or numbers.**

MP3 **16.** Nicholas says that $10 \div 2 = 8$. Is he correct?

Answer _____

✏️ **Justify your answer using words, drawings, or numbers.**

MP2 **17.** Kara partitions 16 dimes into equal groups in 3 different ways. She puts more than 1 dime in each group. She makes 2 or more groups for each way. Describe the groups that Kara made.

Answer _____

✏️ **Justify your answer using words, drawings, or numbers.**

3 Problem Solving: Multiplication/Division and Equal Groups

Essential Question:
How can you use multiplication and division to solve problems involving equal groups?

Words to Know:
equation
unknown

Guided Instruction

In this lesson you will learn how to solve problems involving equal groups.

Understand: Using multiplication to solve problems involving equal groups

> Lindsay has 4 pencil cases. She wants to put 8 pencils in each case. How many pencils does Lindsay need?

The number of pencils Lindsay needs is represented by 4 × 8. Find the product 4 × 8.

One way to find 4 × 8 is to draw a diagram.

Draw 4 pencil cases with 8 pencils in each case.

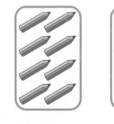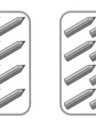

You can count or add to find that there are 32 pencils.

Another way to find 4 × 8 is to multiply.

You can use a symbol for the unknown number to write a multiplication equation that relates the factors to the product. The unknown represents the number of pencils Lindsay needs. To find the value of the unknown number, solve the equation.

4 × 8 = ■
4 × 8 = 32

➤ Lindsay needs 32 pencils.

✏️ Why can you multiply to solve this problem?

Guided Instruction

Understand: Using division to find the number of equal groups

> Mr. Kane asks 21 students to form lines of 7 students each.
> How many lines can the students form?

To solve, separate the 21 students into equal groups.

One way is to use a number line diagram. Start at 21. Draw jumps to show equal groups of 7 until you reach 0.

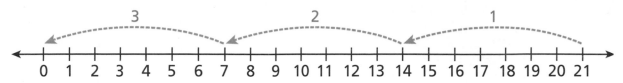

There are 3 equal groups of 7.

Another way is to divide.

$21 \div 7 = \blacksquare$
$21 \div 7 = 3$

> **Remember!**
> Using division to separate:
> The number in all divided by the number in each group is equal to the number of groups.

➡ Mr. Kane's students can form 3 lines.

Understand: Using division to find the number in each group

> Three children share 18 pieces of sidewalk chalk. How many pieces of chalk does each child get?

To solve, make 3 groups of equal shares.

One way is to use a diagram. Draw 3 boxes. Draw 1 line in each box, 1 at a time until you have drawn all 18 lines. Count the 6 lines in each box.

Another way is to divide.

$18 \div 3 = \blacksquare$
$18 \div 3 = 6$

> **Remember!**
> Using division to share:
> The number in all divided by the number of groups is equal to the number in each group.

➡ Each child gets 6 pieces of sidewalk chalk.

Guided Instruction

Connect: **What you know about multiplication and division to solve problems**

Ms. Chavez uses the 4 windows in her bookstore to display 12 new books. She puts the same number of books in each window. How many books are in each window?

Step 1

Decide what information is known and what is unknown.

Known: the number of new books she has —12
            the number of windows she uses —4

Unknown: the number of books in each window

Step 2

Use a diagram to represent the situation. First sketch the windows.

Now represent the 12 books in the 4 windows so that the same number of books is in each window.

Step 3

The diagram shows that you can write and solve a division equation to answer the question.

$12 \div 4 = \blacksquare$

$12 \div 4 = \underline{\hphantom{xxx}}$

➡ There are _____ in each window.

✏ What multiplication fact is represented by your diagram of the 12 books in the 4 windows? Explain why the diagram can show both multiplication and division.

Guided Practice

1. Tony is making a picture frame. He needs 4 pieces of wood, each 9 inches long. How many inches of wood does Tony need in all?

   4 times 9 inches equals how much?
   $4 \times 9 = \blacksquare$

   Use the number line. Represent the 4 pieces of wood, each 9 inches long.

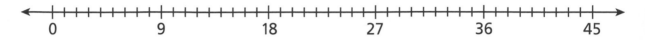

   Answer Tony needs _____ inches of wood.

2. Una and her four friends want to share 40 markers equally. How many markers will each person have?

   40 markers shared equally by 5 persons is the unknown number of markers each person will have.
   $40 \div 5 = \blacksquare$

   Make 5 groups. Show how to share the 40 markers equally.

   ⬭ ⬭ ⬭ ⬭ ⬭

   Answer Each person will have _____ markers.

� Think•Pair•Share

MP2 3. Twenty-seven students sat in 3 rows of 9 chairs to watch a science video. Draw a diagram to represent the situation. Then explain how the diagram represents the two equations $3 \times 9 = 27$ and $27 \div 9 = 3$.

Independent Practice

In exercises 1–3, use the drawing to represent the problem. Then write an equation and solve.

MP4 **1.** Sandy buys 7 bags of pears. Each bag holds 4 pears. How many pears does Sandy buy in all?

✏️ **Show your work.**

$7 \times$ ____ $=$ ____

Answer Sandy buys ____ pears.

MP5 **2.** Joe is packing for a campout. He has 24 flashlight batteries. He puts 8 batteries each into some boxes. How many boxes does he use?

✏️ **Show your work.**

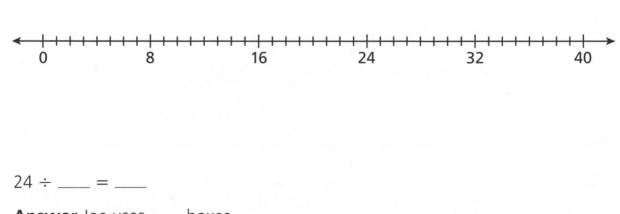

$24 \div$ ____ $=$ ____

Answer Joe uses ____ boxes.

Independent Practice

MP4 **3.** Mrs. McGwin's students are planting flower seeds. If they plant 5 seeds in each of 8 flower pots, how many seeds do they plant in all?

✏️ **Show your work.**

$8 \times$ _____ $= 40$

Answer They plant _____ seeds in all.

MP1 **4.** The third grade class is selling baskets to raise money. The class has 15 baskets to sell.

a. If the class sells 3 baskets each day, how many days will it take to sell all 15 baskets?

■ $= 15 \div 3$

_____ $= 15 \div 3$

Answer It will take _____ days to sell all 15 baskets.

✏️ **Justify your answer using words or drawings.**

b. If the class sells 5 baskets each day, how many days will it take to sell all 15 baskets?

● $= 15 \div 5$

_____ $= 15 \div 5$

Answer It will take _____ days to sell all 15 baskets.

✏️ **Justify your answer using words or drawings.**

Independent Practice

Solve the problems.

MP2 **5.** A group of 10 hikers takes 30 snack bars on their hike. If they share the snack bars equally, how many will each hiker get?

    ✏️ **Show your work.**

Answer _____

MP4 **6.** A group of campers is using 7 rowboats for fishing. Three campers are in each boat. How many campers are fishing?

    ✏️ **Show your work.**

Answer _____

MP5 **7.** A rubber band is 9 centimeters long. It is stretched to be 3 times as long. How long is the stretched rubber band?

    ✏️ **Show your work.**

Answer _____

Independent Practice

MP6 **8.** Mr. Lee ran 35 miles this week. He runs every day from Monday through Friday but does not run on the weekend. This week he ran the same distance every day. How far did Mr. Lee run each day?

 **Show your work.**

Answer _____

MP3 **9.** Alexi drew this picture to show 3 bags with 4 oranges in each bag. What is wrong with Alexi's picture? Correct it.

MP4 **10.** Brie drew this number line to show 3 jumps of 5 inches each. What is wrong with Brie's picture? Correct it.

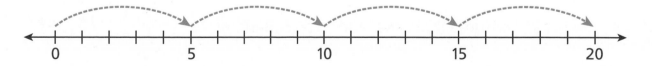

4 Problem Solving: Multiplication/Division and Arrays

Essential Question: How can you use an array to solve a word problem?

Words to Know: array

Guided Instruction

In this lesson you will learn how to solve word problems using arrays.

Understand: Using arrays to solve problems

> The trumpet players in the Youth Band march 6 in a row. When they march, they make 3 full rows. How many trumpet players are in the Youth Band?

To solve this problem, find 3×6.

One way to find 3×6 is to use an array. An array is an arrangement of objects or symbols in equal rows and equal columns.

Use a dot to represent a band member.

Draw 3 rows of 6 dots.

Then add or count to find the total.

There are 18 dots.

Another way to find 3×6 is to use an equation. The equals sign in an equation shows that the two sides of the equation are equal.

■ $= 3 \times 6$ ⟵ ■ represents the value of 3×6.

■ $= 18$ ⟵ Multiply to find the value of ■.

➡ There are 18 trumpet players in the Youth Band.

Remember!
When you do not know the value of a number, use a ■ or other symbol to represent the number.

✏ Explain why you can use an array or an equation to solve the problem.

Guided Instruction

Understand: Representing problem situations with arrays

> Mrs. Stanton uses 28 floor tiles to cover her kitchen floor. If the floor tiles are in rows of 7 each, how many rows are there?

To find the unknown number of rows, find the number of groups of 7 in 28.

You can use an array to solve the problem.

Draw 28 squares to represent the tiles.
Put 7 squares in each row.
Count the number of rows.

You can also use division to find the unknown number of rows.

$28 \div 7 = \blacksquare$
$28 \div 7 = 4$

➡ The floor tiles are in 4 equal rows.

✏ Explain why the array can also represent this multiplication.

$4 \times 7 = 28$

Guided Instruction

Connect: What you know about representing and solving problems

> Ms. Hardy's class has 27 students. Each time the students prepare to leave the classroom, they form 3 equal lines. How many students are in each line?

Step 1

Determine what is known and unknown.

Known: 27 students in all
Known: 3 equal lines of students
Unknown: number of students in each line

Step 2

Make an array to represent the problem.
Show 3 rows for the 3 lines.
Show a total of 27 symbols for the 27 students.

Remember!
Each row must have the same number of symbols.

Step 3

Count the symbols in each row.

There are _____ symbols in each row.

You can also use division to represent and solve the problem.

27 ÷ 3 = _____

➡ There are _____ students in each line.

✎ What multiplication is represented by the array? Explain your thinking.

Guided Practice

Solve the problem. Use the array to help.

1. Jarrod has a collection of 21 sports cards. He wants to share them equally among his 3 brothers. How many sports cards will each brother receive?

You can use division and an array to represent the problem.

$21 \div 3 = \blacksquare$

$21 \div 3 =$ ____

Each brother will receive ____ sports cards.

2. Kayla has a collection of electronic games. She stores them in her game carrier in rows of 5 games each. If Kayla makes 4 rows, how many games are in her collection?

You can use multiplication and an array to represent the problem.

$4 \times 5 = \blacksquare$

$4 \times 5 =$ ____

There are ____ games in her collection.

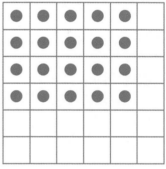

✲ Think•Pair•Share

MP4 **3.** Draw an array to represent 6×8. Then write a word problem that can be solved by finding 6×8.

Independent Practice

Use an array to represent the problem. Then solve.

MP4   **1.** You are setting up 56 chairs for the class play. If you arrange the chairs in 7 rows, how many chairs will be in each row?

$56 \div 7 = \blacksquare$

Draw dots to complete an array that represents the problem.

$56 \div 7 = $ _____

Answer _____ chairs will be in each row.

MP1   **2.** The Ross High School band marches in 6 rows. There are 7 students in each row. How many students are in the band?

$6 \times 7 = \blacksquare$

Draw dots in this grid to make an array that represents the problem.

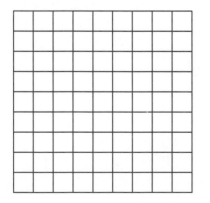

$6 \times 7 = $ _____

Answer There are _____ students in the band.

Independent Practice

MP7 **3.** Lauren has 24 trading cards. She is putting them in an album with the same number of cards on each page. She uses 6 pages for the cards. How many cards are on each page?

$24 \div 6 = \blacksquare$

Use dots in this grid to show the array for this problem.

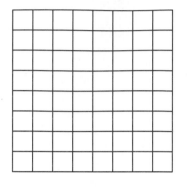

$24 \div 6 =$ ____

Answer Each page of the album has ____ cards.

MP4 **4.** The school cafeteria buys eggs in cartons. If a carton has 6 rows of 6 eggs, how many eggs are in a carton?

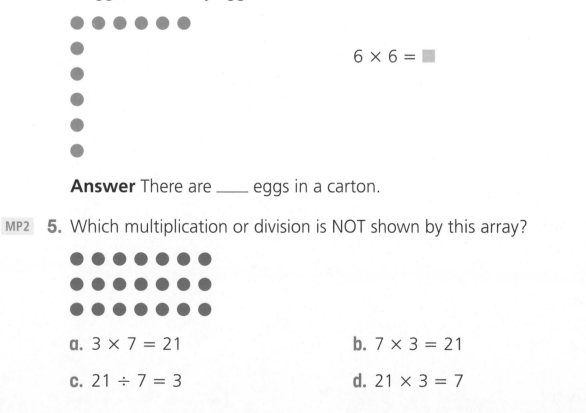

$6 \times 6 = \blacksquare$

Answer There are ____ eggs in a carton.

MP2 **5.** Which multiplication or division is NOT shown by this array?

a. $3 \times 7 = 21$

b. $7 \times 3 = 21$

c. $21 \div 7 = 3$

d. $21 \times 3 = 7$

Independent Practice

Use an array and multiplication or division to solve problems 6–8.

MP4 **6.** Chad's mother made a quilt that is shaped like a rectangle. The quilt has 6 squares across and 3 squares down. How many squares are in the quilt?

✏️ **Show your work.**

Answer _____

MP1 **7.** The neighborhood garden has 56 plants. If there are 7 plants in each row, how many rows of plants are there?

✏️ **Show your work.**

Answer _____

MP5 **8.** There are 28 students in the choir. If they stand in 4 equal rows, how many students are in each row?

✏️ **Show your work.**

Answer _____

Independent Practice

MP5 **9.** Write a problem that can be solved by using this array.

MP4 **10.** Draw as many arrays as you can to represent the product 16. How many different arrays can you draw?

MP2 **11.** Stella drew this array to represent 6 groups of 2 students. What is wrong with Stella's array? Correct it.

5 Find Unknown Numbers in Multiplication and Division Equations

Essential Question:
How can you use multiplication and division equations to find an unknown number?

Guided Instruction

In this lesson, you will learn how to find the value of an unknown number in a multiplication or division equation.

Understand: Finding unknown numbers in multiplication equations

> How can you find an unknown number in a multiplication equation?

The numbers in a multiplication equation are related. You can rewrite a multiplication equation as a division equation.

factor × factor = product   product ÷ factor = factor

When you find the value of the unknown number, you make the equation true because both sides are equal. There are two ways to find an unknown number in a multiplication equation.

Find an unknown first factor.   ■ × 4 = 12

1. Use a multiplication you know. What number times 4 equals 12?	2. Divide the product by the known factor.
■ × 4 = 12	12 ÷ 4 = ■
3 × 4 = 12	12 ÷ 4 = 3
■ = 3	■ = 3

Find an unknown second factor.   3 × ■ = 12

1. Use a multiplication you know. 3 times what number equals 12?	2. Divide the product by the known factor.
3 × ■ = 12	12 ÷ 3 = ■
3 × 4 = 12	12 ÷ 3 = 4
■ = 4	■ = 4

Find an unknown product.   3 × 4 = ■

1. Multiply the factors.	2. Use a division you know.
3 × 4 = ■	■ ÷ 4 = 3
3 × 4 = 12	12 ÷ 4 = 3
■ = 12	■ = 12

➡ You can use multiplication or division to find an unknown number in a multiplication equation.

Understand: Finding unknown numbers in division equations

How can you find the value of an unknown number in a division equation?

A division equation relates a dividend, a divisor, and a quotient. You can rewrite a division equation as a multiplication equation.

dividend ÷ divisor = quotient
quotient × divisor = product

There are two ways to find an unknown number in a division equation. You can use a letter instead of a ■ to represent an unknown number.

Find an unknown dividend. $n \div 4 = 3$

1. Use a division you know.
   What number divided by 4
   equals 3?
   $n \div 4 = 3$
   $12 \div 4 = 3$
   $n = 12$

2. Multiply the quotient by the divisor.
   $3 \times 4 = n$
   $3 \times 4 = 12$
   $n = 12$

Find an unknown divisor. $12 \div n = 3$

1. Use a division you know.
   12 divided by what number
   equals 3?
   $12 \div n = 3$
   $12 \div 4 = 3$
   $n = 4$

2. Use a multiplication you know.
   $3 \times n = 12$
   $3 \times 4 = 12$
   $n = 4$

Find an unknown quotient. $12 \div 3 = n$

1. Divide.
   $12 \div 3 = n$
   $12 \div 3 = 4$
   $n = 4$

2. Use a multiplication you know.
   $n \times 3 = 12$
   $4 \times 3 = 12$
   $n = 4$

➡ You can use multiplication or division to find an unknown number in a division equation.

✏ Explain what it means to find the value of an unknown number in a division equation.

Guided Instruction

Connect: **What you know about multiplication and division equations to solve word problems**

> At the craft fair, a large basket costs $28. This is 4 times as much as a small basket costs.
> How much does a small basket cost?

To solve the problem, find the number that 28 is 4 times as much as.

Step 1

Write an equation to represent the problem.

4 times the cost of a small basket equals $28

$$4 \times \qquad s \qquad = \qquad 28$$

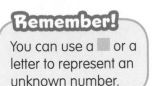

Remember!
You can use a ▇ or a letter to represent an unknown number.

Step 2

Find the factor that makes the equation true. You can use multiplication or division.

Use a multiplication that you know.

$$4 \times s = 28$$

$$4 \times \underline{\quad\quad} = 28$$

Or, divide.

$$s = 28 \div 4$$

$$\underline{\quad\quad} = 28 \div 4$$

➤ A small basket costs $7.

▶ $a \times 5 = 40$

Describe two ways to find the unknown number.

Guided Practice

1. Each box of oranges at the supermarket has 7 rows of oranges with 7 oranges in each row. How many oranges are there altogether?

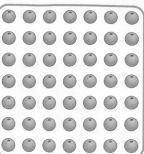

   Write an equation to represent the problem. Then solve to find the unknown number of oranges.

   How many oranges are in 7 rows of 7 oranges each?

   $$o \quad = \quad \underline{\hspace{1cm}} \quad \times \quad \underline{\hspace{1cm}}$$

   $$o \quad = \quad \underline{\hspace{1cm}}$$

   There are _____ oranges altogether.

2. One bag has 36 dog treats. If the treats are shared equally among 9 dogs at the park, how many treats will each dog get?

   How many treats times 9 dogs equals 36?
   Write an equation to represent the problem. Find the unknown number that makes the equation true.

   $$t \quad \times \quad \underline{\hspace{1cm}} \quad = \quad \underline{\hspace{1cm}}$$

   $$\underline{\hspace{1cm}} \quad \times \quad \underline{\hspace{1cm}} \quad = \quad \underline{\hspace{1cm}}$$

   Each dog will get _____ treats.

   Use the same numbers to write a division equation that is true.

   $$\underline{\hspace{1cm}} \div \underline{\hspace{1cm}} = \underline{\hspace{1cm}}$$

☜☝ Think•Pair•Share

MP2 3. What number makes the equation true?

   $$18 \div 6 = \underline{\hspace{1cm}}$$

   What multiplication could you use to check? Explain why you can use multiplication to check division?

Independent Practice

Write the unknown number to complete the equation.

1. $3 \times 5 = \underline{\hspace{1cm}}$

2. $6 \times 9 = \underline{\hspace{1cm}}$

3. $5 \times \underline{\hspace{1cm}} = 25$

4. $4 \times \underline{\hspace{1cm}} = 28$

5. $\underline{\hspace{1cm}} \times 3 = 9$

6. $\underline{\hspace{1cm}} \times 4 = 32$

Write a related division equation to find the unknown number. Then complete the division equation.

7. $2 \times \blacksquare = 12$ $\longrightarrow$ $12 \div \underline{\hspace{1cm}} = \blacksquare$

$12 \div \underline{\hspace{1cm}} = \underline{\hspace{1cm}}$

8. $7 \times \blacksquare = 70$ $\longrightarrow$ $\underline{\hspace{1cm}} \div \underline{\hspace{1cm}} = \blacksquare$

$\underline{\hspace{1cm}} \div \underline{\hspace{1cm}} = \underline{\hspace{1cm}}$

9. $\blacksquare \times 8 = 48$ $\longrightarrow$ $\underline{\hspace{1cm}} \div 8 = \blacksquare$

$\underline{\hspace{1cm}} \div 8 = \underline{\hspace{1cm}}$

10. $\blacksquare \times 4 = 24$ $\longrightarrow$ $\underline{\hspace{1cm}} \div \underline{\hspace{1cm}} = \blacksquare$

$\underline{\hspace{1cm}} \div \underline{\hspace{1cm}} = \underline{\hspace{1cm}}$

11. $5 \times t = 30$ $\longrightarrow$ $\underline{\hspace{1cm}} \div \underline{\hspace{1cm}} = t$

$\underline{\hspace{1cm}} \div \underline{\hspace{1cm}} = \underline{\hspace{1cm}}$

12. $c \times 9 = 81$ $\longrightarrow$ $\underline{\hspace{1cm}} \div \underline{\hspace{1cm}} = c$

$\underline{\hspace{1cm}} \div \underline{\hspace{1cm}} = \underline{\hspace{1cm}}$

Independent Practice

13. Which multiplication equation could you use to find the unknown number?

$$8 \times \blacksquare = 56$$

a. $7 \times 7 = 49$ **b.** $8 \times 7 = 56$

c. $8 \times 8 = 64$ **d.** $8 \times 9 = 72$

14. Which division equation could you use to find the unknown number?

$$3 \times n = 18$$

a. $18 \div 2 = 9$ **b.** $18 \div 9 = 2$

c. $18 \div 1 = 18$ **d.** $18 \div 3 = 6$

15. Which division equation could you use to find the unknown number?

$$63 = y \times 7$$

a. $70 \div 7 = 10$ **b.** $64 \div 8 = 8$

c. $63 \div 7 = 9$ **d.** $60 \div 6 = 10$

Find the unknown number.

16. $4 \times \blacksquare = 12$

     Show your work.

     $\blacksquare = \underline{\quad}$

17. $36 = \blacksquare \times 6$

     Show your work.

     $\blacksquare = \underline{\quad}$

Independent Practice

MP6 **18.** Tell how you would find the unknown number that makes the equation true. Then solve.

$r \times 6 = 54$

_____ $\times\ 6 = 54$

MP6 **19.** Tell how you would find the unknown number that makes the equation true. Then find the unknown number.

$72 \div \blacksquare = 8$

$72 \div$ _____ $= 8$

Solve the problems.

MP4 **20.** Thirty-five nickels are shared equally among 5 friends. How many nickels does each friend get?

▭▶ **Show your work.**

Answer _____

MP1 **21.** At the toy store, a small plush animal costs $8. A large plush animal costs 2 times as much as a small one. How much does a large plush animal cost?

▭▶ **Show your work.**

Answer _____

Independent Practice

MP5 **22.** At the school concert, 64 singers stand in equal rows of 8. How many rows of singers are there? What equation can help you solve the problem?

✏️ **Show your work.**

Answer _____

MP2 **23.** Wei-Yin says that for the equation $30 = \blacksquare \times 3$, the unknown factor is 9. Is he correct?

Answer _____

✏️ **Justify your answer using words, drawings, or numbers.**

MP3 **24.** Maura says that for the equation $6 \times a = 48$, $a = 8$. Is she correct?

Answer _____

✏️ **Justify your answer using words, drawings, or numbers.**

Lesson 6
Apply Commutative and Associative Properties to Multiply

Essential Question:
How can you use properties of multiplication?

Words to Know:
property
Commutative Property of Multiplication
parentheses
Associative Property of Multiplication

Guided Instruction

In this lesson you will learn how to use two properties of multiplication.

Understand: Two numbers can be multiplied in any order

> The students in Ms. Ward's class sit in 4 rows of 6. The students in Mr. Rao's class sit in 6 rows of 4. Which class has more students?

To find which class has more students, multiply to find the number of students in each class. Then compare.

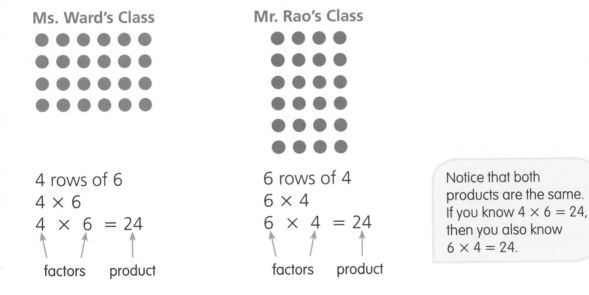

Ms. Ward's Class

4 rows of 6
4×6
$4 \times 6 = 24$
factors   product

Mr. Rao's Class

6 rows of 4
6×4
$6 \times 4 = 24$
factors   product

Notice that both products are the same. If you know $4 \times 6 = 24$, then you also know $6 \times 4 = 24$.

➡ There are 24 students in each class.

When you multiply, the order of the factors does not matter. The product is the same. This is a property, or rule, of multiplication. It is called the Commutative Property of Multiplication. Some people call it the Order Property.

✏ How does the Commutative Property explain why 2×3 and 3×2 have the same product?

Guided Instruction

Understand: Three factors can be grouped in different ways

At a shirt factory, 2 shirts are put in each package. Three packages are put in each box. Two boxes of packages of shirts are delivered to Ms. Roman's store. How many shirts are in the delivery to Ms. Roman's store?

To find the number of shirts in all, multiply $2 \times 3 \times 2$. Use an array to show 2 groups of 3 rows of 2.

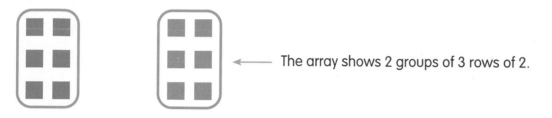

← The array shows 2 groups of 3 rows of 2.

You can group three factors in two different ways to find the product. Put parentheses around the two factors you group together. This shows that you multiply them first.

$2 \times 3 \times 2 = \blacksquare$
$(2 \times 3) \times 2 = \blacksquare$

$6 \times 2 = \blacksquare$
$6 \times 2 = 12$

$2 \times 3 \times 2 = \blacksquare$
$2 \times (3 \times 2) = \blacksquare$

$2 \times 6 = \blacksquare$
$2 \times 6 = 12$

When you multiply three factors, you can group them in two different ways. The product is the same.

This is the Associative Property of Multiplication. Some people call it the Grouping Property.

➡ There are 12 shirts in the delivery to Ms. Roman's store.

When you use the Associative Property, you may not change the order of the factors. To do that, you must use the Commutative Property.

✏ Show how to group the factors $2 \times 1 \times 5$ in two different ways to find their product.

Guided Instruction

Connect: Using the Commutative and Associative Properties

> You can use a property of multiplication to rewrite a multiplication. Tell what the property means and what it lets you do.

Use the Commutative Property to rewrite 3 × 4 and find the product.

You can rewrite 3 × 4 as 4 × ____.

3 × 4 = 12   4 × 3 = 12

The product is ____.

➡ The Commutative Property means that changing the order of the factors does not _____ the product.

The Commutative Property lets you change the order of the _____ in a multiplication.

Use the Associative Property to rewrite 2 × 2 × 4 and find the product.

You can rewrite 2 × 2 × 4 as (2 × 2) × 4 or as 2 × _____.

(2 × 2) × 4 = 4 × 4   2 × (2 × 4) = 2 × 8

(2 × 2) × 4 = 16   2 × (2 × 4) = 16

The product is ____.

➡ The Associative Property means that _____ the grouping of the factors does not change the product. The Associative Property lets you choose which factors to _____ first.

✏ Complete the equations. Tell what property of multiplication you used.

5 × 9 = ____ × 5   _____

3 × 2 × 1 = (____ × 2) × 1   _____

Guided Practice

Draw lines to match the multiplications with the same product.

1. 3×4

2. $5 \times 6 \times 7$

3. $2 \times 4 \times 8$

4. 2×9

a. 9×2

b. $2 + 4 \times 8$

c. 4×3

d. $(2 \times 4) \times 8$

e. $5 \times (6 \times 7)$

5. Use the Associative Property. Show two ways to find the product.

$3 \times 3 \times 2 = \blacksquare$
$(3 \times 3) \times 2 = \blacksquare$

$\underline{\quad} \times 2 = \blacksquare$

$\underline{\quad} \times 2 = \underline{\quad}$

$3 \times 3 \times 2 = \blacksquare$
$3 \times (3 \times 2) = \blacksquare$

$3 \times \underline{\quad} = \blacksquare$

$3 \times \underline{\quad} = \underline{\quad}$

Answer The product is ____.

☺ Think·Pair·Share

MP3 6. Max said he used only the Associative Property to group $3 \times 5 \times 2$ in the three ways shown at the right. Is Max's work correct? Explain your answer.

$(3 \times 5) \times 2$
$3 \times (5 \times 2)$
$(3 \times 2) \times 5$

Independent Practice

Complete the equations. Circle the name of the property you used.

1. $5 \times 1 \times 9 = 5 \times (1 \times \underline{\quad})$

    Commutative Property   Associative Property

2. $9 \times 6 = \underline{\quad} \times 9$

    Commutative Property   Associative Property

For exercises 3–6, find each product.

3. $2 \times (2 \times 4) =$

    $2 \times \underline{\quad} = \underline{\quad}$

4. $(3 \times 2) \times 5 =$

    $\underline{\quad} \times 5 = \underline{\quad}$

5. $6 \times (2 \times 3) =$

    $6 \times \underline{\quad} = \underline{\quad}$

6. $(2 \times 2) \times 7 =$

    $\underline{\quad} \times 7 = \underline{\quad}$

For exercises 7 and 8, use the Commutative Property. Find each unknown product.

7. $1 \times 7 = 7$

    $7 \times 1 = \underline{\quad}$

8. $8 \times 5 = 40$

    $5 \times 8 = \underline{\quad}$

MP3   **9.** Stacy says that $(3 \times 5) \times 4 = 3 \times (5 \times 4)$. Is Stacy correct? What property helps you decide?

     Show your work.

Independent Practice

Find the product. You can use the Associative Property to group the factors.

10. $5 \times 2 \times 3 = \blacksquare$

11. $3 \times 2 \times 3 = \blacksquare$

$5 \times 2 \times 3 = $ ___

$3 \times 2 \times 3 = $ ___

12. $6 \times 1 \times 2 = \blacksquare$

13. $2 \times 2 \times 3 = \blacksquare$

$6 \times 1 \times 2 = $ ___

$2 \times 2 \times 3 = $ ___

14. Which of the following is the same as 3×7?

a. 3×3

b. 3×6

c. 7×3

d. $7 \times 2 \times 3$

15. Which of the following is the same as $(4 \times 9) \times 3$?

a. $4 \times (9 \times 3)$

b. $4 \times (9 \times 2)$

c. $(4 \times 8) \times 3$

d. $(3 \times 9) \times 3$

Independent Practice

MP6 **16.** Explain why you can use the multiplication fact $7 \times 9 = 63$ to find the product of 9×7. Then find the product.

$9 \times 7 = $ _____

MP6 **17.** Explain how you could group $3 \times 2 \times 5$ to multiply. Then find the product.

$3 \times 2 \times 5 = $ _____

Solve the problems.

MP1 **18.** Six groups of 8 students are visiting the science museum. How many students are at the museum?

◼▭▶ **Show your work.**

Answer _____

Independent Practice

MP4 **19.** **a.** There are 5 shelves on a bookshelf. Each shelf holds 9 books. How many books are there in all?

Answer _____

b. There are 9 shelves on a bookshelf. Each shelf holds 5 books. How many books are there in all?

Answer _____

c. Compare the answers to parts a and b. Explain your results.

Answer _____

MP8 **20.** Mr. Smith buys 3 cartons of eggs for his café. Each carton has 2 rows. There are 4 eggs in each row. How many eggs does Mr. Smith buy? Explain your thinking.

➡ **Show your work.**

Answer _____

MP7 **21.** Jillian packs 6 gift mugs in each of 8 small boxes. Aaron packs 8 gift mugs in each of 6 large boxes. Compare the number of mugs they pack.

Answer _____

➡ **Justify your answer using words, drawings, or numbers.**

Apply the Distributive Property to Multiply

Essential Question:
How can you break apart numbers to rewrite multiplication problems?

Words to Know:
Distributive Property

Guided Instruction

In this lesson you will learn about another property of multiplication.

Understand: Breaking apart numbers to multiply

> Bart has 7 packages of pencils. Each package has 6 pencils. How many pencils does Bart have?

To find the total number of pencils, multiply 7×6.

One way to show 7 packages of 6 pencils each is to use an array.

The meaning of multiplication tells you that the number of groups times the number in each group is equal to the number in all.

Draw 7 groups of 6.

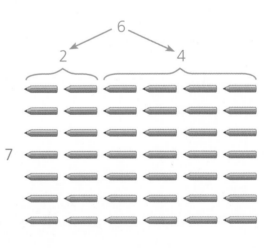

If you do not remember the product for 7×6, you can add $6 + 6 + 6 + 6 + 6 + 6 + 6$.

Another way to find the product is to use multiplication facts you know.
You can show one of the factors as a sum.
Break apart the factor 6 into $2 + 4$.
Change the array to show 7 groups of 2 and 7 groups of 4.

Multiply 7×2 and 7×4 and then add the products.

$7 \times 2 = 14 \qquad 7 \times 4 = 28$

$$14 + 28 = 42$$

▷ Bart has 42 pencils in all.

Understand: Using parentheses with the Distributive Property

Roger has 7 boxes of apples. Each box holds 9 apples.
How many apples does Roger have in all?

To solve, find 7 × 9.

To find the product of 7 × 9, break apart the factor 9 into the sum of the addends 5 + 4. Use parentheses to show the sum of the addends. Parentheses show numbers that belong together.

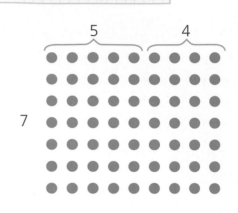

$$7 \times 9 = 7 \times (5 + 4)$$

Multiply each addend by 7 and then add the products. Now you use parentheses to show the factors that you will multiply.

$$7 \times 9 = 7 \times (5 + 4)$$
$$= (7 \times 5) + (7 \times 4)$$

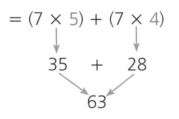

When you multiply a factor by a sum of two addends, you multiply the factor by each of the addends.

$$7 \times 9 = 63$$

▷ Roger has 63 apples in all.

When you break apart a factor so that you can add two simpler multiplications to find a product, you are using the Distributive Property.

✏ How could you use what you just learned about breaking apart one factor to find the product of 7 × 9 another way?

Guided Instruction

Connect: Using the Distributive Property to find a product

> Katya has 9 playlists on her phone. Each playlist has 4 country songs. How many country songs does Katya have in all?

To find the number of country songs Katya has, multiply 9×4. You can use the Distributive Property to rewrite 9×4 as two simpler multiplications. To do this, break apart the factor 9 or the factor 4.

One way to break apart the factor 4 is into $2 + 2$.

$$9 \times 4 = 9 \times (2 + 2)$$
$$= (9 \times 2) + (9 \times 2)$$
$$18 \quad + \quad 18$$
$$\underline{\quad\quad}$$

One way to break apart the factor 9 is into 3 and 6.

$$9 \times 4 = (3 + 6) \times 4$$
$$= (3 \times 4) + (6 \times 4)$$
$$12 \quad + \quad 24$$
$$\underline{\quad\quad}$$

(handwritten)
$(4+5) \times 4$
$(4 \times 4) + (5 \times 4)$
$16 + 20$
36

Whichever factor you break apart, the final product is the same. $9 \times 4 = 36$

▷ Katya has 36 country songs in all.

You can use the Distributive Property to rewrite a multiplication as two simpler multiplications.

✏ You can break apart the factors of 9×4 in other ways. Use the Distributive Property to show two or more other ways.

Guided Practice

1. Use the array to find the product of 4 × 7. Break apart the factor 7.

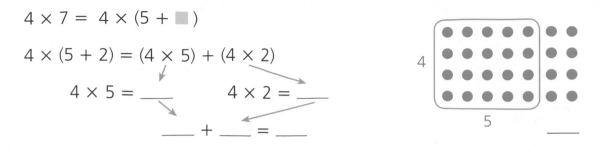

$4 \times 7 = 4 \times (5 + \blacksquare)$

$4 \times (5 + 2) = (4 \times 5) + (4 \times 2)$

$4 \times 5 = \underline{\quad}$　　　　$4 \times 2 = \underline{\quad}$

$\underline{\quad} + \underline{\quad} = \underline{\quad}$

$4 \times 7 = \underline{\quad}$

2. Use the Distributive Property to find the product of 7 × 5. The array may help.

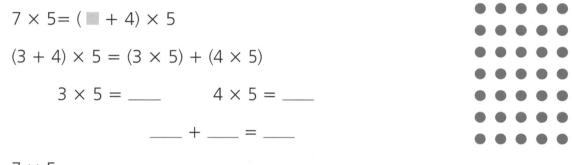

$7 \times 5 = (\blacksquare + 4) \times 5$

$(3 + 4) \times 5 = (3 \times 5) + (4 \times 5)$

$3 \times 5 = \underline{\quad}$　　　　$4 \times 5 = \underline{\quad}$

$\underline{\quad} + \underline{\quad} = \underline{\quad}$

$7 \times 5 = \underline{\quad}$

3. Use the Distributive Property to find 8 × 6. Draw an array if it helps.

$8 \times 6 = (\underline{\quad} + \underline{\quad}) \times 6$

$8 \times 6 = (\underline{\quad} \times 6) + (\underline{\quad} \times 6)$

$8 \times 6 = \underline{\quad} + \underline{\quad}$

$8 \times 6 = \underline{\quad}$

᭡ Think•Pair•Share

MP7　**4.** Show two ways you could use the Distributive Property to find 5 × 9. Explain why the products are the same for each way.

Independent Practice

In exercises 1 and 2, break apart the array. Then show how to use the Distributive Property to find the product.

1. $6 \times 9 = \blacksquare$

2. $7 \times 7 = \blacksquare$

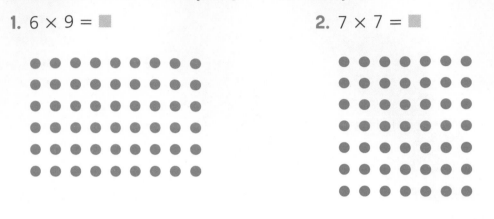

$6 \times 9 = $ _____

$7 \times 7 = $ _____

3. Which of the following is the same as 12×6?

   a. $(9 \times 4) + (3 \times 2)$

   b. $(8 \times 6) + (4 \times 6)$

   c. $(3 \times 4) + (3 \times 2)$

   d. $6 \times (3 + 4)$

4. Choose all of the following that are the same as $(4 \times 3) + (4 \times 5)$.

   a. 8×8

   b. $4 \times (3 + 5)$

   c. 4×8

   d. $4 \times (3 \times 5)$

5. Choose all of the following that have the same total as $(3 \times 5) + (3 \times 6)$.

   a. $3 \times (7 + 4)$

   b. 6×11

   c. $3 \times (10 + 1)$

   d. 3×11

Independent Practice

Draw lines to match.

6. 6 × 9

7. 7 × 8

8. 5 × 7

9. 9 × 4

10. 6 × 4

a. (5 × 8) + (2 × 8)

b. (7 × 4) + (2 × 4)

c. (5 × 4) + (1 × 4)

d. 6 × (6 + 3)

e. (6 × 2) + (3 × 2)

f. 5 × (5 + 2)

Find each product.

11. 7 × 5 = 7 × (3 + 2)

  = (7 × 3) + (7 × ___)

  ___ + ___ = ___

  7 × 5 = ___

12. 6 × 6 = (6 × 3) + (6 × ___)

  ___ + ___ = ___

  6 × 6 = ___

13. 8 × 3 = (2 × 3) + (___ × 3)

  ___ + ___ = ___

  8 × 3 = ___

14. 9 × 8 = (9 × 5) + (9 × ___)

  ___ + ___ = ___

  9 × 8 = ___

Independent Practice

15. Write two ways to find the product of 5 × 8.
Use the Distributive Property.

$5 \times 8 =$ _____

Solve the problems.

MP4 **16.** Vera bought 8 cans of tennis balls.
Each can has 3 tennis balls.
How many tennis balls did Vera buy?

▰▰▶ **Draw an array to justify your answer.**

Answer _____

MP4 **17.** Bill planted 3 rows of pepper plants in his vegetable garden. He
planted 7 plants in each row. How many pepper plants did Bill plant?
Draw an array to model the pepper plants in Bill's garden.

▰▰▶ **Show your work.**

Answer _____

MP6 **18.** Jason buys 8 cartons of oranges. Each carton has 6 oranges in it.
How many oranges does Jason buy altogether?

▰▰▶ **Show your work.**

Answer _____

Independent Practice

MP7 **19.** Evan thinks that 9×8 is the same as $(9 \times 4) + (9 \times 4)$.
Is he correct?

Answer _____

➤ **Justify your answer using words, drawings, or numbers.**

MP3 **20.** Show how to use the Distributive Property to find 6×11.

MP7 **21.** Lauren says that $(4 \times 3) + (2 \times 3)$ is the same as 6×6.
Is she correct?

Answer _____

➤ **Justify your answer using words, drawings, or numbers.**

Divide by Finding an Unknown Factor

Essential Question:
How can you use what you know about how multiplication and division are related to divide?

Words to Know:
fact family

Guided Instruction

In this lesson you will divide using a related multiplication to find an unknown factor.

Understand: Multiplication and division fact families

> Three students are making a large poster. Ms. Peters gives them 21 markers to share equally. How many markers does each student get?

To find how many markers each student gets, divide $21 \div 3$.

One way to find $21 \div 3$ is to use an array.

Draw 21 dots in 3 equal rows.

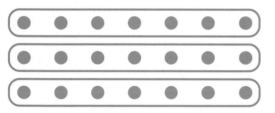

Count to see that there are 7 dots in each row.

Another way to find $21 \div 3$ is to find the value of an unknown factor.

You can use a fact family to find the value of an unknown factor. A fact family shows related multiplication and division facts.

3 times what number is equal to 21? ⟵ Think of a multiplication fact with 21 and 3.

$3 \times \blacksquare = 21$ ⟵ ■ is an unknown factor.

$3 \times 7 = 21$ ⟵ 7 is the unknown factor.

$21 \div 3 = 7$ ⟵ Use the unknown factor to divide.

> Fact Family for 3, 7, and 21:
> $3 \times 7 = 21$ $7 \times 3 = 21$
> $21 \div 3 = 7$ $21 \div 7 = 3$

➡ Each student gets 7 markers.

✏➤ What fact family can you use to find an unknown factor to divide $72 \div 8$?

Guided Instruction

Understand: Using a fact family to find an unknown factor

Sixteen students are on a field trip. The teacher groups them into pairs. How many pairs of students are there?

To find how many pairs, you can divide 16 by 2.

Remember!
A pair is equal to 2.

You can use related multiplication facts to solve division problems.

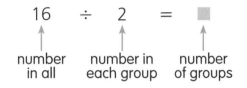
16 ÷ 2 = ▪
number in all   number in each group   number of groups

Think: What number times 2 makes 16?

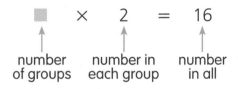
▪ × 2 = 16
number of groups   number in each group   number in all

You can use the fact family for 2, 8, and 16 to help solve the problem.

$2 \times 8 = 16$ $8 \times 2 = 16$
$16 \div 2 = 8$ $16 \div 8 = 2$

Find the unknown factor in the multiplication.

▪ $\times 2 = 16$

Use the unknown factor to complete the related division.

$16 \div 2 = 8$

➡ There are 8 pairs of students.

✎ Why does finding an unknown factor help you divide?

Guided Instruction

Connect: Division equations and finding an unknown factor

Lana wants to store 36 trading cards in plastic sleeves. Each plastic sleeve can hold 4 trading cards. How many plastic sleeves will Lana need?

Step 1

Write a division equation to represent the problem.

$36 \div 4 = a$

Remember!
You can use a letter to represent an unknown number.

Step 2

Think: What number times 4 is equal to 36?

Write the related multiplication.

$a \times 4 = 36$

Step 3

Find the value of the unknown factor in the multiplication.

$\underline{\quad} \times 4 = 36$

Then complete the related division.

$36 \div 4 = \underline{\quad}$

➡ Lana needs 9 plastic sleeves.

✏ Choose a multiplication fact you know. Write the other related multiplication and divisions in the fact family. Explain why they are related.

Complete each fact family.

1. $3 \times 7 = 21$ $21 \div 7 = $ ____   **2.** ___ $\times 5 = 15$ $15 \div 5 = $ ____

___ $\times 3 = 21$ $21 \div 3 = $ ____   ___ $\times 3 = 15$ $15 \div 3 = $ ____

3. $7 \times $ ___ $= 56$ $56 \div 8 = $ ____   **4.** ___ $\times$ ___ $= 64$ $64 \div 8 = $ ____

$8 \times $ ___ $= 56$ $56 \div 7 = $ ____

Solve the problem.

5. The soccer team orders two pizzas with a total of 20 slices. There are 10 players on the team. How many slices will each player get?

This division equation represents the problem. $20 \div 10 = s$

Write a related multiplication equation.   ___ $\times s = $ ____

Find the unknown factor. $10 \times $ ___ $= 20$

Then complete the related division. $20 \div 10 = $ ____

Complete the fact family for 2, 10, and 20.

___ $\times 10 = 20$ $20 \div 10 = $ ____

___ $\times 2 = 20$ $20 \div 2 = $ ____

Answer Each player will get ___ slices.

Think•Pair•Share

MP7 **6.** Amy makes triangles to show multiplication and division fact families. Complete the fact family triangle for 4, 9, and 36. How can you use the triangle to help you multiply and divide?

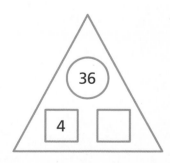

Independent Practice

Complete each fact family.

1. ___ × ___ = 42

   ___ × ___ = 42

   42 ÷ 7 = ___

   42 ÷ 6 = ___

2. ___ × ___ = 27

   ___ × ___ = 27

   27 ÷ 9 = ___

   27 ÷ 3 = ___

3. ___ × ___ = 40

   ___ × ___ = 40

   40 ÷ 8 = ___

   40 ÷ 5 = ___

4. ___ × ___ = 63

   ___ × ___ = 63

   63 ÷ 9 = ___

   63 ÷ 7 = ___

To divide, find the unknown factor.

5. 42 ÷ 7 = ■   ⟶   What number times 7 equals 42?

   ___ × 7 = 42

   42 ÷ 7 = ___

6. 64 ÷ 8 = ■   ⟶   What number times 8 equals 64?

   ___ × 8 = 64

   64 ÷ 8 = ___

7. 63 ÷ 7 = ■   ⟶   What number times 7 equals 63?

   ___ × 7 = 63

   63 ÷ 7 = ___

8. 50 ÷ 10 = ■   ⟶   What number times 10 equals 50?

   ___ × 10 = 50

   50 ÷ 10 = ___

Independent Practice

9. Which multiplication fact could you use to find the unknown number?

$36 \div 9 = \blacksquare$

a. $4 \times 8 = 32$

b. $5 \times 7 = 35$

c. $4 \times 9 = 36$

d. $5 \times 9 = 45$

10. Which multiplication fact could you use to find n?

$24 \div 3 = n$

a. $7 \times 3 = 21$

b. $8 \times 3 = 24$

c. $9 \times 3 = 27$

d. $10 \times 3 = 30$

For exercises 11 and 12, find the unknown number.

11. $63 \div 7 = m$

Show your work.

Answer $63 \div 7 =$ _____

12. $48 \div 8 = m$

Show your work.

Answer $48 \div 8 =$ _____

Independent Practice

MP6 **13.** Tell how you would find *a*. Then solve.

$a = 49 \div 7$

Answer _____ $= 49 \div 7$

MP8 **14.** Ethan knows that $6 \times 9 = 54$. How can he use that fact to solve the following equation?

$54 \div 9 = d$

Answer $54 \div 9 =$ _____

Solve the problems.

MP2 **15.** Zoey has flower plants to sell at the spring fair. She has 72 plants and 9 boxes. How many plants can she put in each box?

✏ **Show your work.**

Answer _____

Independent Practice

MP5 16. Six tacos from the Lunch Place cost $18. How much does 1 taco cost?

✏ **Show your work.**

Answer _____

MP3 17. C.J. does not know the answer to 54 ÷ 9. Can C.J. correctly find the answer in each of the following ways? Explain why or why not for each way.

✏ **Justify your answer using words, drawings, or numbers.**

a. He can make an array to show that 6 rows of 9 makes 54. So 54 divided by 9 is 6.

b. He knows that 6 × 9 = 54, so 54 divided by 9 must be 6.

Answer _____

For exercises 1 and 2, find the product. You can use the drawing.

1. $4 \times 4 = $ ■

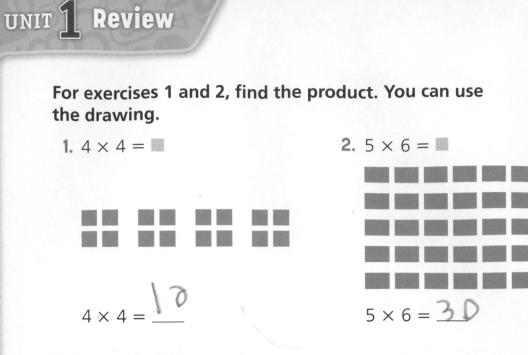

$4 \times 4 = $ __10__

2. $5 \times 6 = $ ■

$5 \times 6 = $ __30__

For exercises 3 and 4, find the quotient. Make a drawing to justify your answer.

3. $15 \div 3 = $ __5__

4. $32 \div 4 = $ __8__

5. Which multiplication equation could you use to find the unknown number?

$$7 \times \blacksquare = 35$$

a. $7 \times 5 = 35$ ✓

b. $7 \times 6 = 42$

c. $7 \times 7 = 49$

d. $7 \times 8 = 56$

6. Which division equation could you use to find the unknown number?

$$4 \times n = 20$$

a. $20 \div 10 = 2$

b. $20 \div 5 = 4$ ✓

c. $20 \div 2 = 10$

d. $20 \div 1 = 20$

For exercises 7 and 8, find the unknown product.

7. $3 \times 6 = 18$

$6 \times 3 = $ __18__

8. $9 \times 6 = 54$

$6 \times 9 = $ __54__

For exercises 9 and 10, use the Associative Property to group the factors. Find the unknown product. Show your work.

9. $2 \times 5 \times 4 = \blacksquare$

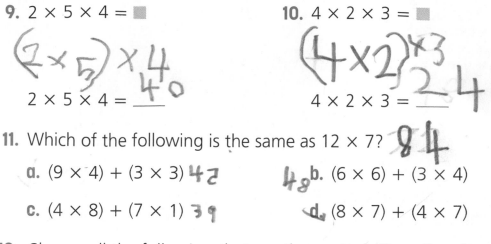

$(2 \times 5) \times 4$
40

$2 \times 5 \times 4 = \underline{40}$

10. $4 \times 2 \times 3 = \blacksquare$

$(4 \times 2) \times 3$
$2 4$

$4 \times 2 \times 3 = \underline{24}$

11. Which of the following is the same as 12×7? 84

   a. $(9 \times 4) + (3 \times 3)$ 42

   48 **b.** $(6 \times 6) + (3 \times 4)$

   c. $(4 \times 8) + (7 \times 1)$ 39

   d. $(8 \times 7) + (4 \times 7)$

12. Choose all the following that are the same as $(3 \times 4) + (3 \times 4)$.

   a. 6×4

   b. 6×8

   c. $(6 \times 2) + (6 \times 2)$

   d. $(2 \times 2) + (4 \times 4)$

For exercises 13 and 14, complete the fact family.

13. $\underline{} \times 7 = 28$ $28 \div 7 = \underline{}$

   $\underline{} \times 4 = \underline{}$ $\underline{} \div 4 = \underline{}$

14. $\underline{} \times 9 = 27$ $27 \div 9 = \underline{}$

   $\underline{} \times 3 = \underline{}$ $\underline{} \div 3 = \underline{}$

For exercises 15 and 16, find the unknown number. Show your work.

15. $64 \div 8 = n$

16. $42 \div 6 = m$

Solve the problems.

MP1 **17.** A group of 8 people take 16 water bottles on their hike. If they share the water bottles equally, how many water bottles will each person get?

✏️➤ **Show your work.**

Answer _____

MP1 **18.** There are 48 people in a marching band. If they stand in 6 equal rows, how many people will stand in each row?

✏️➤ **Show your work.**

Answer _____

MP3 **19.** Tamara drew this array to represent 4 rows of 5 marbles. What is wrong with Tamara's array? Correct it.

● ● ● ● ●
● ● ● ● ●
● ● ● ● ●

MP7 **20.** Mr. Kent has 28 students in his gym class. He wants the students to sit in rows with the same number of students in each row. What are two ways Mr. Kent can arrange the 28 students?

Answer _____

_____

✏️➤ **Justify your answer using words, drawings, or numbers.**

Progress ✓ Check

Look at how the math concepts and skills you have learned and will learn connect.

It is very important for you to understand the math concepts and skills from the prior grade level so that you will be able to develop an understanding of operations and algebraic thinking / number and operations in base ten in this unit and be prepared for next year. To practice your skills, go to sadlierconnect.com.

UNIT **2**

GRADE 2		GRADE 3		GRADE 4
I Can...	Before Unit 2	**Can I ?**	After Unit 2	**I Will...**
	☐	Fluently multiply and divide within 100	☐	Multiply multi-digit whole numbers by one-digit whole numbers
Solve one- and two-step word problems by adding and subtracting within 100	☐	Solve two-step problems using the four operations	☐	Solve multistep word problems using the four operations
Use drawings and equations to represent word problems	☐	Check reasonableness of answers to problems using mental math and estimation	☐	Represent multistep word problems using equations
	☐	Represent two-step word problems using equations	☐	
	☐	Identify arithmetic patterns	☐	Generate and analyze patterns
Understand place value in two-digit and three-digit numbers	☐	Round whole numbers to the nearest 10 or 100	☐	Round multi-digit whole numbers to any place
Fluently add and subtract within 100	☐	Fluently add and subtract within 1000	☐	Fluently add and subtract multi-digit whole numbers
Add up to four two-digit numbers				
Add and subtract within 1000				
	☐	Multiply one-digit numbers by multiples of 10	☐	Multiply multi-digit whole numbers by one-digit whole numbers
				Multiply two two-digit numbers

In this unit your child will:

- Fluently multiply and divide.

- Solve two-step problems.

- Check answers for reasonableness.

- Represent two-step word problems using equations.

- Identify arithmetic patterns.

- Round whole numbers to the nearest 10 or 100.

- Fluently add or subtract numbers within 1,000.

- Multiply one-digit numbers by multiples of 10.

In third grade, your child will solve word problems using addition, subtraction, multiplication, and division. Support your child by using the following problem-solving model:

- **Read** Read the problem with your child. Focus on the facts and the questions. Ask: *What facts do you know? What do you need to find out?*

- **Plan** Outline a plan with your child. Plan how to solve the problem. Ask: *What operation* (addition, subtraction, multiplication, or division) *will you use? Do you need to use 1 step or 2 steps? Will you draw a picture? How have you solved similar problems?*

- **Solve** Follow the plan to solve the problem with your child. Ask: *Did you answer the question? Did you label your answer?*

- **Check** Test that the solution is reasonable. Ask: *How can you solve the problem a different way? Is the answer the same? How can you estimate to check your answer?*

Ways to Help Your Child

Your child will likely have daily homework assignments. Establishing a homework routine can help promote good study habits. Schedule a consistent time for doing homework. The homework routine should also include a homework space that is quiet and comfortable, free from distractions. You may want to use a kitchen or dining room table so that you can easily monitor your child and provide assistance as needed.

Conversation Starters: Estimation is another strategy your child will use in third grade. Talk about situations in which you need to use estimation. For example: planning a family celebration for twenty people. Ask questions such as: *How many people can sit at a table? About how many tables would we need? How many people would eat hamburgers? About how many packages of hamburgers would we need?*

ONLINE
For more Home Connect activities, continue online at sadlierconnect.com

Focus on Operations and Algebraic Thinking / Number and Operations in Base Ten

Essential Question:
How does understanding place value help you add, subtract, and multiply?

Multiply and Divide Fluently within 100

Essential Question:
What strategies can you use to multiply and divide with one-digit numbers?

Words to Know:
strategy
Zero Property
Identity Property
   of Multiplication

Guided Instruction

In this lesson you will learn to use different strategies to multiply and divide.

Understand: How multiplication and division are related

> You have used an array to show equal groups. What does an array tell you about multiplication and division?

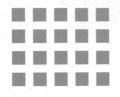

This array shows 4 equal groups of 5.
You can write 4 × 5 = 20.

Turn the array to show 5 equal groups of 4.
You can write 5 × 4 = 20.

You can also write 4 × 5 as

$$\begin{array}{r} 4 \\ \times\ 5 \\ \hline 20 \end{array}$$

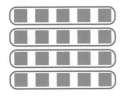

The array shows that 20 can be divided into 4 equal groups of 5.
You can write 20 ÷ 4 = 5.

The turned array shows that 20 can be divided into 5 equal groups of 4.
You can write 20 ÷ 5 = 4.

You can also write 20 ÷ 4 as

$$4\overline{)20}$$ with 5 above

➡ The arrays show that multiplication and division are related, because they undo each other.

The relationship between multiplication and division is a strategy or method you can use when you multiply or divide. When you know 4 × 5 = 20, you also know that 20 ÷ 4 = 5.

The Commutative Property is another strategy you can use to multiply. This tells you that when you know 4 × 5 = 20, you also know that 5 × 4 = 20.

You can use the relationship between multiplication and division again to undo 5 × 4 = 20 to find 20 ÷ 5 = 4.

Remember!
The Commutative Property says that changing the order of factors does not change the product.

Guided Instruction

Understand: How to use properties of multiplication to learn facts

> The multiplication table shows all 100 products of two 1-digit numbers. You need to learn all of these facts this year. How can using a property of multiplication help?

The left column and the top row show factors. To find a product of two factors, move across a row and down a column until you reach a box where the row and the column meet. The number in that box is the product of those two factors.

The red row and column show that $7 \times 3 = 21$.

×	0	1	2	3	4	5	6	7	8	9
0	0	0	0	0	0	0	0	0	0	0
1	0	1	2	3	4	5	6	7	8	9
2	0	2	4	6	8	10	12	14	16	18
3	0	3	6	9	12	15	18	21	24	27
4	0	4	8	12	16	20	24	28	32	36
5	0	5	10	15	20	25	30	35	40	45
6	0	6	12	18	24	30	36	42	48	54
7	0	7	14	21	28	35	42	49	56	63
8	0	8	16	24	32	40	48	56	64	72
9	0	9	18	27	36	45	54	63	72	81

The Commutative Property helps you learn two facts at the same time.

Notice that the green row and column show that $3 \times 7 = 21$. For every multiplication fact with two different factors, there is another fact with the order of the factors changed.

×	0	1	2	3	4	5	6	7	8	9
0	0	0	0	0	0	0	0	0	0	0
1	0	1	2	3	4	5	6	7	8	9
2	0	2	4	6	8	10	12	14	16	18
3	0	3	6	9	12	15	18	21	24	27
4	0	4	8	12	16	20	24	28	32	36
5	0	5	10	15	20	25	30	35	40	45
6	0	6	12	18	24	30	36	42	48	54
7	0	7	14	21	28	35	42	49	56	63
8	0	8	16	24	32	40	48	56	64	72
9	0	9	18	27	36	45	54	63	72	81

The Zero Property says that if you multiply any number by 0, the product is 0.

The purple row and column use the Zero Property. The product for all facts that have 0 as a factor is 0.

×	0	1	2	3	4	5	6	7	8	9
0	0	0	0	0	0	0	0	0	0	0
1	0	1	2	3	4	5	6	7	8	9
2	0	2	4	6	8	10	12	14	16	18
3	0	3	6	9	12	15	18	21	24	27
4	0	4	8	12	16	20	24	28	32	36
5	0	5	10	15	20	25	30	35	40	45
6	0	6	12	18	24	30	36	42	48	54
7	0	7	14	21	28	35	42	49	56	63
8	0	8	16	24	32	40	48	56	64	72
9	0	9	18	27	36	45	54	63	72	81

The Identity Property of Multiplication says that if you multiply any number by 1, the product is that number.

The orange row and column use the Identity Property. The product for all facts with 1 as a factor is the other factor itself.

×	0	1	2	3	4	5	6	7	8	9
0	0	0	0	0	0	0	0	0	0	0
1	0	1	2	3	4	5	6	7	8	9
2	0	2	4	6	8	10	12	14	16	18
3	0	3	6	9	12	15	18	21	24	27
4	0	4	8	12	16	20	24	28	32	36
5	0	5	10	15	20	25	30	35	40	45
6	0	6	12	18	24	30	36	42	48	54
7	0	7	14	21	28	35	42	49	56	63
8	0	8	16	24	32	40	48	56	64	72
9	0	9	18	27	36	45	54	63	72	81

➤ Using a property is a strategy that helps save time and work while you learn all the multiplication facts.

Guided Instruction

Connect: Using what you know to multiply and divide within 100

> What are some other strategies you can use for multiplying and dividing within 100?

You can skip count by 2s or by 5s, so you can multiply by 2 or 5.

Look at the red and blue rows and columns. The numbers you see in the red column and row are the numbers you would use to count by 2s: 2, 4, 6, 8, 10, 12, 14, 16, and 18. The numbers you see in the blue column and row are the numbers you would use to count by 5s: 5, 10, 15, 20, 25, 30, 35, 40, and 45.

×	0	1	2	3	4	5	6	7	8	9
0	0	0	0	0	0	0	0	0	0	0
1	0	1	2	3	4	5	6	7	8	9
2	0	2	4	6	8	10	12	14	16	18
3	0	3	6	9	12	15	18	21	24	27
4	0	4	8	12	16	20	24	28	32	36
5	0	5	10	15	20	25	30	35	40	45
6	0	6	12	18	24	30	36	42	48	54
7	0	7	14	21	28	35	42	49	56	63
8	0	8	16	24	32	40	48	56	64	72
9	0	9	18	27	36	45	54	63	72	81

You know that division undoes multiplication. You can use a multiplication table to find quotients. First find the divisor in the top row of factors. Next move down the column until you find the dividend. Then move left to the column of factors. The factor you find is the quotient.

To find $42 \div 7$, go to the 7 in the top row of factors. Move down until you find 42. Then move left to the column of factors where you find 6. $42 \div 7 = 6$

×	0	1	2	3	4	5	6	7	8	9
0	0	0	0	0	0	0	0	0	0	0
1	0	1	2	3	4	5	6	7	8	9
2	0	2	4	6	8	10	12	14	16	18
3	0	3	6	9	12	15	18	21	24	27
4	0	4	8	12	16	20	24	28	32	36
5	0	5	10	15	20	25	30	35	40	45
6	0	6	12	18	24	30	36	42	48	54
7	0	7	14	21	28	35	42	49	56	63
8	0	8	16	24	32	40	48	56	64	72
9	0	9	18	27	36	45	54	63	72	81

You know how to use the Distributive Property to find a product. To find 6×8, start by breaking apart 8.

$6 \times 8 = 6 \times (5 + 3)$ ⟵ Break 8 apart into $5 + 3$.

$\quad\quad\quad = (6 \times 5) + (6 \times 3)$ ⟵ Multiply both addends by 6.

$\quad\quad\quad = 30 + 18$ ⟵ Add the two products.

$\quad\quad\quad = 48$ ⟵ The product of 6×8.

> Using 5 as one of the addends means you will use a 5s fact.

➤ Some strategies for multiplying and dividing are skip counting, undoing multiplication, and using the Distributive Property.

✏ Choose a fact that you are not sure of. Explain a strategy that you can use to learn it.

Guided Practice

Multiply. Use the Zero Property and the Identity Property.

1. $5 \times 0 =$ _____   **2.** $1 \times 9 =$ _____   **3.** $1 \times$ _____ $= 0$

Multiply. Skip count by 2s or 5s to help.

4. $5 \times 7 =$ _____   **5.** $7 \times 2 =$ _____   **6.** $2 \times$ _____ $= 18$

Divide. Write the related multiplication.

7. $28 \div 7 =$ _____   The related multiplication is _____.

8. $36 \div 4 =$ _____   The related multiplication is _____.

9. $56 \div 8 =$ _____   The related multiplication is _____.

10. $81 \div 9 =$ _____   The related multiplication is _____.

Multiply or divide. Use any strategy you like.

11. $1 \times 5 =$ _____   **12.** $3 \times 5 =$ _____   **13.** $5 \times$ _____ $= 25$

14. $\begin{array}{r} 6 \\ \times\ 2 \\ \hline \end{array}$ **15.** $\begin{array}{r} 6 \\ \times\ 0 \\ \hline \end{array}$ **16.** $\begin{array}{r} 6 \\ \times\ 3 \\ \hline \end{array}$

17. $10 \div 2 =$ _____   **18.** $15 \div 3 =$ _____   **19.** $12 \div 3 =$ _____

20. $2\overline{)14}$ **21.** $2\overline{)12}$ **22.** $2\overline{)16}$

᪥ Think•Pair•Share

MP1 **23.** Explain two strategies you can use to find $42 \div 7$.
What is the quotient?

Independent Practice

1. Use the array. Write four related multiplications and divisions.

____ × ____ = ____

____ × ____ = ____

____ ÷ ____ = ____

____ ÷ ____ = ____

2. Which property says that $8 \times 0 = 0$?

a. Associative Property   **b.** Commutative Property

c. Distributive Property   **d.** Zero Property

3. Which property says that $8 \times 9 = 9 \times 8$?

a. Associative Property   **b.** Commutative Property

c. Distributive Property   **d.** Zero Property

Find the product.

4. $1 \times 9 =$ ____   **5.** $9 \times 2 =$ ____

6. $3 \times 9 =$ ____   **7.** $5 \times 9 =$ ____

8. $9 \times 8 =$ ____   **9.** $0 \times 9 =$ ____

10. $9 \times 6 =$ ____   **11.** $9 \times 9 =$ ____

12. Which multiplication could you use to find n?

$$24 \div 3 = n$$

a. $8 \times 3 = 24$ **b.** $6 \times 4 = 24$

c. $4 \times 6 = 24$ **d.** $1 \times 24 = 24$

13. Which division could you use to find n?

$$3 \times n = 12$$

a. $12 \div 1 = 12$ **b.** $12 \div 2 = 6$

c. $12 \div 3 = 4$ **d.** $12 \div 6 = 2$

Independent Practice

Divide. Write the related multiplication.

14. $18 \div 3 =$ _____   The related multiplication is _____.

15. $45 \div 5 =$ _____   The related multiplication is _____.

16. $64 \div 8 =$ _____   The related multiplication is _____.

17. $72 \div 9 =$ _____   The related multiplication is _____.

Find the product.

18. $8 \times 0 =$ _____

19. $5 \times 1 =$ _____

20. $8 \times 6 =$ _____

21. $6 \times 3 =$ _____

22. $9 \times 5 =$ _____

23. $7 \times 6 =$ _____

24. $\begin{array}{r} 4 \\ \times\ 2 \\ \hline \end{array}$

25. $\begin{array}{r} 0 \\ \times\ 6 \\ \hline \end{array}$

26. $\begin{array}{r} 4 \\ \times\ 4 \\ \hline \end{array}$

27. $\begin{array}{r} 8 \\ \times\ 7 \\ \hline \end{array}$

28. $\begin{array}{r} 7 \\ \times\ 1 \\ \hline \end{array}$

29. $\begin{array}{r} 2 \\ \times\ 5 \\ \hline \end{array}$

Find the quotient.

30. $24 \div 6 =$ _____

31. $35 \div 7 =$ _____

32. $42 \div 6 =$ _____

33. $63 \div 7 =$ _____

34. $45 \div 9 =$ _____

35. $48 \div 8 =$ _____

36. $3\overline{)12}$

37. $2\overline{)8}$

38. $1\overline{)9}$

39. $3\overline{)21}$

40. $6\overline{)54}$

41. $8\overline{)56}$

Independent Practice

MP6 **42.** Tell how you would find m. Then solve.
$$m = 7 \times 9$$

Answer _____ $= 7 \times 9$

MP7 **43.** Marcus knows that $2 \times 7 = 14$. How can he use that fact to find the answer to 4×7?

Answer $4 \times 7 =$ _____

MP8 **44.** Simone knows that 8 groups of 6 make 48. How can she find $48 \div 6$?

Answer $48 \div 6 =$ _____

Solve the problems.

MP2 **45.** The school band has 9 rows, with 9 students in each row. How many students are in the band?

⬛▶ **Show your work.**

Answer _____

Independent Practice

MP1 46. For a long camping trip, the Rubio family packed 42 apples. Mr. and Mrs. Rubio and their four children will each eat one apple a day. How many days will it take the Rubio family to eat all the apples?

➡ **Show your work.**

Answer _____

MP7 47. Rey says that for the equation 472 =? × 472, the unknown is 1. Is he correct?

Answer _____

➡ **Justify your answer using words, drawings, or numbers.**

MP3 48. Chiyo knows that 2 × 8 = 16. She uses this fact to find that 16 = 8 ÷ 2. Is her answer correct? Explain your thinking.

Answer _____

➡ **Justify your answer using words, drawings, or numbers.**

Problem Solving:
Two-Step Problems

Essential Question:
How can you use two steps to solve a problem?

Words to Know:
operations
estimation
compatible numbers

Guided Instruction

In this lesson you will learn how to solve word problems with two steps.

Understand: Solving a two-step word problem

> The Maroni family bought 3 lunches for $5 each and 1 lunch for $7. How much did the lunches cost in all?

Read to find the information and the question.

> 3 lunches cost $5 each and 1 lunch cost $7.
> What is the cost of all the lunches?

Plan how to find the answer.

Draw a diagram to represent the problem.

Total cost of the lunches			
$5	$5	$5	$7

You can use the diagram and two operations to find the total cost.

> First find the cost of the three $5 lunches. Multiply. $\leftarrow 3 \times \$5$
> Then add the cost of the $7 lunch. $\leftarrow + \$7$

Solve the problem.

> $3 \times \$5 = \$15$
> $\$15 + \$7 = \$22$

> You use two steps to find the answer, so this is a two-step word problem.

➡ The lunches cost $22 in all.

Check your work. Make sure your solution answers the question in the problem.

You can work backward to check whether the answer is reasonable.

Start at the end and work back to the beginning.

> $\$22 - (\$7 + \$5 + \$5 + \$5)$ should equal 0.
> $\$22 - \$22 = 0$

The check shows that the answer is reasonable.

Guided Instruction

Understand: Checking that an answer is reasonable

> Greenmount School has 627 students. One day, 48 students are absent. Another 103 students are on a field trip. How many students are at the school that day?

First read to find the information you will need to solve the problem. Ask the question in your own words.

> The school has 627 students. 48 are absent. 103 are on a field trip. How many students are at the school?

Next plan what you will do and how you will find the answer.

Use a diagram to represent the problem.

Find the number of students that are not at the school. Add. ← 48 + 103
Then subtract the sum from 627. ← 627 − (48 + 103)

627 students		
_____ absent	103 on trip	?

Write an equation. Let ■ be the number of students at the school. Solve to find the answer.

$$■ = 627 − (48 + 103)$$

$$■ = 627 − \_\_\_\_\_$$

$$■ = 476$$

➡ There are _____ students at the school that day.

Check your work. Use estimation with compatible numbers, to see whether the answer makes sense. Compatible numbers are numbers that are easy to add and subtract.

Estimate: 627 − (48 + 103) should be close to

$$600 − (50 + 100) = 600 − 150 = 450$$

> 627 is close to 600.
> 48 is close to 50.
> 103 is close to 100.

Compare the answer and the estimate.

476 is close to 450, so the answer _____ sense.

Guided Instruction

Connect: Why checking your answer is important when solving a problem

> Kimi made 20 popcorn balls for a party. She ate 2 popcorn balls and put the rest in bags of 3 each. How many bags of popcorn balls does Kimi have?

Step 1

Read to find what the problem is asking. Then find the information you need.

Kimi made ____ popcorn balls.

Kimi ate ____ popcorn balls.

Kimi put the rest in bags of ____ each.

How many _____ does she have?

Step 2

Plan how to use two steps to find the answer.

First find the number of popcorn balls Kimi put into bags of 3 each. Draw a diagram.

Then find the number of bags.

20 popcorn balls	
ate 2	? left to put in bags of 3

Step 3

Solve the problem.

$20 - 2 =$ ____

$18 \div 3 =$ ____

➡ Kimi has ____ bags of popcorn balls.

Step 4

Explain how to check your answer.

1. Riley has 9 crayons. Terrell has twice as many crayons as Riley. How many crayons do they have in all?

   a. Read to understand. What is the question?

   _____

   b. Explain how you plan to solve the problem.

   _____

   c. Then solve to find the answer.

   Riley and Terrell have _____ crayons in all.

   d. Check to show that your answer makes sense. Explain your reasoning.

ᵚᵂ Think•Pair•Share

MP1 2. Write a two-step word problem. Then find the answer. Check that your answer is reasonable.

Independent Practice

Follow the steps to solve the problems.

MP4 **1.** On a vacation, the Jones family travels 722 miles in three days.
They travel 328 miles the first day and 115 miles the second day.
How many miles do they travel on the third day?

  a. Read. What information is in the problem?

  b. Plan. What will you do?

  c. Solve. What is your answer?

> Remember to label your answer.

  Answer The family traveled _____ on the third day.

  d. Check. Explain why your answer is reasonable.

MP1 **2.** Taylor has 4 packages of stickers. Each package has 10 stickers in it.
Leah has 14 fewer stickers than Taylor. How many stickers does
Leah have?

  a. Read. Underline the information you need.

  b. Plan. What will you do?

  c. Solve. What is your answer?

  Answer Leah has _____ stickers.

  d. Check. Explain why your answer is reasonable.

Independent Practice

MP2 **3.** At a basketball tournament, each of the 8 teams has 9 players and a coach. There are 100 bottles of water. How many bottles of water are left over after each player and coach get 1 bottle?

   a. Read to find the information in the problem.

   b. Plan what you will do.

   c. Solve to find the answer.

> What label will you use for your answer?

   Answer There will be _____ of water left over.

   d. Explain why your answer makes sense.

MP1 **4.** Mikhail has 48 stamps. His uncle gives him 15 more. The pages in his small stamp book have spaces for 9 stamps. How many pages can he fill with the stamps he has now?

   a. As you read, underline the information you need.

   b. What is your plan?

   c. Solve to answer the question.

   Answer Mikhail can fill _____ with his stamps.

   d. Explain why your answer is reasonable.

Independent Practice

MP2　**5.** Trane has 145 marbles. He gives 20 to Katie, 52 to Gwen, and 31 to Yusef. He keeps the rest. Who has the most marbles?

    a. Trane

    b. Katie

    c. Gwen

    d. Yusef

Solve the problems. Check that your answer is reasonable.

MP4　**6.** Erica planted 9 zinnias each in 2 big pots. She planted another 49 zinnias, one in each small pot. How many zinnias did she plant in all?

    ▭▶ **Show your work.**

Answer _____

MP6　**7.** For the school play, most of the chairs are in rows of 10 each, with one row of 8 chairs. If there are 78 chairs altogether, how many rows are there?

    ▭▶ **Show your work.**

Answer _____

MP3 **8.** Mr. Cook bakes 6 pans of fruit bars for a bake sale. He cuts each pan into 9 bars. He eats one bar and wraps 5 to go in his freezer. He puts the rest in a box to take to the bake sale. How many fruit bars does Mr. Cook take to the bake sale?

✏ **Show your work.**

Answer _____

MP1 **9.** When Sean adds 202 + 124 + 192, he finds that the sum is 518. To check his work, he estimates that the sum is about 600. He sees that his estimate does not agree with his answer. Which is correct, Sean's answer or his estimate?

Answer _____

✏ **Justify your answer using words, drawings, or numbers.**

MP3 **10.** Farah and her aunt are making 3 batches of jam. Each batch makes 7 jars of jam. To be sure there are enough jars, Farah's aunt wants to have 2 extra jars ready for each batch. How many jars does Farah need to get ready for the 3 batches?

✏ **Show your work.**

Answer _____

Problem Solving: Use Equations

Essential Question:
How can you use
an equation to solve
a problem?

Guided Instruction

In this lesson you will learn how to write an equation to represent a word problem.

Understand: Writing an equation for a two-step word problem

Reid buys a box of crayons for 75¢ and 3 stickers for 8¢ each. What is the total cost of these items?

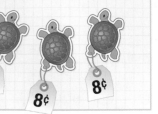

Read to find the information and the question.

> The crayons cost 75¢ and the stickers each cost 8¢.
> What is the total cost of the items?

Plan how to find the answer. Write an equation.

> total cost of items = cost of crayons + cost of stickers ← Start with words.
> t =   75¢   + (3 × 8¢) ← Represent the words.

Solve the equation to find the total cost.

> $t = 75¢ + (3 × 8¢)$
> $t = 75¢ + 24¢$ ← Multiply 3 × 8.
> $t = 99¢$ ← Add 75 + 24.

➤ The total cost of the items is 99¢.

Estimate to check your answer.

> 75¢ is close to 80¢.
> 8¢ + 8¢ + 8¢ is 24¢, which is close to 20¢.
> 80¢ + 20¢ = 100¢.

Comparing 100¢ and 99¢ shows that the estimate and the answer are very close to each other.

This means that 99¢ is a reasonable answer.

Guided Instruction

Understand: Using diagrams in solving two-step word problems

> Sabrena bikes 3 miles a day. Her goal is to bike 25 miles. After 6 days, how many more miles must Sabrena bike to meet her goal?

After you read, describe the problem in words.

> number of miles more
> equals 25 miles minus 6 days times 3 miles a day

Use the words to write an equation.

Represent the words with numbers and symbols.

$m = 25 - (6 \times 3)$ ← Use *m* to represent the number of miles more

Solve the equation to find the answer.

$m = 25 - (6 \times 3)$

$m = 25 - 18$ ← Multiply 6×3.

$m = 7$ ← Subtract: $25 - 18$.

➡ Sabrena must bike _____ more miles to meet her goal.

Draw a number line to check your answer.

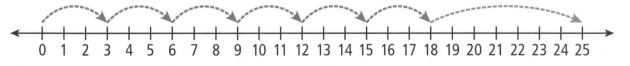

6 times 3 equals 18, and 18 plus 7 equals 25.

✏ Look at the problem. Find another way to solve it.

Guided Instruction

Connect: **Using a diagram and writing an equation**

> The 68 rocks in John's rock collection are stored in 5 boxes. Four small boxes hold 8 rocks each. The fifth box is larger and holds the rest of the rocks. How many rocks are in the fifth box?

Step 1

Read the problem again and underline the information you need.

Step 2

Draw a diagram to help plan your work.

| 68 | | | | | ← number of rocks in all |

4 boxes of 8 rocks → | 8 | 8 | 8 | 8 | *r* | ← number of rocks in larger box

The diagram shows how you can write an equation.

number of rocks in larger box = number of rocks in all − 4 boxes of 8 rocks

r = 68 − (4 × 8)

Step 3

Solve the equation to find the answer.

$r = 68 - (4 \times 8)$

$r = 68 - \underline{}$

$r = \underline{}$

➡ There are _____ in the fifth box.

> What label should you use for your answer?

Step 4

Check that your answer is reasonable.

Estimate. 68 is close to ___. 8 is close to 10, and 4 × 10 = ___.

70 − 40 = ___
Compare 30 and 36.
36 is close to 30, so 36 is a _____ answer.

1. The Durands are driving 900 miles to visit their cousins. The first day they drive 385 miles. The second day they drive 319 miles. How many miles do they have left to drive?

   a. Read the problem again. Underline information and the question.

   b. Explain how you plan to solve the problem.

   _____

   c. Solve to find the answer.

   d. Explain how you can check to show that your answer makes sense.

   Answer The Durands have _____ left to drive.

⚊⚊ **Think•Pair•Share**

MP7 **2.** One way to solve a two-step problem is to find and solve the two one-step problems that are inside the two-step problem. Look at problem 1. Explain what the two one-step problems are and solve them. Compare your answer with your answer to problem 1.

Independent Practice

Circle the letter of the correct answer.

1. Xavier shoots 75 baskets on Monday and 110 baskets on Tuesday. His goal is to shoot a total of 500 baskets by the end of the week. How many baskets does he have left to shoot?

   Which equation could you use to solve this problem?

   a. $75 + 110 = b + 500$

   b. $110 - 75 + b = 500$

   c. $75 + 100 - b = 500$

   d. $75 + 110 + b = 500$

2. In Natalie's class, August has 3 times as many birthdays as February. September has 2 fewer birthdays than August. There are 4 birthdays in February. How many birthdays are in September?

   Which equation could you use to solve this problem?

   a. $3 \times 4 = s$

   b. $(3 \times 4) - 2 = s$

   c. $(3 \times 4) + 2 = s$

   d. $3 \times 4 \times 2 = s$

3. Taren bikes 2 miles to school each day, and 2 miles back home. How many miles does Taren bike in 5 days?

   Which equation could you use to solve this problem?

   a. $5 \times (2 + 2) = t$

   b. $5 \times (2 - 2) = t$

   c. $2 + (2 \times t) = 5$

   d. $2 + 5 + t = 10$

Independent Practice

As you read each problem, underline information you need. Follow the steps to solve. Show your work.

MP2 **4.** Jia-li needs 32 trading cards to fill her album. Each of 4 friends gives her 6 cards. How many more cards does Jia-li need?

a. What information helps you write an equation?

_____

b. Write and solve an equation.

c. Check your answer. Does it make sense? Explain.

Answer Jia-li needs ____ more cards.

MP1 **5.** Five hundred seventy-nine students are at school today. Three hundred fifteen students rode the bus, ninety-four rode to school in a car, and the rest walked to school. How many students walked to school today?

a. What information can you use to write an equation?

b. Write and solve an equation to find the answer.

c. Check to show that your answer is reasonable.

Answer Today, ____ students walked to school.

Independent Practice

Write an equation to solve. Tell how you checked your answer.

MP4 **6.** A delivery truck was carrying 136 packages. At the next stop, 25 packages were dropped off and 13 packages were picked up. How many packages did the truck carry then?

✏️➤ **Show your work.**

Answer The truck carried _____ after the stop.

MP6 **7.** Ana filled 9 baskets with blueberries at the farm. Jeremiah filled three times as many baskets as Ana. How many baskets of blueberries did they fill together?

✏️➤ **Show your work.**

Answer Jeremiah and Ana together filled _____ with blueberries.

Independent Practice

MP5 **8.** For a food drive, Jack collected 3 cans of food from each of 8 neighbors. His goal is 30 cans of food. How many more cans does he need?

✏️ **Show your work.**

Answer Jack needs ____ more cans of food.

MP7 **9.** Lillian is shopping for a bicycle. The red bike costs $79 more than the blue bike. The blue bike costs $18 less than the yellow bike. The yellow bike costs $125. How much does the red bike cost?

✏️ **Show your work.**

Answer The red bike costs _____.

Identify and Explain Arithmetic Patterns

Essential Question:
How can you identify and explain arithmetic patterns?

Words to Know:
pattern
odd
even
rule

Guided Instruction

In this lesson you will work with arithmetic patterns, including patterns in the multiplication and addition tables.

Understand: Patterns in the multiplication table

Look at the multiplication table.
What patterns do you see?

×	0	1	2	3	4	5	6	7	8	9
0	0	0	0	0	0	0	0	0	0	0
1	0	1	2	3	4	5	6	7	8	9
2	0	2	4	6	8	10	12	14	16	18
3	0	3	6	9	12	15	18	21	24	27
4	0	4	8	12	16	20	24	28	32	36
5	0	5	10	15	20	25	30	35	40	45
6	0	6	12	18	24	30	36	42	48	54
7	0	7	14	21	28	35	42	49	56	63
8	0	8	16	24	32	40	48	56	64	72
9	0	9	18	27	36	45	54	63	72	81

Remember that the numbers in the blue boxes at the top and the left are factors. Use them to identify a row or a column.

Look at the 1 column and the 1 row. The numbers are the same. Every column has a matching row with the same numbers. This is just one pattern that you can see in the multiplication table.

Look at the 3 row. The difference between 2 numbers next to each other in that row is 3. Notice that 3 is the factor for that row. This kind of pattern is true for all rows.

Look at the 6 column. The difference between 2 numbers above and below each other in that column is 6. Notice that 6 is the factor for that column. This kind of pattern is true for all columns.

Look at the 7 row. Start with the 1 column. The product 7 × 1 is odd. An odd number always has one left over when broken into equal addends. Look at the 2 column. The product 7 × 2 is even. An even number can be broken down into two equal addends. This pattern continues across the row.

➡ There are many number patterns in the multiplication table.

✏ Find another pattern in the multiplication table.

Guided Instruction

Understand: Patterns in the addition table

Look at the addition table.
What patterns do you see?

+	0	1	2	3	4	5	6	7	8	9
0	0	1	2	3	4	5	6	7	8	9
1	1	2	3	4	5	6	7	8	9	10
2	2	3	4	5	6	7	8	9	10	11
3	3	4	5	6	7	8	9	10	11	12
4	4	5	6	7	8	9	10	11	12	13
5	5	6	7	8	9	10	11	12	13	14
6	6	7	8	9	10	11	12	13	14	15
7	7	8	9	10	11	12	13	14	15	16
8	8	9	10	11	12	13	14	15	16	17
9	9	10	11	12	13	14	15	16	17	18

The numbers in the green boxes at the top and the left are addends. Use them to identify a row or a column.

Look at the 1 column and the 1 row. The numbers are the same. Every column has a matching row.

Look at the 3 row. Each number is ____ greater than the one before it. This pattern is true for all rows and columns.

Look at the 6 column. Each number is 1 _____ than the one after it. This pattern is true for all rows and columns.

Look at the 7 row. The first number is _____, the next one is

_____, and this pattern continues across the row. You can find this pattern in any row or column with an odd addend.

➡ There are many number patterns in the addition table.

✏➤ Find another pattern in the addition table.

Understand: Rules for patterns

Look at the 6 row. What pattern do you see? Describe its rule.

A rule for a pattern tells what number to start with and how to find the next number in the pattern.

The pattern in the 6 row shows that the row starts with 6, and each number is 1 more than the one before it.

➡ The pattern rule is: Start with 6. Add 1.

Guided Instruction

Connect: Patterns and multiplying by 9

Some students think that learning the facts for the 9s multiplications is difficult. How can using patterns make it easier to learn the 9s facts?

Complete this table to look for patterns in the 9s multiplications.

9s fact	Sum of the digits in the product	Digit in tens place in the product	Digit in ones place in the product
9 × 1 = 09	0 + 9 = 9	0	9
9 × 2 = 18	1 + 8 = 9	1	8
9 × 3 = 27	2 + 7 = ____	2	7
9 × 4 = 36	3 + 6 = ____		
9 × 5 = 45	4 + 5 = ____		
9 × 6 = 54			
9 × 7 = 63			
9 × 8 = 72			
9 × 9 = 81			

The sum of the digits in the products for all the 9s facts is ____.

The pattern of the digits in the tens place for the 9s facts is that the

digits increase by ____ for each multiplication.

The pattern of the digits in the ones place for the 9s is that the digits

are 1 _____ for each multiplication.

For any 9s fact, the digit in the _____ place is 1 less than the factor you multiply by 9.

➡ The patterns in the 9s multiplications show relationships that make them easier to remember.

✏ Explain how you can use these patterns to find 9 × 7.

Guided Practice

Use the addition table for exercises 1–4.

1. Complete the addition table.

+	0	1	2	3	4	5	6	7	8	9
0	0	1	2	3	4	5	6	7		
1	1	2	3	4	5	6	7	8		
2	2	3	4	5	6	7	8	9		
3	3	4	5	6	7	8	9	10		
4	4	5	6	7	8	9	10	11		
5	5	6	7	8	9	10	11	12		
6										
7										
8										
9										

2. Describe two patterns you see in the addition table.

3. How can you use the addition table to find the sum of 5 + 9 two different ways?

4. Look at the row and column for 0. What can you say about the sum of any number and 0? Explain.

ᐁᐁ Think•Pair•Share

MP7 5. The house numbers on the south side of East Street form a pattern. Write the next three house numbers. Explain how you decided on the next three house numbers.

| 4 | 8 | 12 | 16 | | | |

Independent Practice

1. Complete the multiplication table for factors to 10.

×	0	1	2	3	4	5	6	7	8	9	10
0	0	0	0	0	0	0	0	0	0	0	
1	0	1	2	3	4	5	6	7	8	9	
2	0	2	4	6	8	10	12	14	16	18	
3	0	3	6	9	12	15	18	21	24	27	
4	0	4	8	12	16	20	24	28	32	36	
5	0	5	10	15	20	25	30	35	40	45	
6	0	6	12	18	24	30	36	42	48	54	
7	0	7	14	21	28	35	42	49	56	63	
8	0	8	16	24	32	40	48	56	64	72	
9	0	9	18	27	36	45	54	63	72	81	
10											

MP7 2. What pattern do you see in the 10 row and the 10 column? Describe the pattern. Then name the pattern rule.

Rule: _____

Multiply. Then draw lines to match each pair of products.

3. $4 \times 9 =$ ____

4. $5 \times 7 =$ ____

5. $1 \times 8 =$ ____

6. $3 \times 6 =$ ____

a. $8 \times 1 =$ ____

b. $6 \times 3 =$ ____

c. $7 \times 5 =$ ____

d. $9 \times 0 =$ ____

e. $9 \times 4 =$ ____

MP8 7. Use exercises 3–6. What do you notice about each pair of products? What property of multiplication does this show?

Independent Practice

Use the multiplication table for exercises 8–11.

8. Complete the multiplication table for the factors 3 and 9.

×	0	1	2	3	4	5	6	7	8	9
0	0	0	0		0	0	0	0	0	
1	0	1	2		4	5	6	7	8	
2	0	2	4		8	10	12	14	16	
3										
4	0	4	8		16	20	24	28	32	
5	0	5	10		20	25	30	35	40	
6	0	6	12		24	30	36	42	48	
7	0	7	14		28	35	42	49	56	
8	0	8	16		32	40	48	56	64	
9										

9. Use the multiplication table or skip-counting to find each product.

$0 \times 3 =$ _____ $6 \times 3 =$ _____ $0 \times 9 =$ _____ $6 \times 9 =$ _____

$1 \times 3 =$ _____ $7 \times 3 =$ _____ $1 \times 9 =$ _____ $7 \times 9 =$ _____

$2 \times 3 =$ _____ $8 \times 3 =$ _____ $2 \times 9 =$ _____ $8 \times 9 =$ _____

$3 \times 3 =$ _____ $9 \times 3 =$ _____ $3 \times 9 =$ _____ $9 \times 9 =$ _____

$4 \times 3 =$ _____ $10 \times 3 =$ _____ $4 \times 9 =$ _____ $10 \times 9 =$ _____

$5 \times 3 =$ _____ $5 \times 9 =$ _____

MP7 10. What patterns do you see for the products of 3 and the factors 0–9?

MP8 11. What patterns do you see for the products of 9 and the factors 0–9?

Independent Practice

Complete the pattern. Then name the pattern rule.

12. 7, 14, 21, ____, ____, ____, ____

Rule: _____

13. 8, 16, 24, ____, ____, ____, ____

Rule: _____

14. 42, 36, 30, ____, ____, ____, ____

Rule: _____

MP8 **15.** Jean says that the product of two odd numbers is always odd. Is Jean's statement correct?

✏️ **Complete parts a, b, and c to show your work.**

a. Find the product of two odd numbers: 3 × 5.

b. Break apart the product into two addends. Can you break apart the product into two equal addends?

c. Find the products of other pairs of odd numbers. Can you break them apart into two equal addends?

Answer  _____

Circle the correct answer.

MP6 **16.** Which statement explains why 6 times a number is always even?

    a. You can break apart the product into three equal addends.

    b. You can break apart the product into two equal addends.

    c. You cannot break apart the product into three equal addends.

    d. You cannot break apart the product into two equal addends.

Independent Practice

Solve the problems.

MP7 **17.** Mrs. Gonzalez puts whole-wheat rolls on racks to cool. She puts 12 rolls on the first rack, 18 rolls on the second rack, 24 rolls on the third rack, 30 rolls on the fourth rack, and 36 rolls on the fifth rack. If the pattern continues, how many rolls will Mrs. Gonzalez put on the sixth rack?

✏️ **Show your work.**

Answer _____

MP3 **18.** Addison uses the multiplication table to find the product of an even number and any other number. He says that sometimes the product is even and sometimes the product is odd. What mistake might Addison have made?

Answer _____

✏️ **Justify your answer using words, drawings, or numbers.**

MP8 **19.** Kwan says that the product of 9 times an odd number is always odd. Is Kwan's statement correct?

Answer _____

✏️ **Justify your answer using words, drawings, or numbers.**

13 Round Whole Numbers to the Nearest 10 or 100

Essential Question:
How can you round whole numbers?

Words to Know:
round

Guided Instruction

In this lesson you will round whole numbers to the nearest 10 or 100.

Understand: **Rounding two-digit numbers to the nearest 10**

> There are 38 third graders at recess. There are 54 fourth graders at recess. About how many students from both grades are at recess?

You can estimate to solve this problem. The word *about* in the question shows that an exact answer is not needed.

One way to estimate is to round numbers before you calculate an answer. Rounding a 2-digit number to the nearest 10 gives a number with 0 in the ones place.

> A 10 is a number you count when you skip count by 10. The 10s are 10, 20, 30 40, 50, 60, 70, 80, and 90.

Locate 38 and 54 on the number line.

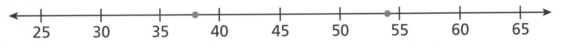

The number line shows which 10 each number is closest to.

38 is closer to 40 than to 30.
38 rounds to 40.

54 is closer to 50 than to 60.
54 rounds to 50.

Now add 40 + 50 to estimate the answer: 40 + 50 = 90.

➡ About 90 students from both grades are at recess.

You can use these rules to round two-digit numbers.

> If the ones digit is 1, 2, 3, or 4, round to the lesser 10.
> If the ones digit is 5 or greater, round to the greater 10.

To round 68 using the rules, think:

> 68 is between 60 and 70. The ones digit is 8, so round to the greater 10. 68 rounds to 70.

Guided Instruction

Understand: Rounding three-digit numbers to the nearest 100

> Mr. Klein's class counted birds for a science project. They counted 126 blue jays, and 271 robins. To the nearest 100, estimate how many birds the class counted?

The problem asks you to estimate to the nearest 100, so you need to round each number to the nearest 100. This gives numbers with 0 in both the ones place and the tens place.

You can use a number line to round the numbers to the nearest 100.

> A 100 is a number you count when you skip count by 100. The 100s are 100, 200, 300, 400, 500, 600, 700, 800, and 900.

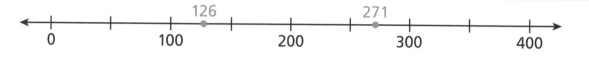

Round each number to the nearest 100.

126 is closer to 100 than 200.
126 rounds to 100.

271 is closer to 300 than to 200.
271 rounds to 300.

Now add 100 + 300 to estimate the answer.

100 + 300 = _____ ← You can use mental math.

➡ Mr. Klein's class counted about 400 birds.

You can use these rules to round three-digit numbers.

If the tens digit is 1, 2, 3, or 4, round to the lesser 100.
If the tens digit is 5 or greater, round to the greater 100.

To round 325 using the rules, think:

325 is between 300 and 400.
The tens digit is 2, so round to the lesser 100.

325 rounds to _____.

✏ Why does rounding let you use mental math to make an estimate?

Guided Instruction

Connect: Rounding a three-digit number to the nearest 10

Some friends made a table of the number of jumping jacks they did last week. They want to round to the nearest 10 to estimate how many jumping jacks they did in all. About how many jumping jacks is that?

Our Jumping Jacks	
Marta	125
Liz	152
Kate	136

One way to round to the nearest 10 is to use a number line. Locate the numbers from the problem on the number line.

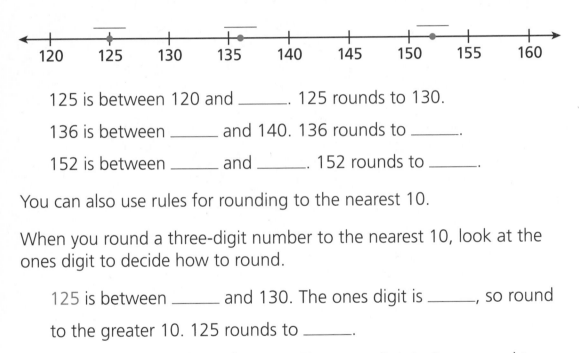

125 is between 120 and _____. 125 rounds to 130.

136 is between _____ and 140. 136 rounds to _____.

152 is between _____ and _____. 152 rounds to _____.

You can also use rules for rounding to the nearest 10.

When you round a three-digit number to the nearest 10, look at the ones digit to decide how to round.

125 is between _____ and 130. The ones digit is _____, so round to the greater 10. 125 rounds to _____.

136 is between 130 and _____. The ones digit is 6, so round to the _____ 10. 136 rounds to _____.

152 is between _____ and _____. The ones digit is _____, so round to the _____ 10. 152 rounds to _____.

To solve the problem, add. 130 + 140 + 150 = _____

➡ The friends did about _____ jumping jacks in all.

Guided Practice

Round to the nearest 10.

1. 18 _____
2. 25 _____
3. 49 _____
4. 99 _____
5. 7 _____
6. 5 _____
7. 3 _____
8. 64 _____
9. 65 _____
10. 12 _____
11. 55 _____
12. 88 _____
13. 137 _____
14. 272 _____
15. 398 _____

Round to the nearest 100.

16. 373 _____
17. 105 _____
18. 624 _____
19. 99 _____
20. 650 _____
21. 575 _____
22. 50 _____
23. 409 _____
24. 14 _____
25. 220 _____
26. 468 _____
27. 813 _____

Think•Pair•Share

MP3 **28.** Ismael says that 85 rounds to 100. Gabriella says that 85 rounds to 90. Explain why both students' answers could be correct.

Independent Practice

Use the chart for questions 1–14.

0	1	2	3	4	5	6	7	8	9	10
10	11	12	13	14	15	16	17	18	19	20
20	21	22	23	24	25	26	27	28	29	30
30	31	32	33	34	35	36	37	38	39	40
40	41	42	43	44	45	46	47	48	49	50
50	51	52	53	54	55	56	57	58	59	60
60	61	62	63	64	65	66	67	68	69	70
70	71	72	73	74	75	76	77	78	79	80
80	81	82	83	84	85	86	87	88	89	90
90	91	92	93	94	95	96	97	98	99	100

1. Use a marker or crayon. Lightly shade all the numbers that round to the greater 10.

2. Complete the rules for rounding two-digit numbers. Write **lesser** or **greater**.

   Rules for Rounding Two-Digit Numbers

   a. If a number has a 1, 2, 3, or 4 in the ones place, round to the

      _____ 10.

   b. If a number has a 5, 6, 7, 8, or 9 in the ones place, round to

      the _____ 10.

Round to the nearest 10.

3. 6 _____   4. 32 _____   5. 78 _____

6. 37 _____   7. 15 _____   8. 8 _____

9. 84 _____   10. 63 _____   11. 1 _____

12. 56 _____   13. 95 _____   14. 49 _____

15. 557 _____   16. 243 _____   17. 185 _____

Independent Practice

18. Complete the rules for rounding three-digit numbers. Write **lesser** or **greater**.

Rules for Rounding Three-Digit Numbers

a. If a number has a 1, 2, 3, or 4 in the tens place, round to the

_____ 100.

b. If a number has a 5, 6, 7, 8, or 9 in the tens place, round to the

_____ 100.

Round to the nearest 100.

19. 702 _____

20. 425 _____

21. 241 _____

22. 329 _____

23. 650 _____

24. 889 _____

25. 855 _____

26. 174 _____

27. 817 _____

28. 438 _____

29. 499 _____

30. 977 _____

Round to the nearest 10 and the nearest 100.

200   250   300   350   400   450   500   550   600   650   700

31. 422 nearest 10 _____

nearest 100 _____

32. 672 nearest 10 _____

nearest 100 _____

33. 259 nearest 10 _____

nearest 100 _____

34. 475 nearest 10 _____

nearest 100 _____

35. 272 nearest 10 _____

nearest 100 _____

36. 650 nearest 10 _____

nearest 100 _____

37. 495 nearest 10 _____

nearest 100 _____

38. 302 nearest 10 _____

nearest 100 _____

Independent Practice

Solve the problems.

MP1 **39.** Janine walks several days each week. If she walked 35 miles in April and 42 miles in May, about how far did she walk in all? Estimate.

▰▶ **Show your work.**

Answer _____

MP8 **40.** Tamika is making a list of animals she has seen. Her list has 27 birds, 13 reptiles, and 42 mammals. About how many animals has she seen?

▰▶ **Show your work.**

Answer _____

MP6 **41.** Len buys and sells posters. At the beginning of the year, he had 63 posters. He bought 29 posters and sold 37 posters. About how many posters does he have now?

▰▶ **Show your work.**

Answer _____

Independent Practice

MP6 **42.** Ms. Asato's class raised $322 in autumn and $569 in winter for a charity. About how much money did the class raise in all?

 **Show your work.**

Answer _____

MP3 **43.** Jonas rounded 249 to the nearest ten and said it was 250. He rounded 249 to the nearest hundred and said it was 300. Was this correct?

Answer _____

Justify your answer using words, drawings, or numbers.

MP1 **44.** Mrs. Moore drives 161 miles on Friday and 179 miles on Saturday. To estimate how far she drove, first she estimated to the nearest 10 before finding the total. Then she estimated to the nearest 100 before finding the total. Which method gives the closer estimate?

Answer _____

Justify your answer using words, drawings, or numbers.

Add and Subtract Fluently within 1,000

Essential Question:
How can you add and
subtract within 1,000?

Words to Know:
Associative Property
of Addition
Commutative Property
of Addition

Guided Instruction

In this lesson you will use strategies to add and subtract within 1,000.

Understand: Using place-value methods to add and subtract

> At the school fair, the students bought 172 veggie burgers and 265 hamburgers. How many burgers did the students buy in all? How many more hamburgers than veggie burgers did the students buy?

To find how many burgers in all, add $172 + 265$. Two strategies are: adding in each place first and using expanded form.

Add in Each Place First

```
  172
+ 265
  300  ← Add the hundreds.
  130  ← Add the tens.
    7  ← Add the ones.
  437  ← Add everything.
```

Use Expanded Form

```
  172 → 100 +  70 + 2
+ 265 → 200 +  60 + 5
        300 + 130 + 7  ← Add each place.

              430 + 7  ← Add 100s and 10s.

                  437  ← Add on the ones.
```

➡ The students bought 437 burgers in all.

To find how many more hamburgers than veggie burgers the students buy, you subtract. Two strategies are to ungroup first and to use expanded form.

Ungroup First

```
   1 16
   2 6̸ 5  ← Ungroup hundreds
 − 1 7 2     and tens.
      9 3
```

Use Expanded Form

```
  265 → 200 +  60 + 5 →   100 + 160 + 5
− 172 → 100 +  70 + 2 → − 100 +  70 + 2
                                 90 + 3

                                    93
```

➡ The students buy 93 more hamburgers than veggie burgers.

Guided Instruction

Understand: Using properties of addition to find sums

A strategy for finding sums is to use properties of addition.

When you add, changing the grouping of addends does not change the sum. This property is called the Associative Property of Addition.

When you add, changing the order of addends does not change the sum. This property is called the Commutative Property of Addition.

Find the sum of 57 and 94.

$57 + 94$
$(50 + 7) + (90 + 4)$ ← Decompose into 10s and 1s.
$50 + (7 + 90) + 4$ ← Use the Associative Property to change the grouping.
$50 + (90 + 7) + 4$ ← Use the Commutative Property to change the order.
$(50 + 90) + (7 + 4)$ ← Use the Associative Property to change the grouping.

$140 \quad + \quad 11$ ← Add the 10s. Add the 1s.

151 ← Add to find the sum.

➡ The sum of 57 and 94 is 151.

> When you can add and subtract quickly and accurately, you can use both of these strategies to calculate mentally.

Understand: Adding on to subtract

You can add on to subtract because of the relationship between addition and subtraction.

Find $179 - 37$.

37 ← Start with the number being subtracted.
$37 + \quad 3 = 40$ ← Add on to go to the next 10.
$40 + \quad 60 = 100$ ← Add on to go to the next 100.
$100 + \underline{\quad 79} = 179$ ← Add on to go to the number being subtracted from.
$\qquad 142$ ← The sum of the add-ons is the difference.

➡ The difference $179 - 37$ is 142.

Guided Instruction

Connect: Add and subtract three-digit numbers

The school librarian bought 473 books this year. He bought 419 books last year. How many books did the librarian buy in all? How many more books did he buy this year?

To answer the first question, you can add.

Find the sum.   473 + 419 = ■

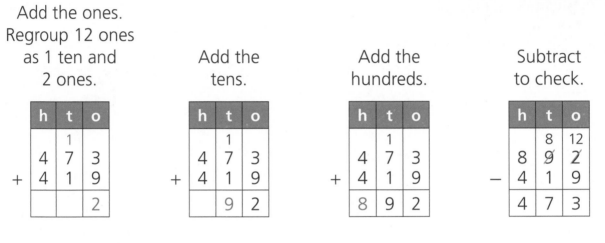

Add the ones. Regroup 12 ones as 1 ten and 2 ones.   Add the tens.   Add the hundreds.   Subtract to check.

➡ The librarian bought ____ books in all.

To answer the second question, you can subtract.

Find the difference: 473 − 419 = ■.

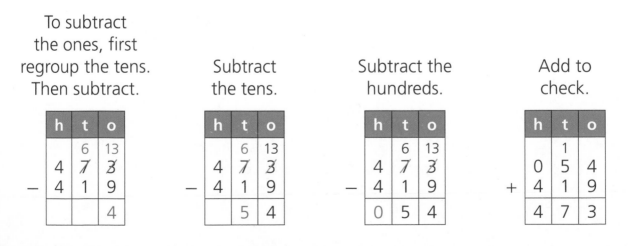

To subtract the ones, first regroup the tens. Then subtract.   Subtract the tens.   Subtract the hundreds.   Add to check.

➡ The librarian bought 54 more books this year.

Guided Practice

Add. Check your work.

1.

	h	t	o
	6	0	2
+	3	7	3

2.

	h	t	o
	4	3	9
+	1	4	2

3.

	h	t	o
	3	9	0
+	4	5	9

4.

	h	t	o
	5	6	8
+	2	9	8

Subtract. Check your work.

5.

	h	t	o
	5	9	8
−	2	9	7

6.

	h	t	o
	2	4	3
−	1	2	5

7.

	h	t	o
	9	3	5
−	6	4	8

8.

	h	t	o
	8	5	9
−	7	6	4

Think•Pair•Share

MP4 **9.** Explain why you can subtract to check addition and you can add to check subtraction.

Independent Practice

Use any strategy you like to find the sum.

1. 475 + 305 = _____

2. 174 + 29 = _____

3. 312 + 298 = _____

4. 623 + 377 = _____

5. 286 + 241 = _____

6. 747 + 173 = _____

Add. Check your work.

7. 408
   +436

8. 281
   +405

9. 271
   +352

10. 192
   +339

11. 545
   +375

12. 397
   +228

13. 457
   +462

14. 273
   +140

15. 609
   +329

16. 512
   +127

17. 315
   +587

18. 826
   + 38

19. 128
    205
   +137

20. 540
    100
   +139

21. 162
    145
   +285

Independent Practice

Use any strategy you like to find the difference.

22. $325 - 210 = $ _____   **23.** $830 - 140 = $ _____

24. $762 - 451 = $ _____   **25.** $794 - 392 = $ _____

26. $276 - 254 = $ _____   **27.** $685 - 176 = $ _____

Subtract. Check your work.

28. $\begin{array}{r} 64 \\ -27 \\ \hline \end{array}$ **29.** $\begin{array}{r} 75 \\ -18 \\ \hline \end{array}$ **30.** $\begin{array}{r} 41 \\ -25 \\ \hline \end{array}$

31. $\begin{array}{r} 408 \\ -104 \\ \hline \end{array}$ **32.** $\begin{array}{r} 519 \\ -235 \\ \hline \end{array}$ **33.** $\begin{array}{r} 635 \\ -294 \\ \hline \end{array}$

34. $\begin{array}{r} 235 \\ -\ 45 \\ \hline \end{array}$ **35.** $\begin{array}{r} 776 \\ -\ 59 \\ \hline \end{array}$ **36.** $\begin{array}{r} 866 \\ -371 \\ \hline \end{array}$

37. $\begin{array}{r} 526 \\ -371 \\ \hline \end{array}$ **38.** $\begin{array}{r} 645 \\ -293 \\ \hline \end{array}$ **39.** $\begin{array}{r} 107 \\ -\ 45 \\ \hline \end{array}$

40. $\begin{array}{r} 599 \\ -192 \\ \hline \end{array}$ **41.** $\begin{array}{r} 909 \\ -427 \\ \hline \end{array}$ **42.** $\begin{array}{r} 352 \\ -278 \\ \hline \end{array}$

Independent Practice

MP6 **43.** Explain how to compute the sum of 382 + 130.

MP8 **44.** Explain how to compute the difference of 382 − 130.

Solve the problems.

MP2 **45.** Last month Mrs. Turner's class collected 349 cans for recycling. This month the class collected 570 cans for recycling. How many cans did the class collect in all? Explain why your answer is reasonable.

 ➤ **Show your work.**

Answer _____

MP6 **46.** Southwest Elementary has 739 students. If 392 students are boys, how many are girls? Explain why your answer is reasonable.

 ➤ **Show your work.**

Answer _____

MP8 **47.** Four hundred twenty-eight students came to the school fair the first day, and 355 students came the second day. How many students attended during the two days?

▸ **Show your work.**

Answer _____

MP3 **48.** Ramona says that 135 + 279 equals the same sum as 279 + 135. Is Ramona's statement correct?

Answer _____

▸ **Justify your answer using words, drawings, or numbers.**

MP1 **49.** Jarred subtracted 540 − 365 and got a difference of 275. Give the correct answer and explain Jarred's error.

Answer _____

▸ **Justify your answer using words, drawings, or numbers.**

Multiply One-Digit Whole Numbers by Multiples of 10

Essential Question:
How can you multiply a number by a multiple of 10?

Words to Know:
multiple

Guided Instruction

In this lesson you will multiply one-digit numbers by multiples of 10.

Understand: What a multiple of 10 is

> You know how to multiply a one-digit number by another one-digit number. The number 10 is the first two-digit number. What happens when you multiply 3×10?

When you multiply, you find the total of a number of equal groups.

number of groups × number in each group = number in all

$$3 \qquad \times \qquad 10 \qquad = \qquad n$$

To think about finding 3×10, you can draw an array.

The array shows that 3 groups of 10 is equal to 30: $3 \times 10 = 30$.

The product, 30, is called a multiple of 10. It is a number found by multiplying by 10.

When you skip count by 10s to 90, you name multiples of 10.

10, 20, 30, 40, 50, 60, 70, 80, 90

$1 \times 10 = 10$
$2 \times 10 = 20$
$3 \times 10 = 30$
$4 \times 10 = 40$
$5 \times 10 = 50$
$6 \times 10 = 60$
$7 \times 10 = 70$
$8 \times 10 = 80$
$9 \times 10 = 90$

Notice the pattern. When you multiply a one-digit factor by 10, the tens digit of the product is the same as that factor.
Multiplying a one-digit factor by 10 is the same as moving that digit to the tens place and putting a 0 in the ones place.

➡ When you multiply 3×10, you get 30. The 3 moves to the tens place and a 0 goes in the ones place.

Guided Instruction

Understand: Multiplying by a multiple of 10

> There are desks for 30 students in each of the 4 third-grade classrooms. How many desks are there in the 4 classrooms?

To answer this question, you need to multiply 4×30.

number of groups × number in each group = number in all

     4   ×   30   = d

One way to think about finding 4×30 is to draw an array.

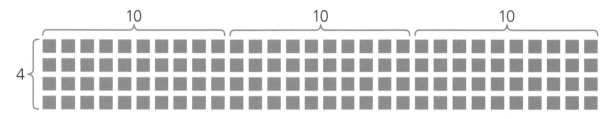

You can count all 120 squares in the array.

Another way to think about this problem is to think about groups of tens. There are 4 groups of 3 tens.

     4 groups of 3 tens = _____ tens

         $4 \times 30 =$ _____

▶ There are 120 desks in the 4 classrooms.

There is a faster way to multiply with multiples of 10.

     $4 \times 30 = 120$

Notice that you can find 120 by multiplying 4×3 and putting a 0 to the right. When you do this, you are moving the product of 4×3 one place to the left and there is a 0 in the ones place.

✏ Find the product of 6×20 two different ways.

Guided Instruction

Connect: Using properties when multiplying by a multiple of 10

> How can the properties of multiplication help you understand multiplying a one-digit number by a multiple of 10?

To answer this question, look at the problem on page 129 again. You found the number of desks in 4 classrooms with 30 desks in each classroom. You used this diagram to visualize the problem.

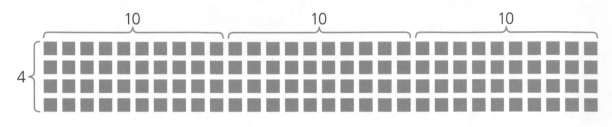

You can use the Distributive Property to find the product.

$4 \times 30 = 4 \times (10 + 10 + 10)$
$= (4 \times 10) + (4 \times 10) + (4 \times 10)$
$= 40 + 40 + 40$
$4 \times 30 = 120$

You can use the Associative Property to find the product.

$4 \times 30 = 4 \times (3 \times 10)$ ← Rename 30 as 3×10.
$= (4 \times 3) \times 10$ ← Use the Associative Property to change the grouping.
$= 12 \times 10$ ← Multiply 4×3.
$4 \times 30 = 120$ ← Multiply 12×10.

▶ The properties of multiplication show what happens when a number is multiplied by a multiple of 10.

✏ Find the product of 6×20 using the Distributive Property and using the Associative Property.

Guided Practice

Complete the multiplication equations to find the product.

1. 3 groups of 7 tens = ____ tens

   $3 \times 70 =$ ____

2. 2 groups of 8 tens = ____ tens

   $2 \times 80 =$ ____

3. 5 groups of 2 tens = ____ tens

   $5 \times 20 =$ ____

4. 4 groups of 6 tens = ____ tens

   $4 \times 60 =$ ____

5. 3 groups of 9 tens = ____ tens

   $3 \times 90 =$ ____

6. 7 groups of 6 tens = ____ tens

   $7 \times 60 =$ ____

7. Draw a diagram to represent 2×70. Then find the product. Show your work.

Think•Pair•Share

MP4 8. Use what you know about multiplying multiples of 10 to show that 2×80 equals 8×20. Then find the product.

Independent Practice

Find the unknown factor to complete the equations.

1. 2 groups of ____ tens = 12 tens

   $2 \times$ ____ $= 120$

2. 3 groups of ____ tens = 21 tens

   $3 \times$ ____ $= 210$

3. 1 group of ____ tens = 5 tens

   $1 \times$ ____ $= 50$

4. 9 groups of ____ tens = 36 tens

   $9 \times$ ____ $= 360$

5. 4 groups of ____ tens = 32 tens

   $4 \times$ ____ $= 320$

6. 9 groups of ____ tens = 81 tens

   $9 \times$ ____ $= 810$

Find the product. You can use place-value models.

7. $4 \times 80 =$ ____

8. $9 \times 40 =$ ____

9. $7 \times 10 =$ ____

10. $0 \times 30 =$ ____

11. $6 \times 90 =$ ____

12. $7 \times 70 =$ ____

13. $40 \times 2 =$ ____

14. $20 \times 5 =$ ____

15. $70 \times 5 =$ ____

16. $90 \times 5 =$ ____

Circle the correct answer.

17. What is the product of 8 × 40?

   a. 32

   b. 320

   c. 3,200

   d. 32,000

18. What is the product of 60 × 5?

   a. 300,000

   b. 30,000

   c. 3,000

   d. 300

19. What is the next number in the pattern?
   40, 80, 120, 160, _____

   a. 160

   b. 180

   c. 200

   d. 220

MP1 20. Circle all computations that do NOT help you find the product of 9 × 70.

   a. 9 × 7

   b. 7 × 9

   c. (7 + 9) × 10

   d. 9 + 9 + 9 + 9 + 9 + 9

Independent Practice

MP8 **21.** Explain how to compute the product of 20 × 3.

MP7 **22.** Explain how to find the product of 4 × 60.

Solve the problems.

MP1 **23.** At the animal shelter, each box of dog food holds 30 cans. How many cans of dog food are in 6 boxes?

> **Show your work.**

Answer _____

MP2 **24.** Each sheet of stickers holds 60 stickers. If Roxanne has 8 sheets, how many stickers does she have?

> **Show your work.**

Answer _____

MP6 **25.** Two hundred students from the school are going on a field trip. How many buses will the school need if only 40 students can ride on each bus?

✏️ **Show your work.**

Answer _____

MP3 **26.** Maiko says that 6 times 50 is 30. Give the correct answer and explain her error.

Answer _____

✏️ **Justify your answer using words, drawings, or numbers.**

MP2 **27.** Kyle says that 5 × 80 is the same as 80 + 80 + 80 + 80 + 80. Is his thinking correct?

Answer _____

✏️ **Justify your answer using words, drawings, or numbers.**

For exercises 1 and 2, use the number pattern below.

7	14	21	28			

1. Write the next three numbers in the pattern.

2. What is the pattern rule? _____

For exercises 3–8, add or subtract.

3.
$$\begin{array}{r} 358 \\ +436 \\ \hline \end{array}$$

4.
$$\begin{array}{r} 562 \\ +49 \\ \hline \end{array}$$

5.
$$\begin{array}{r} 261 \\ 305 \\ +387 \\ \hline \end{array}$$

6.
$$\begin{array}{r} 489 \\ -286 \\ \hline \end{array}$$

7.
$$\begin{array}{r} 725 \\ -698 \\ \hline \end{array}$$

8.
$$\begin{array}{r} 806 \\ -378 \\ \hline \end{array}$$

9. Mike knows that $4 \times 6 = 24$. How can Mike use $4 \times 6 = 24$ to find the product of 8×6?

10. Raisa knows that 7 groups of 9 make 63. How can Raisa use that information to find the quotient of 63 and 9?

Answer $63 \div 9 = $ ____

11. What is 35 rounded to the nearest ten?

    a. 10

    b. 30

    c. 35

    d. 40

12. What is 549 rounded to the nearest hundred?

    a. 600

    b. 550

    c. 500

    d. 100

For exercises 13–15, find the product.

13. $3 \times 50 =$ ____

14. $1 \times 90 =$ ____

15. $70 \times 4 =$ ____

MP4 16. Katsu runs 2 miles each day. His goal is to run a total of 20 miles. After 7 days, how many miles does Katsu have left to run in order to meet his goal?

Choose the equation you can use to solve the problem?

a. $2 + 7 + n = 20$

b. $2 \times 7 + n = 20$

c. $4 \times 7 + n = 20$

d. $2 + 7 \times n = 20$

Answer _____

MP7 17. What do you notice about the numbers highlighted in green in the multiplication table? Explain the pattern using a multiplication property.

×	0	1	2	3	4	5	6	7	8	9
0	0	0	0	0	0	0	0	0	0	0
1	0	1	2	3	4	5	6	7	8	9
2	0	2	4	6	8	10	12	14	16	18
3	0	3	6	9	12	15	18	21	24	27
4	0	4	8	12	16	20	24	28	32	36
5	0	5	10	15	20	25	30	35	40	45
6	0	6	12	18	24	30	36	42	48	54
7	0	7	14	21	28	35	42	49	56	63
8	0	8	16	24	32	40	48	56	64	72
9	0	9	18	27	36	45	54	63	72	81

Solve the problems.

MP4 **18.** Yvette has 8 books. Darcie has twice as many books as Yvette. How many books do they have in all?

✏️ **Show your work.**

Answer _____

MP3 **19.** Tariq says that a reasonable estimate for the quotient of 55 ÷ 7 is 8. Is Tariq correct?

Answer _____

✏️ **Justify your answer using words, drawings, or numbers.**

MP8 **20.** Dr. Wu studies birds and goes bird watching. He counts 329 birds on the first day and 441 birds on the second day. How many birds does Dr. Wu count altogether? Explain your reasoning.

✏️ **Show your work.**

Answer _____

Progress ✓ Check

Look at how the math concepts and skills you have learned and will learn connect.

It is very important for you to understand the math concepts and skills from the prior grade level so that you will be able to develop an understanding of fractions in this unit and be prepared for next year. To practice your skills, go to sadlierconnect.com.

GRADE 2	Before Unit 3	GRADE 3	After Unit 3	GRADE 4
I Can...		**Can I ?**		**I Will...**
Partition shapes into two, three, or four equal shares	☐	Understand that fractions name equal parts of a whole	☐	Add and subtract fractions with like denominators
Describe equal shares as halves, thirds, or fourths	☐	Understand the meaning of the numerator of a fraction	☐	Add and subtract mixed numbers with like denominators
Describe a whole as two halves, three thirds, or four fourths	☐	Understand the meaning of the denominator of a fraction	☐	Solve word problems involving addition and subtraction of fractions
Represent whole numbers as lengths on a number line	☐	Represent unit fractions on a number line	☐	Multiply a fraction by a whole number
	☐	Represent fractions on a number line	☐	Solve word problems by multiplying fractions by whole numbers
	☐	Find equivalent fractions	☐	Explain why fractions are equivalent
	☐	Express whole numbers as fractions	☐	Express a fraction with a denominator of 10 as an equivalent fraction with a denominator of 100
	☐	Compare fractions with the same numerator	☐	Compare two fractions with different numerators and different denominators
	☐	Compare fractions with the same denominator	☐	

HOME◆CONNECT...

A pizza pie is a great example to use with your child about fractions. Most pizza pies are pre-sliced with eight equal slices. In this example, the pizza is the whole that can be partitioned into equal parts. The slices of the pizza pie are the equal parts of the whole pizza pie. One slice of pizza represents a unit fraction, in this case $\frac{1}{8}$.

Use the following math vocabulary to talk about ways you could share this pizza pie.

- A **fraction** is a number that describes parts of a whole. A fraction contains a numerator and a denominator.

$$\frac{\text{numerator}}{\text{denominator}}$$ tells how many equal parts you are talking about
tells how many equal parts are in the whole

- A fraction that shows 1 equal part of a whole is known as a **unit fraction**. A unit fraction has 1 as the numerator. Example: $\frac{1}{8}$

Activity: Make a set of fraction strips with your child using three strips of paper in three different colors. Choose one colored strip to represent one whole. Choose a second colored strip, fold it, and cut it into two equal pieces to represent halves ($\frac{1}{2}$). Label each piece as $\frac{1}{2}$. Repeat this process of folding, cutting, and labeling equal pieces for fourths ($\frac{1}{4}$). Explore the fraction strips and find relationships among the unit and equivalent fractions.

In this unit your child will:

- Understand that fractions name equal parts of a whole.

- Understand the meaning of the numerator of a fraction.

- Understand the meaning of the denominator of a fraction.

- Represent unit fractions on a number line.

- Represent fractions on a number line.

- Find equivalent fractions.

- Express whole numbers as fractions.

- Compare fractions with the same numerator.

- Compare fractions with the same denominator.

Ways to Help Your Child

Make time to talk with your child's teacher. Ask about your child's level of progress, and find out if there are ways that you can assist with his or her learning at home. If your child needs extra practice, your support can really make a difference.

ONLINE

For more Home Connect activities, continue online at sadlierconnect.com

Focus on Number and Operations—Fractions

Essential Question:
How are fractions and whole numbers alike?

Lesson 16 — Understand Unit Fractions as Quantities

Essential Question:
What are unit fractions?

Words to Know:
fraction
unit fraction
numerator
denominator

Guided Instruction

In this lesson you will learn about fractions and unit fractions.

Understand: The meaning of a unit fraction

For art class Jenna partitions a square into four equal parts in different ways. Then she shades one part of each square. Here are Jenna's drawings.

What number does the shaded part in each of Jenna's drawings represent?

A fraction is a number. When a whole is partitioned, or divided, into equal parts, a unit fraction represents the quantity, or amount, in one of those equal parts.

All fractions have this form:

numerator ← number of equal parts in the fraction
denominator ← number of equal parts in the whole

A unit fraction has this form:

1 ← 1 equal part in the fraction
denominator ← number of equal parts in the whole

Look at Jenna's drawings.
Each square has 1 equal part that is shaded.
Each square has 4 equal parts.

1 equal part in the fraction ⟶ $\frac{1}{4}$
4 equal parts in the whole ⟶

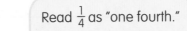

Read $\frac{1}{4}$ as "one fourth."

▷ The shaded part in each of Jenna's drawings represents the unit fraction $\frac{1}{4}$.

Guided Instruction

Understand: The numerator in a unit fraction

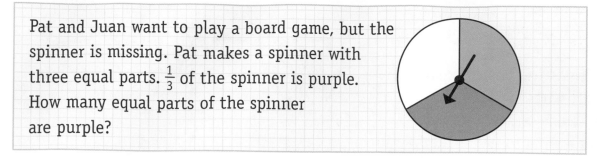

Pat and Juan want to play a board game, but the spinner is missing. Pat makes a spinner with three equal parts. $\frac{1}{3}$ of the spinner is purple. How many equal parts of the spinner are purple?

Use what you know about the form of a unit fraction.

In $\frac{1}{3}$ the numerator, 1, means one of three equal parts.

➡ So one equal part of the spinner is purple.

Understand: The denominator in a unit fraction

Manny cut out $\frac{1}{8}$ of a red paper strip.
Here is what his cutout looked like.

Draw a model of the whole paper strip.

Use what you know about the denominator of a unit fraction. In $\frac{1}{8}$ the denominator means that the whole is partitioned into 8 equal parts.

Draw a model of a strip with 8 equal parts that are the same as Manny's cutout.

➡ Here is a model of the whole paper strip.

$\frac{1}{8}$	$\frac{1}{8}$	$\frac{1}{8}$	$\frac{1}{8}$	$\frac{1}{8}$	$\frac{1}{8}$	$\frac{1}{8}$	$\frac{1}{8}$

✏ Draw a spinner that is $\frac{1}{4}$ green.

Guided Instruction

Connect: What you know about unit fractions

Mr. Smith buys poster board for his daughter, Jill.
He partitions the poster board into equal parts.
Jill paints one of the parts.
Use the drawing to name the fraction of the poster board Jill paints.

Jill's Poster Board

paint	

You can name the fraction because you know that the whole is partitioned into equal parts.

Step 1

Identify the denominator.

Count the number of equal parts in the whole poster board.

There are 6 equal parts in the whole poster board.

So the denominator of the fraction is 6.

> **Remember!**
> The denominator tells how many equal parts are in the whole.

Step 2

Identify the numerator.

Count the number of equal parts with paint.

There is 1 equal part with paint.

So the numerator of the fraction is 1.

Write the numerator and denominator to show the fraction.

$$\frac{\boxed{}}{\boxed{}}$$

> **Remember!**
> The numerator tells how many equal parts are in the fraction.

 Jill paints $\frac{1}{6}$ of the poster board.

Each model represents a whole. Write a unit fraction for the shaded part of each model.

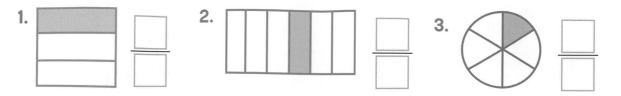

1.

2.

3.

Use the model at the right for exercises 4–6.

4. Draw lines in the square to show fourths.

5. How many equal parts are in your model? _____

6. Write a unit fraction that represents

one equal part of your model. _____

Solve the problem.

7. Rita makes a flower garden and divides it into three equal sections. She plants $\frac{1}{3}$ of the garden with yellow flowers. Draw a model to show the fraction of the garden Rita plants with yellow flowers.

✿ Think•Pair•Share

MP3 **8.** Amal says that $\frac{1}{4}$ of a rectangle is shaded. Cadence says that $\frac{1}{2}$ of a rectangle is shaded. Jim says that 1 rectangle is shaded. Describe what each student used as the whole.

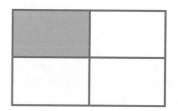

Independent Practice

Each figure represents one whole. Write the unit fraction that the shaded part of each figure represents.

1. 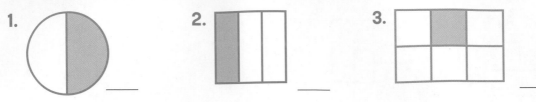 ___

2. ___

3. ___

4. Look at the shaded part of each model. Which model represents the fraction $\frac{1}{3}$?

a.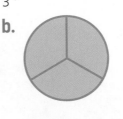

b.

c.

d.

5. Which fraction does the shaded part of the circle represent?

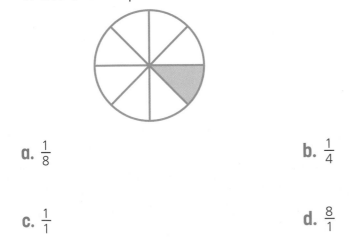

a. $\frac{1}{8}$

b. $\frac{1}{4}$

c. $\frac{1}{1}$

d. $\frac{8}{1}$

Independent Practice

Partition each figure into the given number of equal parts.
Shade one part. Then write the fraction for the shaded part.

6. 2 equal parts

Answer _____

7. 4 equal parts

Answer _____

8. Show two different ways to partition a square into thirds.
Shade 1 equal part of each square. Write the fraction that
one equal part represents.

Answer _____

Answer _____

9. This square is $\frac{1}{6}$ of a whole.
Draw a model of the whole.
Label each unit fraction.

Independent Practice

10. Think of two unit fractions.

   a. Write the fractions.   ____   ____

   b. Tell how the two fractions are alike.

   _____

   c. Tell how the two fractions are different.

   _____

Solve the problems.

MP4 **11.** Steve writes a letter to his grandparents. He folds the paper into 6 equal parts. He draws a picture on 1 part. What fraction of the paper does Steve draw on?

   ▆▆▶ **Show your work.**

   Answer _____

MP6 **12.** Mina has a rope. She wants to cut it into 8 equal parts. What fraction of the rope will each part be?

   ▆▆▶ **Show your work.**

   Answer _____

Independent Practice

Solve the problems.

MP5 **13.** The Thompson family eats a whole pot pie for dinner.

- The pot pie is cut into equal parts.

- Each part is $\frac{1}{3}$ of the pot pie.

- Each person eats 1 part.

How many people are in the Thompson family?

✏ **Show your work.**

Answer _____

MP3 **14.** Jorge has a large sheet of paper. He cuts it into pieces to make airplanes. Each piece is $\frac{1}{8}$ of the whole sheet. If it takes one piece to make an airplane, how many airplanes can Jorge make?

Answer _____

✏ **Justify your answer using words, drawings, or numbers.**

MP2 **15.** Teresa cuts a ribbon into equal pieces. She gives one piece to each of her friends: Tomás, Nick, and Linda. Teresa takes the last piece for herself. "We each get $\frac{1}{3}$ of the ribbon," she said. Does Teresa's statement make sense?

Answer _____

✏ **Justify your answer using words, drawings, or numbers.**

Understand Fractions as Quantities

Guided Instruction

In this lesson you will learn about fractions with numerators greater than 1.

Understand: Using unit fractions to form other fractions

Mindy draws three identical rectangles and partitions each rectangle into fourths. Then she shades different parts of each rectangle.

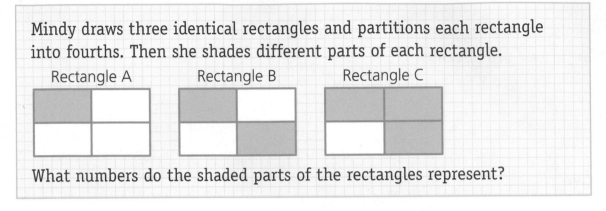

Rectangle A   Rectangle B   Rectangle C

What numbers do the shaded parts of the rectangles represent?

The numbers are fractions. Use what you know about a fraction.

$$\frac{\text{numerator}}{\text{denominator}}$$ ← number of equal parts in the fraction
← number of equal parts in the whole

Mindy's rectangles are divided into 4 equal parts. She shades a different number of parts in each rectangle.

In Rectangle A, count to find that 1 equal part is shaded.

$\frac{1}{4}$ ← 1 equal part in the fraction
← 4 equal parts in the whole

> The shaded part of Rectangle A represents the fraction $\frac{1}{4}$.

In Rectangle B, count to find that 2 equal parts are shaded.

$\frac{2}{4}$ ← 2 equal parts in the fraction
← 4 equal parts in the whole

> The shaded part of Rectangle B represents the fraction $\frac{2}{4}$.

In Rectangle C, count to find that 3 equal parts are shaded.

$\frac{3}{4}$ ← 3 equal parts in the fraction
← 4 equal parts in the whole

> The shaded part of Rectangle C represents the fraction $\frac{3}{4}$.

When you counted, you found the number of unit fractions of $\frac{1}{4}$ that are in $\frac{1}{4}$, in $\frac{2}{4}$, and in $\frac{3}{4}$.

➡ The shaded parts of the figures represent the numbers $\frac{1}{4}$, $\frac{2}{4}$, and $\frac{3}{4}$.

Guided Instruction

Connect: What you know about fractions

Marc ordered a pizza with mushrooms on some of the slices. The pizza was cut into equal slices. Use the picture to name the fraction of the pizza that has mushrooms.

Each slice is an equal part, so you can write a fraction to answer the question.

Step 1

Identify the denominator.

Count the number of equal parts in the whole pizza.

There are 8 equal parts in the pizza.

So the denominator of the fraction is ____.

Step 2

Identify the numerator.

Count the number of equal parts with mushrooms.

There are 3 equal parts with mushrooms.

So the numerator of the fraction is ____.

Use the numerator and denominator to write the fraction. $\frac{\Box}{\Box}$

➡ The part of the pizza that has mushrooms is $\frac{3}{8}$.

Another way to name the fraction is to count the unit fractions. For this problem, the slices are the unit fractions.

Count 3 slices or 3 unit fractions of $\frac{1}{8}$ to get $\frac{3}{8}$.

✏ Use the picture to name the fraction of the pizza that has no mushrooms.

Guided Practice

Each model represents a whole. Count the unit fractions to name the shaded part of each model.

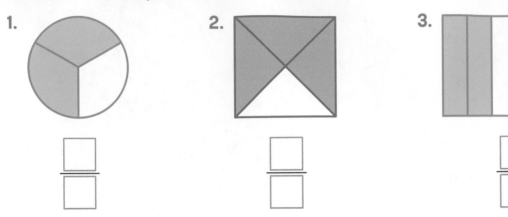

1.   2.   3.

Each model represents one whole. Shade the model to represent the fraction.

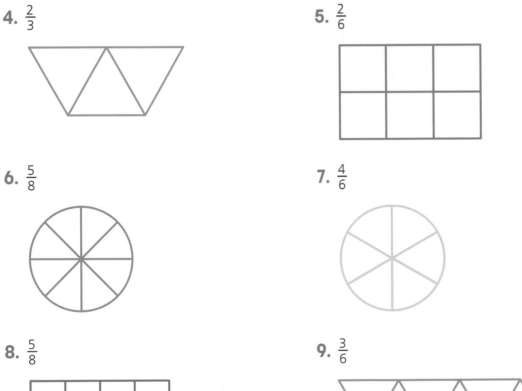

4. $\frac{2}{3}$ 5. $\frac{2}{6}$

6. $\frac{5}{8}$ 7. $\frac{4}{6}$

8. $\frac{5}{8}$ 9. $\frac{3}{6}$

10. Shade $\frac{2}{6}$ of each shape.

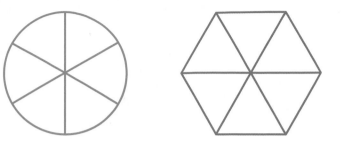

Use the model at the right for exercises 11–13.

11. Divide the rectangle into equal parts to show eighths.

12. How many equal parts did you make? ____

13. Shade 7 equal parts. Write the fraction for the

parts you shaded. ____

Solve the problem.

14. Jaime designed a flag. He colored $\frac{3}{4}$ of the flag blue and $\frac{1}{4}$ of the flag green. Draw a picture that shows the flag that Jaime designed.

🦅 **Think·Pair·Share**

MP4 **15.** Keiko says that three $\frac{1}{8}$ unit fractions are shaded in the figure. Jordan says that $\frac{3}{8}$ of the figure is shaded. Explain why both students' answers are correct.

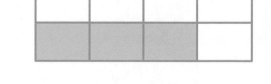

Independent Practice

Each figure represents one whole. Write the fraction that the shaded part of each figure represents.

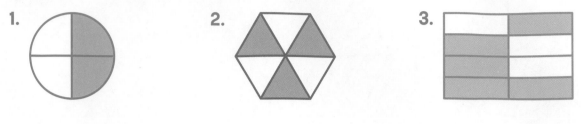

1. _____ 2. _____ 3. _____

4. In which model do the shaded parts represent the fraction $\frac{3}{8}$?

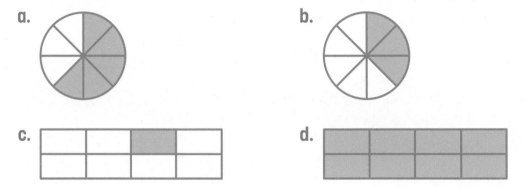

a. b. c. d.

5. Which fraction does the shaded part of the rectangle represent?

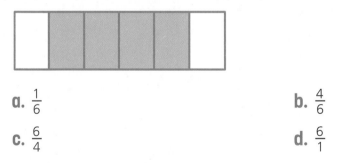

a. $\frac{1}{6}$ b. $\frac{4}{6}$

c. $\frac{6}{4}$ d. $\frac{6}{1}$

6. Which fraction does the shaded part of the square represent?

a. $\frac{4}{8}$ b. $\frac{3}{4}$

c. $\frac{5}{6}$ d. $\frac{4}{4}$

Independent Practice

Partition each figure into the given number of equal parts. Shade two parts. Then write the fraction for the shaded part.

7. 4 equal parts

Answer _____

8. 3 equal parts

Answer _____

9. Show two different ways to partition a square into fourths. Shade 3 equal parts of each square. Write the fraction that the 3 equal parts represent.

Answer _____

Answer _____

Make a drawing to represent the fraction.

10. $\frac{5}{6}$

11. $\frac{4}{8}$

Independent Practice

MP6 **12.** Explain two ways to find the fraction of the square that is green.

One way is to

Another way is to

MP4 **13.** Write a unit fraction and another fraction with the same denominator. How are they alike? How are they different?

Solve the problems.

MP7 **14.** Sarah says that $\frac{2}{3}$ of each figure is shaded. Do you agree? Explain your answer.

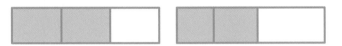

MP4 **15.** Omar is using a board to make a plaque with the letters of his name on it. He divides the board into 6 equal parts. He writes each letter of his name on a different part. What fraction of the board has a letter from Omar's name on it? What fraction of the board does not have a letter from Omar's name?

➡ **Show your work.**

Answer _____

Independent Practice

Solve the problems.

MP4 **16.** Mrs. Turan makes some pita breads for her family's dinner.

- Each pita bread is cut into equal slices.

- Each slice is $\frac{1}{4}$ of the pita bread.

- Each person in the family eats 3 slices.

- There are 4 people in the family.

How many pita breads does Mrs. Turan make?

Answer _____

✏ Justify your answer using words, drawings, or numbers.

MP2 **17.** The Green family's garden is divided into 8 equal size plots. The Greens plant vegetables in 5 of the plots and flowers in the other plots. What fraction of the garden has flowers?

✏ Show your work.

Answer _____

MP7 **18.** Katya is making designs by shading the same amount in each square. Make a different design in the blank square that represents the same fraction shaded as in Katya's designs.

Answer

✏ Justify your answer using words.

Understand Fractions on the Number Line

Essential Question:
How can I represent a fraction on a number line?

Words to Know:
number line

Guided Instruction

In this lesson you will learn how to represent a fraction on a number line.

Understand: Representing a unit fraction on a number line

Tyler knows that $\frac{1}{4}$ is a number. How can he locate $\frac{1}{4}$ on the number line?

To do this, you can find the whole and make equal parts on the number line.

Step 1

Find the whole on the number line. The whole is the distance from 0 to 1.

Step 2

Divide the whole into 4 equal parts. Make 4 parts because the denominator is 4. The size of each part is $\frac{1}{4}$.

Step 3

Look at the first $\frac{1}{4}$ part. It has one endpoint at 0. Its size is $\frac{1}{4}$. So its other endpoint is located at the point for $\frac{1}{4}$.

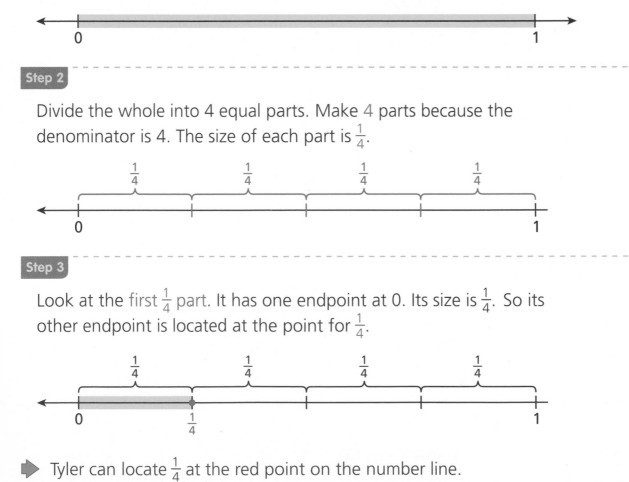

▶ Tyler can locate $\frac{1}{4}$ at the red point on the number line.

Guided Instruction

Understand: Representing a fraction on a number line

Fumi knows that $\frac{7}{6}$ is a number. How can she locate $\frac{7}{6}$ on the number line?

You can find the whole and use equal parts to locate $\frac{7}{6}$.

Step 1

Find the whole. The whole is the distance from 0 to 1.

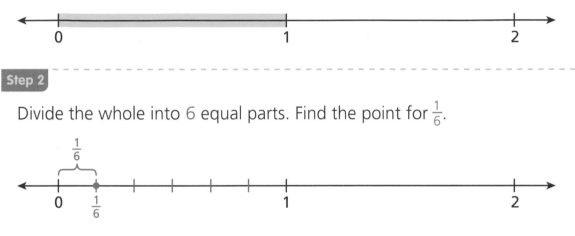

Step 2

Divide the whole into 6 equal parts. Find the point for $\frac{1}{6}$.

Step 3

Count unit fractions of $\frac{1}{6}$ until you reach $\frac{7}{6}$. $\frac{7}{6}$ is the same as seven $\frac{1}{6}$ unit fractions.

➡️ Fumi can locate $\frac{7}{6}$ at the red point on the number line.

✏️ Compare finding $\frac{7}{6}$ on the number line with finding 7 on the number line.

Guided Instruction

Connect: Using number lines to identify fractions

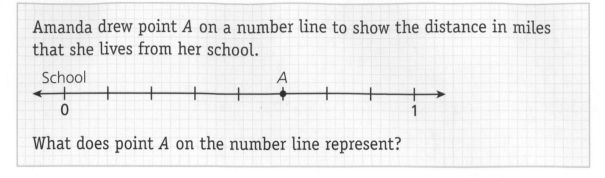

Amanda drew point *A* on a number line to show the distance in miles that she lives from her school.

What does point *A* on the number line represent?

Point *A* represents a fraction. Use the meaning of a fraction to identify the fraction.

Step 1

Count the number of parts between 0 and 1.

There are 8 equal parts.

Step 2

Since there are 8 equal parts, label the number line in _____.

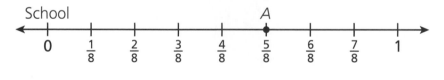

Step 3

Identify the fraction at point *A*.

The fraction at point *A* is $\dfrac{\square}{\square}$.

➡ Point *A* represents $\frac{5}{8}$ mile, the distance Amanda lives from her school.

✏ Identify the fraction at point *B* to find the distance in miles that Amanda lives from the park.

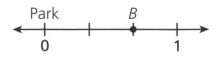

1. Write the missing fractions on the number line.

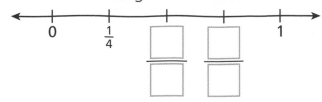

Use the number line for exercises 2 and 3.

2. Into how many parts is the number line equally divided? ____

3. What fraction is represented by point *A*? ____

Use the number line for exercises 4 and 5.

4. Into how many parts is the number line equally divided? ____

5. What fraction is represented by point *B*? ____

Solve the problem.

6. Will draws a number line to represent a fraction.

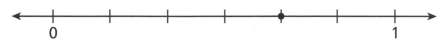

What fraction does the point on Will's number line represent?

_____

Think•Pair•Share

MP4 **7.** Work with a partner. Represent a fraction with a point on the number line. Have your partner identify the fraction for the point and explain how he or she arrived at the answer.

Independent Practice

1. Write the missing fractions on the number line.

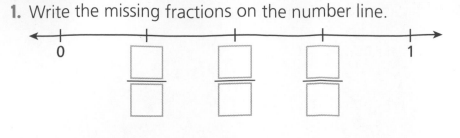

2. Write the missing fractions on the number line.

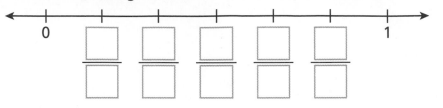

3. On which number line does a point represent the fraction $\frac{6}{8}$?

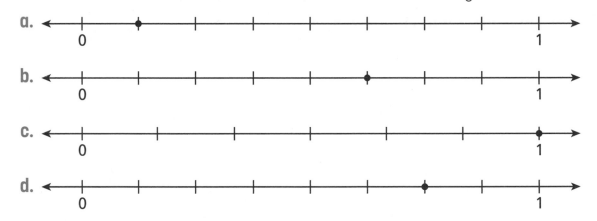

4. Which fraction does the point on the number line represent?

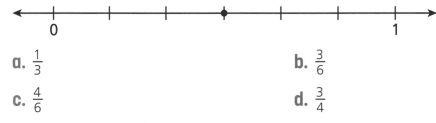

a. $\frac{1}{3}$ **b.** $\frac{3}{6}$

c. $\frac{4}{6}$ **d.** $\frac{3}{4}$

5. Which fraction does the point on the number line represent?

a. $\frac{1}{4}$ **b.** $\frac{1}{2}$

c. $\frac{5}{8}$ **d.** $\frac{3}{4}$

Independent Practice

Use the number line for exercises 6 and 7.

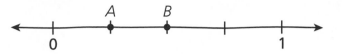

6. What fraction is represented by point *A*?

Answer _____

7. What fraction is represented by point *B*?

Answer _____

Use the number line for exercises 8 and 9.

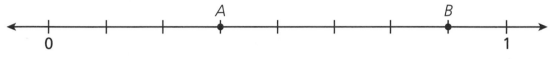

8. What fraction is represented by point *A*?

Answer _____

9. What fraction is represented by point *B*?

Answer _____

Draw a number line. Use a point to locate the given fraction.

10. $\frac{3}{4}$

11. $\frac{3}{6}$

Independent Practice

MP6 **12.** Compare your number lines in exercises 10 and 11. How are they alike? How are they different?

MP1 **13.** Point *L* on the number line represents $\frac{6}{8}$. Which point represents 1?

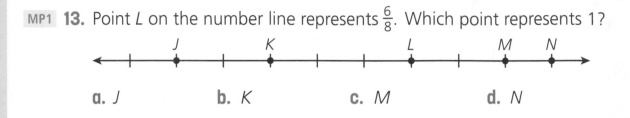

a. *J*   b. *K*   c. *M*   d. *N*

Solve the problems.

MP4 **14.** Hudson buys some muffins. He draws a number line to show what fraction of the muffins he buys are blueberry muffins.

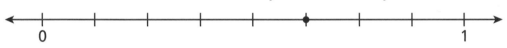

What fraction of the muffins Hudson buys are blueberry muffins?

Answer _____

MP4 **15.** Ella makes a strawberry milk shake. She drinks $\frac{3}{4}$ of it. Draw a number line to show how much of the milk shake Ella drinks. Then find what fraction of the milkshake Ella has left.

Answer _____

Independent Practice

Solve the problems.

MP2 **16.** Lily has 8 cups of milk. She used 2 cups of milk for a recipe. What fraction of the milk is left? Use a number line to represent the problem. Explain your reasoning.

Answer _____

MP4 **17.** Victor has a rope that is 3 yards long. He cut off 1 yard of the rope. What fraction of the rope is left? Use a number line.

Answer _____

MP1 **18.** Ariana's necklace has 6 beads. The necklace broke and all the beads fell off. She could only find 5 of the beads. What fraction of the beads did she lose? Use a number line.

Answer _____

Understand Equivalent Fractions

Essential Question:
How can I use a number line to understand that two fractions are equivalent?

Words to Know:
equivalent fractions

Guided Instruction

In this lesson you will learn how to find equivalent fractions.

Understand: Equivalent fractions on a number line

> Nuts come in bags that weigh $\frac{1}{6}$ pound. Ashton wants to buy $\frac{1}{3}$ pound of nuts. How many bags weighing $\frac{1}{6}$ pound does Ashton need to buy?

You can use number lines to find fractions that have different names but are at the same point on the number line. These are called equivalent fractions.

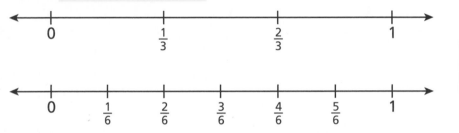

Notice that the distance from 0 to 1 is the same on both number lines.

Find $\frac{1}{3}$ on the number line on top. Find the equivalent fraction in sixths directly below it on the number line on the bottom.

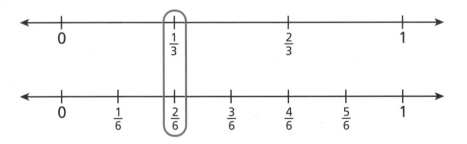

➡ $\frac{1}{3} = \frac{2}{6}$, so Ashton needs to buy two bags weighing $\frac{1}{6}$ pound each.

▬▶ Find $\frac{2}{3}$ on the top number line above.

What fraction is directly below it?
Write an equation to show that the fractions are equivalent.

Guided Instruction

Connect: How you can use equivalent fractions

Yolanda and Tony shared a pizza. Yolanda ate $\frac{1}{4}$ of the pizza and Tony ate $\frac{2}{8}$ of the pizza. Did Yolanda and Tony eat the same amount of pizza?

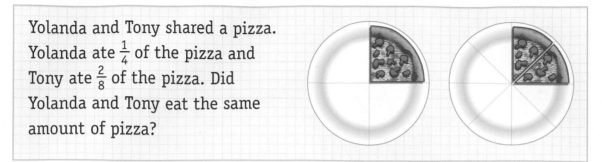

You can use number lines to find the answer.

Step 1

Draw a number line in fourths.

$$0 \quad \frac{1}{4} \quad \frac{2}{4} \quad \frac{3}{4} \quad 1$$

Step 2

Draw a number line in eighths.

$$0 \quad \frac{1}{8} \quad \frac{2}{8} \quad \frac{3}{8} \quad \frac{4}{8} \quad \frac{5}{8} \quad \frac{6}{8} \quad \frac{7}{8} \quad 1$$

Remember!

To compare fractions using number lines, the distance from 0 to 1 must be the same on both number lines.

Step 3

Find $\frac{1}{4}$ on the number line in Step 1. Find the equivalent fraction in eighths directly below it on the number line in Step 2. $\frac{1}{4} = \frac{2}{8}$

▶ Yolanda and Tony ate the same amount of pizza.

✏ What if Yolanda eats $\frac{1}{2}$ of a small pizza and Tony eats $\frac{1}{2}$ of a large pizza? Do they eat the same amount of pizza? Explain your answer.

Guided Practice

Find and circle equivalent fractions on each pair of number lines.

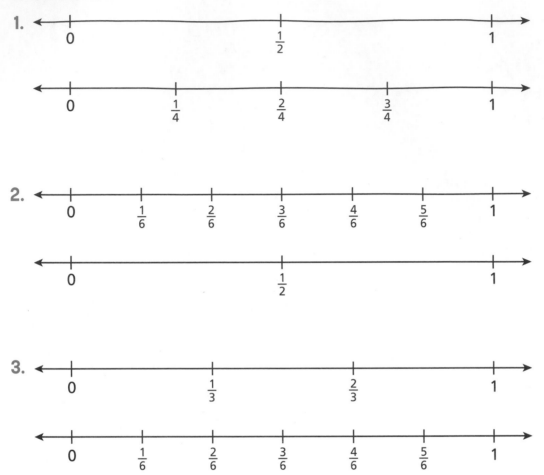

1.

2.

3.

Solve the problem.

4. Sharona buys $\frac{3}{4}$ yard of ribbon. Use the number lines to find an equivalent fraction for how many yards of ribbon Sharona buys.

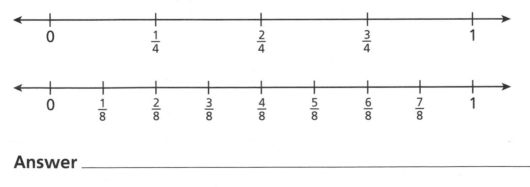

Answer _____

Guided Practice

5. Colin walks $\frac{2}{6}$ mile from his house to the library. Use the number lines to find an equivalent fraction for how many miles Colin walked.

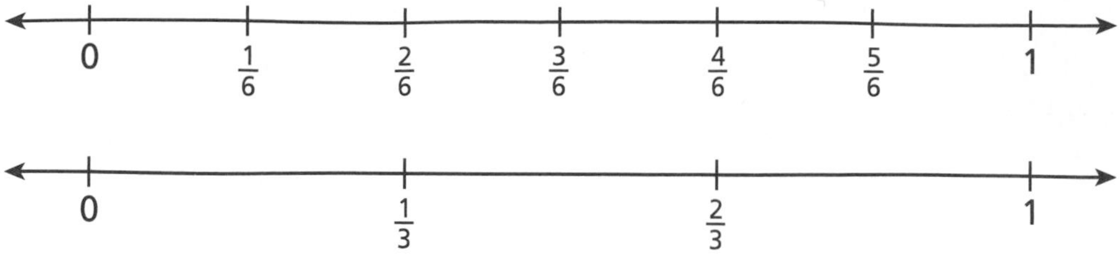

Answer ______________________________

6. Jill buys $\frac{4}{8}$ pound of trail mix. Use the number lines to find an equivalent fraction for how many pounds of trail mix Jill buys.

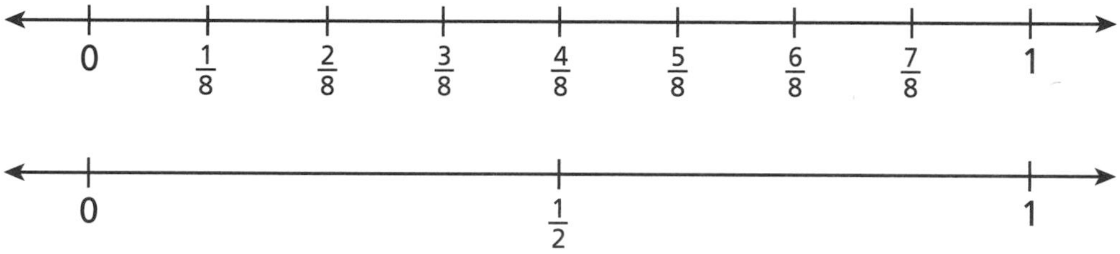

Answer ______________________________

Think•Pair•Share

MP4 **7.** Francesco looks at the number lines below. He says that no fractions between 0 and 1 shown on these number lines are equivalent. Do you agree? Explain your answer.

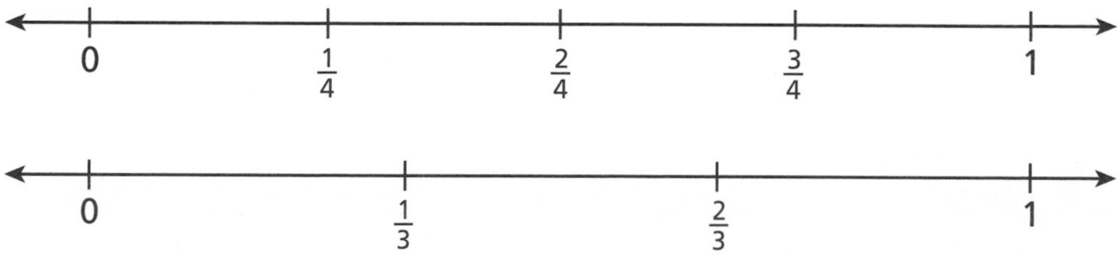

Independent Practice

Plot each fraction on a number line. Determine if the fractions are equivalent.

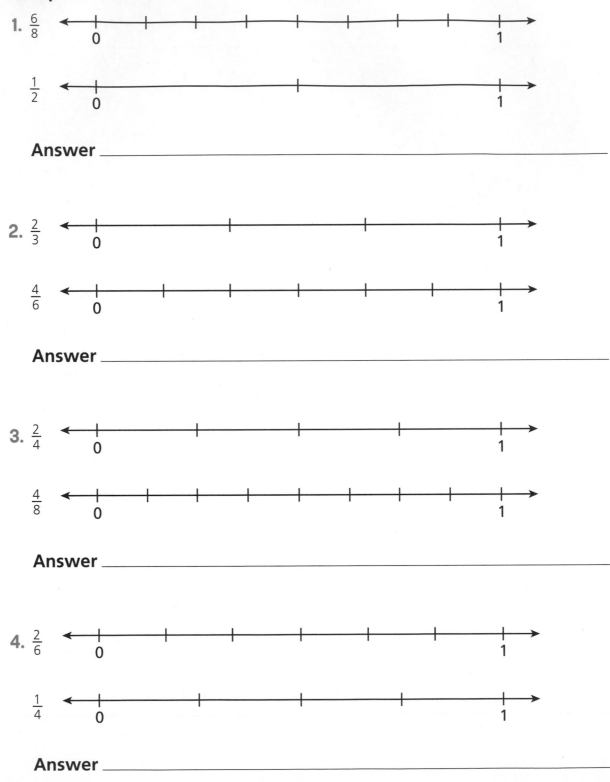

1. $\frac{6}{8}$

   $\frac{1}{2}$

Answer _____

2. $\frac{2}{3}$

   $\frac{4}{6}$

Answer _____

3. $\frac{2}{4}$

   $\frac{4}{8}$

Answer _____

4. $\frac{2}{6}$

   $\frac{1}{4}$

Answer _____

Independent Practice

Use these number lines to find equivalent fractions.

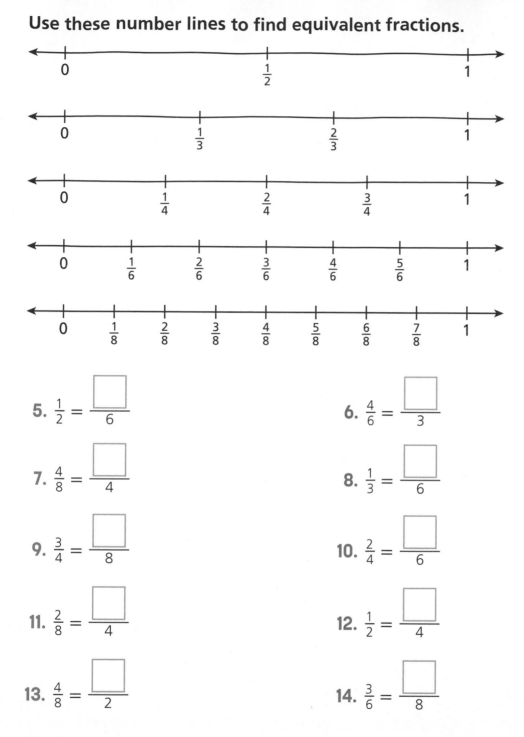

5. $\frac{1}{2} = \frac{\boxed{}}{6}$

6. $\frac{4}{6} = \frac{\boxed{}}{3}$

7. $\frac{4}{8} = \frac{\boxed{}}{4}$

8. $\frac{1}{3} = \frac{\boxed{}}{6}$

9. $\frac{3}{4} = \frac{\boxed{}}{8}$

10. $\frac{2}{4} = \frac{\boxed{}}{6}$

11. $\frac{2}{8} = \frac{\boxed{}}{4}$

12. $\frac{1}{2} = \frac{\boxed{}}{4}$

13. $\frac{4}{8} = \frac{\boxed{}}{2}$

14. $\frac{3}{6} = \frac{\boxed{}}{8}$

15. Explain why you can use the number lines above to find equivalent fractions.

Answer _____

Independent Practice

Use the number lines on page 171 to solve the problems.

16. Justin shaded 2 parts of a square. Which fraction is equivalent to the shaded part of the square?

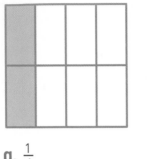

a. $\frac{1}{4}$ b. $\frac{1}{2}$

c. $\frac{6}{8}$ d. $\frac{3}{4}$

17. Maria shaded 2 parts of a circle. Which fraction is equivalent to the shaded part of the circle?

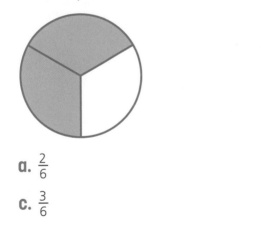

a. $\frac{2}{6}$ b. $\frac{1}{3}$

c. $\frac{3}{6}$ d. $\frac{4}{6}$

18. Liam shaded 2 parts of a parallelogram. Which fraction is equivalent to the shaded part of the parallelogram?

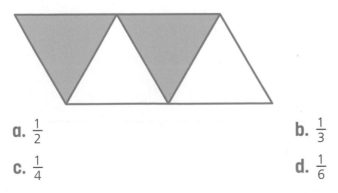

a. $\frac{1}{2}$ b. $\frac{1}{3}$

c. $\frac{1}{4}$ d. $\frac{1}{6}$

Independent Practice

Use the number lines on page 171 to solve the problems.

MP3 **19.** Sandria shades 3 parts of a rectangle. She says that the shaded part of the rectangle represents more than one fraction. Do you agree?

Answer _____

✏ **Justify your answer using words, drawings, or numbers.**

MP3 **20.** Joe cuts a pizza into 8 equal slices. He gives 2 slices to each of his friends: Brent, Lisandra, and Paco. Joe also takes 2 slices for himself. "We each get $\frac{1}{3}$ of the pizza," he said. Is Joe right?

Answer _____

✏ **Justify your answer using words, drawings, or numbers.**

MP4 **21.** Place the following fractions on the number line: $\frac{1}{2}$, $\frac{1}{4}$, $\frac{2}{4}$, $\frac{3}{4}$, $\frac{1}{8}$, $\frac{2}{8}$, $\frac{3}{8}$, $\frac{4}{8}$, $\frac{5}{8}$, $\frac{6}{8}$, and $\frac{7}{8}$.

Explain why there is more than one fraction at some of the points on the number line.

Answer _____

✏ **Justify your answer using words, drawings, or numbers.**

Essential Question:
How can I use area models to write equivalent fractions?

Guided Instruction

In this lesson you will learn how to find equivalent fractions.

Understand: Using fraction strips to find equivalent fractions

> Eda wants to use fraction strips to find some equivalent fractions for $\frac{1}{2}$. How can she do this?

To find equivalent fractions, look for lengths that are the same.

Line up the fraction strips under the 1.

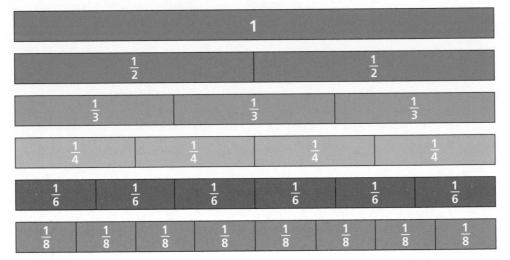

Start with a $\frac{1}{2}$ strip.

Find sets of strips that are exactly the same length as the $\frac{1}{2}$ strip. Look at the set of fraction strips or pull out some to compare.

Fraction strips showing $\frac{2}{4}$, $\frac{3}{6}$, and $\frac{4}{8}$ have the same length as the $\frac{1}{2}$ fraction strip.

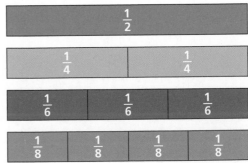

➡ Eda finds that $\frac{2}{4}$, $\frac{3}{6}$, and $\frac{4}{8}$ are equivalent fractions for $\frac{1}{2}$ because they are all the same length.

Guided Instruction

Understand: Using number lines to find equivalent fractions

Jorge wants to use number lines to find some equivalent fractions for $\frac{1}{2}$. How can he do this?

To find equivalent fractions, look for numbers that are at the same place on the number line.

Draw number lines with halves, thirds, fourths, sixths, and eighths.

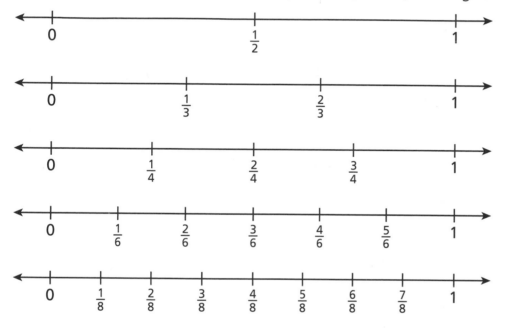

Find the fractions that are at the same place as $\frac{1}{2}$ on the number line. Draw a line going straight down from $\frac{1}{2}$. The fractions it crosses are equivalent to $\frac{1}{2}$.

The fractions $\frac{2}{4}$, $\frac{3}{6}$, and $\frac{4}{8}$ are equivalent to $\frac{1}{2}$. Each point is the same distance from 0.

➡ Jorge finds that _____ are equivalent fractions for $\frac{1}{2}$ because they are all at the same place on the number line.

✏ Why is there no equivalent fraction for $\frac{1}{2}$ that has 3 as its denominator?

Guided Instruction

Connect: Using models to represent equivalent fractions

Henry and his sister Lucy made a small lasagna. Henry ate $\frac{1}{4}$ of the lasagna and Lucy ate $\frac{2}{8}$ of the lasagna. Did Henry and Lucy eat the same amount of lasagna?

To find out whether Henry and Lucy ate the same amount of lasagna, check whether $\frac{1}{4}$ and $\frac{2}{8}$ are equivalent fractions.

Step 1

Draw a rectangle to represent the lasagna. Show the part of the lasagna that Henry ate. Divide the rectangle into fourths. Shade $\frac{1}{4}$ of the rectangle.

Step 2

Draw another rectangle of the same size to represent the lasagna. Show the part of the lasagna that Lucy ate. Divide the rectangle into eighths. Shade $\frac{2}{8}$ of the rectangle.

Step 3

Compare the amounts shaded in each rectangle.

The amounts shaded are the same, so $\frac{1}{4} = \frac{2}{8}$.

▶ Lucy and Henry ate the same amount of lasagna.

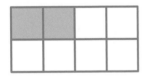 Why is it important to draw rectangles that are the same size?

Guided Practice

Use the fraction strips. Find an equivalent fraction.

1. $\frac{1}{3} =$ _____

2. $\frac{2}{4} =$ _____

3. $\frac{4}{6} =$ _____

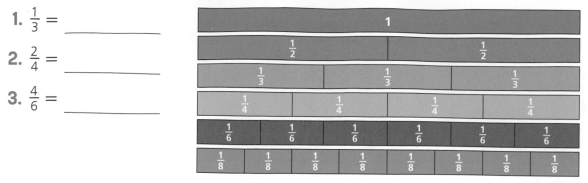

Use the number lines. Find an equivalent fraction.

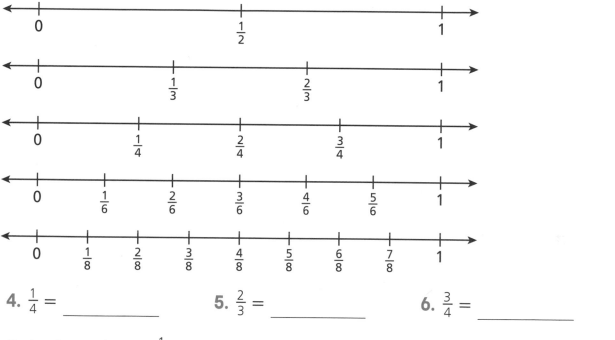

4. $\frac{1}{4} =$ _____

5. $\frac{2}{3} =$ _____

6. $\frac{3}{4} =$ _____

7. Doriano planted $\frac{1}{6}$ of his garden with green peppers and $\frac{1}{6}$ with red peppers. He said that he planted $\frac{1}{3}$ of the garden with peppers. Use the models to show why Doriano's thinking is correct.

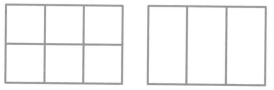

☝☝ Think•Pair•Share

MP3 8. Compare using fraction strips, number lines, and rectangles as models to find equivalent fractions. Tell which one you like to use and why.

Independent Practice

Use the fraction strips for the problems on this page.

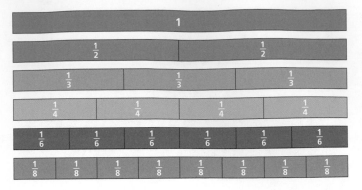

Complete the equivalent fraction.

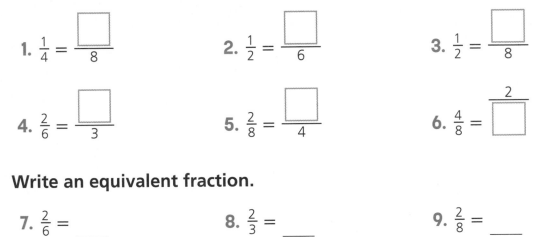

1. $\frac{1}{4} = \frac{\boxed{}}{8}$

2. $\frac{1}{2} = \frac{\boxed{}}{6}$

3. $\frac{1}{2} = \frac{\boxed{}}{8}$

4. $\frac{2}{6} = \frac{\boxed{}}{3}$

5. $\frac{2}{8} = \frac{\boxed{}}{4}$

6. $\frac{4}{8} = \frac{2}{\boxed{}}$

Write an equivalent fraction.

7. $\frac{2}{6} =$ _____

8. $\frac{2}{3} =$ _____

9. $\frac{2}{8} =$ _____

10. $\frac{4}{8} =$ _____

11. $\frac{6}{8} =$ _____

12. $\frac{1}{3} =$ _____

13. Find 3 equivalent fractions for $\frac{1}{2}$.

_____   _____   _____

14. Why is there no equivalent fraction for $\frac{3}{4}$ that has a denominator of 3?

15. Describe any pattern you notice in the set of fraction strips.

Independent Practice

Use the number lines for the problems on this page.

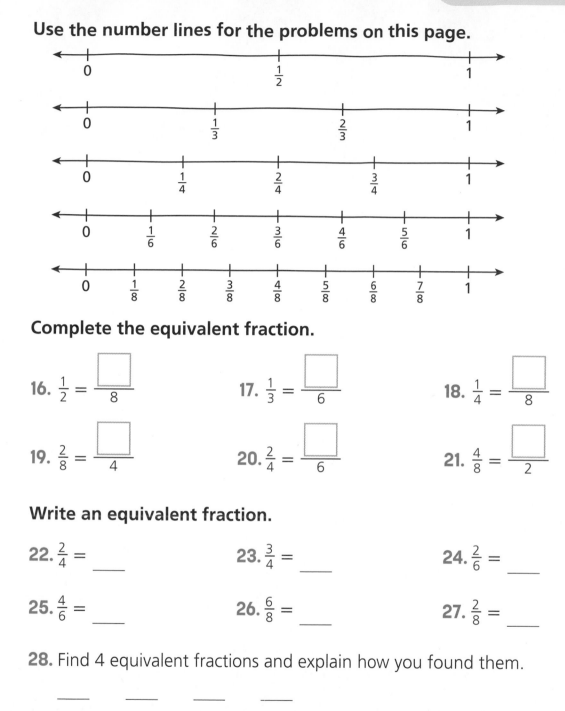

Complete the equivalent fraction.

16. $\frac{1}{2} = \frac{\square}{8}$

17. $\frac{1}{3} = \frac{\square}{6}$

18. $\frac{1}{4} = \frac{\square}{8}$

19. $\frac{2}{8} = \frac{\square}{4}$

20. $\frac{2}{4} = \frac{\square}{6}$

21. $\frac{4}{8} = \frac{\square}{2}$

Write an equivalent fraction.

22. $\frac{2}{4} = $ ____

23. $\frac{3}{4} = $ ____

24. $\frac{2}{6} = $ ____

25. $\frac{4}{6} = $ ____

26. $\frac{6}{8} = $ ____

27. $\frac{2}{8} = $ ____

28. Find 4 equivalent fractions and explain how you found them.

____   ____   ____   ____

29. Describe any pattern you notice in the number lines.

Independent Practice

For each question, circle any figures that have a shaded part equivalent to the given fraction.

30. $\frac{1}{2}$

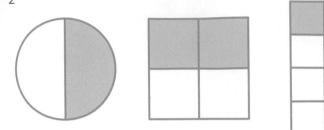

31. $\frac{1}{3}$

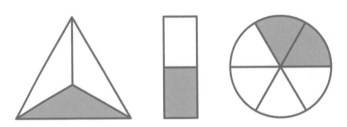

32. $\frac{1}{4}$

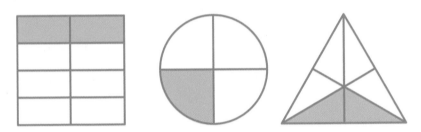

MP1 **33.** Explain how you decided which figure is not equal to $\frac{1}{2}$ in exercise 30.

MP3 **34.** Explain how you decided which figure is not equal to $\frac{1}{4}$ in exercise 32.

Independent Practice

Solve the problems.

MP2 **35.** Jaime and Serena are painting a room. So far Jaime has painted $\frac{2}{6}$ of one wall. Serena has painted the same amount of that wall. Write an equivalent fraction to represent how much of the wall Serena has painted.

Answer _____

✏️ **Justify your answer using words, drawings, or numbers.**

MP4 **36.** Sophie, Ethan, and Ava each have a garden.

Sophie's Garden		Ethan's Garden		Ava's Garden	
roses	tulips	roses	daffodils	tulips	roses
		tulips	pansies		
daffodils	pansies	pansies	tulips	roses	daffodils
		daffodils	roses		

Which two people have the same amount of roses planted in their gardens?

Answer _____

✏️ **Justify your answer using words, drawings, or numbers.**

MP7 **37.** Bobby only has a $\frac{1}{4}$-cup measuring cup. He needs to measure $\frac{4}{8}$ cup of flour. Explain how he can do it with the $\frac{1}{4}$-cup measuring cup.

Answer _____

✏️ **Justify your answer using words, drawings, or numbers.**

Relate Whole Numbers and Fractions

Essential Question:
How can I relate whole numbers and fractions?

Words to Know:
  whole number

Guided Instruction

In this lesson you will learn to express whole numbers as fractions and recognize fractions that are equivalent to whole numbers.

Understand: Recognizing fractions equivalent to whole numbers

Naomi is using wooden dowels to make axles for two model cars she is building. She cuts each dowel in half and makes four pieces.

How many dowels did Naomi use?

Naomi made 4 halves. To find the number of dowels, find the whole number that is equivalent to $\frac{4}{2}$.

Use a number line. Count 4 unit fractions of $\frac{1}{2}$.

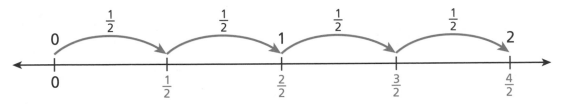

The number line shows that the whole number 2 is equivalent to $\frac{4}{2}$.

➡ Naomi used 2 dowels.

Another way to find the whole number that a fraction is equivalent to is to divide the numerator by the denominator.

$\frac{4}{2} \longrightarrow 4 \div 2 = 2$

$\frac{4}{2}$ is equivalent to 2

✏ How can you use a number line to find the whole number that is equivalent to $\frac{8}{4}$?

Guided Instruction

Understand: Expressing a whole number as a fraction

Burnell, Candace, and Jake are sharing equal parts of 2 seed pots.

You need to write 2 as a fraction in thirds.
Each person gets $\frac{1}{3}$ of a seed pot.
How many thirds are in the 2 seed pots?

Label the parts of the seed pots.

Count the number of thirds in the 2 seed pots.
There are 3 thirds in the first seed pot and
3 thirds in the second seed pot.

3 thirds + 3 thirds = 6 thirds

➡ The 2 seed pots contain 6 thirds. $2 = \frac{6}{3}$

Another way to express a whole number as a
fraction is to multiply the whole number by the
denominator you want. Use the product as the
numerator with the denominator you want.

Remember!
The denominator of a fraction tells how many parts the whole is divided into.

Express 6 as a fraction in fourths.
The denominator you want is 4.
$6 \times 4 = 24$.
6 is equivalent to $\frac{24}{4}$.

✏ How can you use a number line to find the number of thirds in 2?

Guided Instruction

Connect: Writing 1 as a fraction

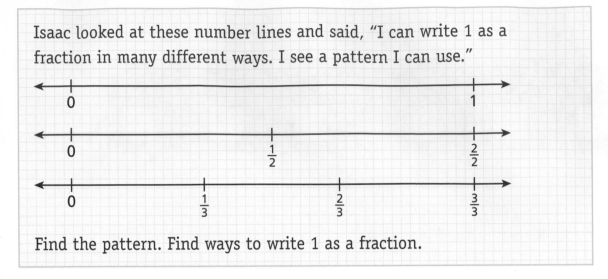

Isaac looked at these number lines and said, "I can write 1 as a fraction in many different ways. I see a pattern I can use."

Find the pattern. Find ways to write 1 as a fraction.

Find a pattern for writing 1 as fraction in different ways. Look at the fractions at the same place on the number lines as 1. Each numerator is the same as the denominator.

Write the fractions.

$$1 = \frac{2}{2} = \frac{3}{\Box}$$

Continue the pattern:

$$\frac{4}{4} = \frac{\Box}{5} = \frac{9}{\Box}$$

➡ The pattern is that the numerator and denominator are the same. Some ways to write 1 as a fraction are $\frac{2}{2}$, $\frac{3}{3}$, $\frac{5}{5}$, $\frac{10}{10}$, and $\frac{47}{47}$.

Connect: Writing a whole number as a fraction with 1 as the denominator

How can Alana write 8 as a fraction with 1 in the denominator?

The denominator tells how many parts in the whole. To have a denominator of 1, the whole can have only 1 part. The fraction $\frac{8}{1}$ shows there are 8 parts in the fraction and each part is 1 whole.

➡ Alana can write 8 as $\frac{8}{1}$. To write a whole number as a fraction with 1 as the denominator, use the whole number as the numerator.

Guided Practice

Use the number line to find the whole number for each fraction.

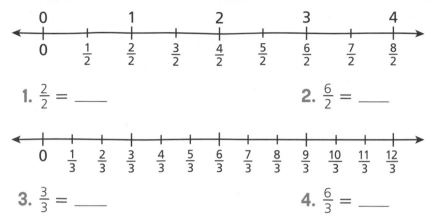

1. $\frac{2}{2} =$ ____

2. $\frac{6}{2} =$ ____

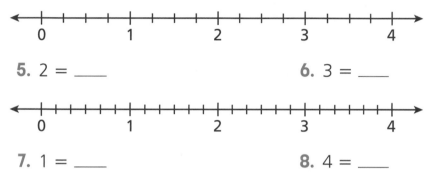

3. $\frac{3}{3} =$ ____

4. $\frac{6}{3} =$ ____

Use the number line to find the fraction for each whole number.

5. $2 =$ ____

6. $3 =$ ____

7. $1 =$ ____

8. $4 =$ ____

Solve the problem.

9. Makaela plants $\frac{3}{4}$ of her herb garden with basil and $\frac{1}{4}$ with sage. Explain why the fraction strips show that the whole garden is planted with basil and sage.

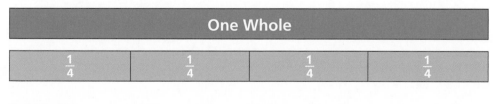

Answer _____

⁂ Think•Pair•Share

MP3 **10.** Work with a partner. Explain how you can find whole numbers for $\frac{8}{8}$, $\frac{16}{8}$, $\frac{24}{8}$, and $\frac{32}{8}$. Share your ideas with your class.

Lesson 21 Relate Whole Numbers and Fractions

Independent Practice

Write the fraction and whole number for the parts that are shaded.

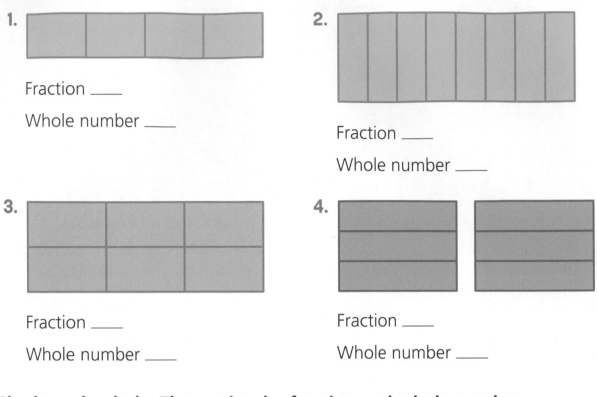

1.

Fraction ＿＿

Whole number ＿＿

2.

Fraction ＿＿

Whole number ＿＿

3.

Fraction ＿＿

Whole number ＿＿

4.

Fraction ＿＿

Whole number ＿＿

Shade each whole. Then write the fraction and whole number for the parts that are shaded.

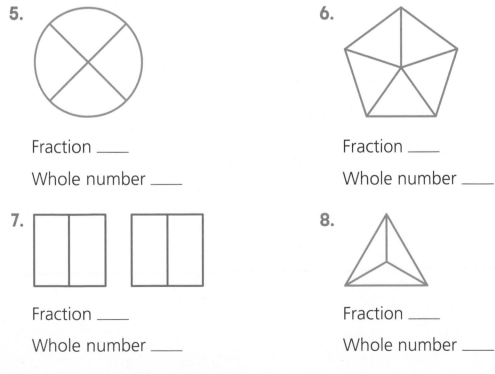

5.

Fraction ＿＿

Whole number ＿＿

6.

Fraction ＿＿

Whole number ＿＿

7.

Fraction ＿＿

Whole number ＿＿

8.

Fraction ＿＿

Whole number ＿＿

Independent Practice

9. Which whole number does the point on the number line represent?

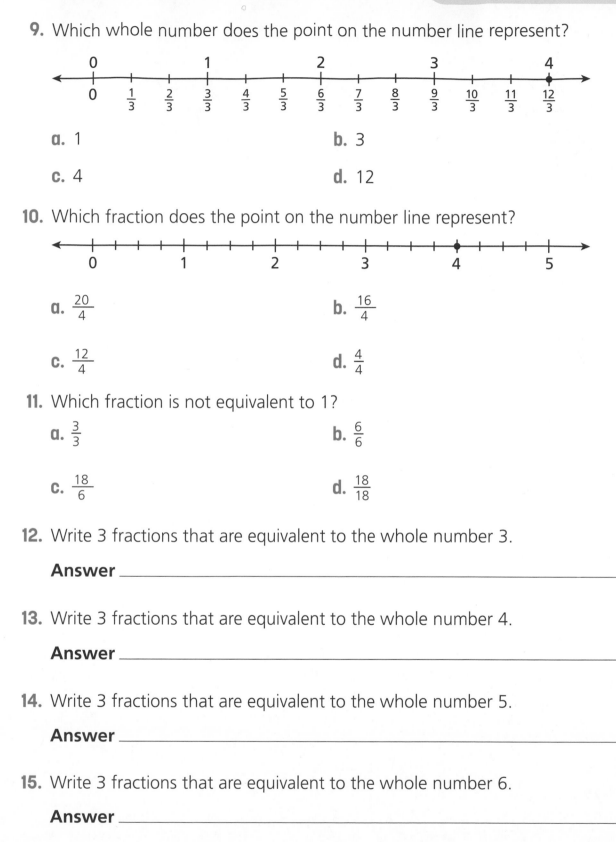

a. 1

b. 3

c. 4

d. 12

10. Which fraction does the point on the number line represent?

a. $\frac{20}{4}$

b. $\frac{16}{4}$

c. $\frac{12}{4}$

d. $\frac{4}{4}$

11. Which fraction is not equivalent to 1?

a. $\frac{3}{3}$

b. $\frac{6}{6}$

c. $\frac{18}{6}$

d. $\frac{18}{18}$

12. Write 3 fractions that are equivalent to the whole number 3.

Answer _____

13. Write 3 fractions that are equivalent to the whole number 4.

Answer _____

14. Write 3 fractions that are equivalent to the whole number 5.

Answer _____

15. Write 3 fractions that are equivalent to the whole number 6.

Answer _____

Independent Practice

Solve the problems.

MP4 **16.** Lauren bakes 2 lasagnas. She cuts each lasagna into sixths. How many pieces does she have? Draw or use fraction strips to express 2 as a fraction in sixths. Write the equivalent fractions.

Answer _____

MP5 **17.** Marco makes 6 personal pizzas. He cuts each pizza into thirds. How many pieces does he have? Draw a number line to express 6 as a fraction in thirds. Write the equivalent fractions.

Answer _____

MP6 **18.** Joanie bakes 3 pies. She cuts each pie into eighths. How many pieces does she have? Draw a model to express 3 as a fraction in eighths. Write the equivalent fractions.

Answer _____

Independent Practice

MP4 **19.** Mrs. Becker bakes an apple pie for her family. Mr. Becker eats $\frac{2}{8}$, Josh eats $\frac{3}{8}$, Randi eats $\frac{1}{8}$, and Mrs. Becker eats $\frac{1}{8}$. Did they eat the whole pie?

Answer _____

✏️ **Justify your answer using words, drawings, or numbers.**

MP2 **20.** Liat, Kevin, and Chandler each baked corn bread in the same size pan. The pictures show how each person cuts the corn bread in the pan.

Liat's Pan   Kevin's Pan   Chandler's Pan

Chandler says he bakes the most corn bread. Do you agree?

Answer _____

✏️ **Justify your answer using words, drawings, or numbers.**

MP3 **21.** Parker says that the shading in the figure represents the fraction $\frac{3}{3}$. Maddie says the shading in the figure represents the fraction $\frac{6}{6}$. Who do you agree with?

Answer _____

✏️ **Justify your answer using words, drawings, or numbers.**

Compare Fractions: Same Denominator

Guided Instruction

In this lesson you will learn to compare two fractions that have the same denominator.

Understand: Comparing fractions on a number line

Tamara is ordering a large pizza with mushrooms on $\frac{5}{8}$ of the slices and pineapple on $\frac{3}{8}$ of the slices. Does the pizza have more mushrooms or more pineapple?

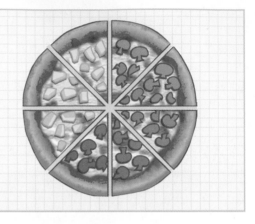

Compare $\frac{5}{8}$ and $\frac{3}{8}$ to answer the question.

Look at the number line.

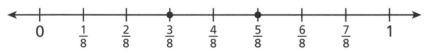

$\frac{5}{8}$ is to the right of $\frac{3}{8}$ on the number line, so $\frac{5}{8}$ is greater than $\frac{3}{8}$.

To show this comparison, write $\frac{5}{8} > \frac{3}{8}$.

$\frac{3}{8}$ is to the left of $\frac{5}{8}$ on the number line, so $\frac{3}{8}$ is less than $\frac{5}{8}$.

To show this comparison, write $\frac{3}{8} < \frac{5}{8}$.

Remember!
> means is greater than and < means is less than.

➡ The pizza has more mushrooms.

✏ How can you compare $\frac{5}{8}$ and $\frac{3}{8}$ using fraction models?

Guided Instruction

Understand: Using fraction strips to compare fractions with the same denominator

> Bryce bought $\frac{2}{4}$ pound of American cheese and $\frac{3}{4}$ pound of Swiss cheese. Compare the amounts of cheese that Bryce bought.

You can use fraction strips to represent $\frac{2}{4}$ pound and $\frac{3}{4}$ pound.

Step 1

Use two $\frac{1}{4}$ fraction strips for $\frac{2}{4}$.

Use three $\frac{1}{4}$ fraction strips for $\frac{3}{4}$.

	1			
American cheese	$\frac{1}{4}$	$\frac{1}{4}$	$\frac{1}{4}$	$\frac{1}{4}$
Swiss cheese	$\frac{1}{4}$	$\frac{1}{4}$	$\frac{1}{4}$	$\frac{1}{4}$

Step 2

Compare the lengths.

The length of the fraction strips for $\frac{3}{4}$ is greater than the length of the fraction strips for $\frac{2}{4}$.

The length of the fraction strips for $\frac{2}{4}$ is less than the length of the fraction strips for $\frac{3}{4}$.

Step 3

Compare the fractions. Use < and >.

$$\frac{3}{4} > \frac{2}{4} \qquad \frac{2}{4} < \frac{3}{4}$$

➡ Bryce bought more Swiss cheese than American cheese.
Bryce bought less American cheese than Swiss cheese.

✏ Why can you compare two fractions two ways?

Guided Instruction

Connect: Reasoning about fractions with the same denominator

Uma has to compare $\frac{2}{6}$ and $\frac{4}{6}$, but she does not have any fraction strips or number lines to use. How can Uma compare the fractions?

To compare fractions with the same denominator, use what you know about the fractions.

The denominators tell you that the parts that make up each fraction are the same size. The numerators tell you how many parts you are comparing. You can compare the fractions by comparing the numerators.

Compare $\frac{2}{6}$ and $\frac{4}{6}$.

2 ____ 4   4 ____ 2

$\frac{2}{6}$ ____ $\frac{4}{6}$ $\frac{4}{6}$ ____ $\frac{2}{6}$

You can write the comparison of two numbers two ways.

▶ Uma can compare $\frac{2}{6}$ and $\frac{4}{6}$ by comparing the numerators.

Connect: Reasoning about the size of the whole

In which two rectangles can you compare the fractions represented by the shaded parts?

Rectangle A   Rectangle B   Rectangle C

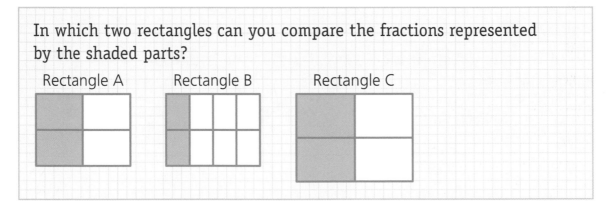

To compare fractions, the wholes must be the same size.

Each rectangle represents the whole for a fraction. Rectangle C is larger than Rectangles A and B. Rectangles A and B are the same size, so the wholes are the same size.

▶ The fractions represented by the shaded parts in Rectangles A and B can be compared. $\frac{2}{4} > \frac{2}{8}$ and $\frac{2}{8} < \frac{2}{4}$.

Guided Practice

Use the number line to compare the fractions. Write < or >.

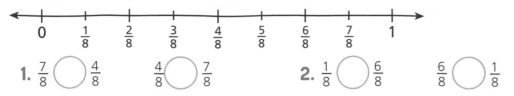

1. $\dfrac{7}{8} \bigcirc \dfrac{4}{8}$ $\dfrac{4}{8} \bigcirc \dfrac{7}{8}$ 2. $\dfrac{1}{8} \bigcirc \dfrac{6}{8}$ $\dfrac{6}{8} \bigcirc \dfrac{1}{8}$

Use the models to compare the fractions. Write < or >.

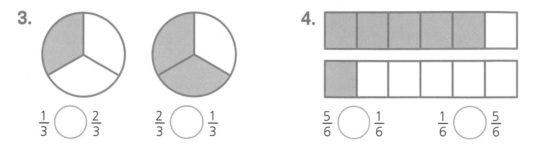

3. $\dfrac{1}{3} \bigcirc \dfrac{2}{3}$ $\dfrac{2}{3} \bigcirc \dfrac{1}{3}$ 4. $\dfrac{5}{6} \bigcirc \dfrac{1}{6}$ $\dfrac{1}{6} \bigcirc \dfrac{5}{6}$

Solve the problem.

5. Molly bought $\dfrac{1}{4}$ yard of blue ribbon and $\dfrac{3}{4}$ yard of red ribbon. Compare the amounts of ribbon Molly bought. Make a drawing to support your answer.

Answer _____

ⵙⵙ Think·Pair·Share

MP4 6. Work with a partner. Arrange 3 rows of fraction strips on a desk. In row one, place one $\dfrac{1}{3}$ fraction strip. In row two, place two $\dfrac{1}{3}$ fraction strips. In row three, place three $\dfrac{1}{3}$ fraction strips.

• Write the fractions that the fraction strips represent in order from least to greatest.

• What do you notice about the denominators?

• What do you notice about the numerators?

• How do the numerators relate to the number of fraction strips?

Independent Practice

Use the number line to compare the fractions. Write < or >.

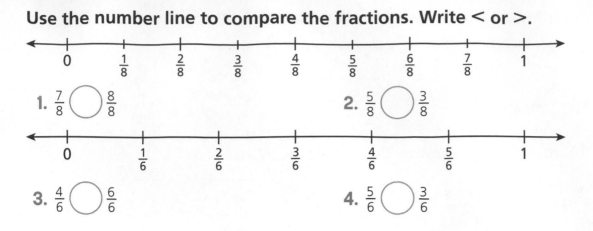

1. $\frac{7}{8}$ ◯ $\frac{8}{8}$
2. $\frac{5}{8}$ ◯ $\frac{3}{8}$

3. $\frac{4}{6}$ ◯ $\frac{6}{6}$
4. $\frac{5}{6}$ ◯ $\frac{3}{6}$

Use the models to compare the fractions. Write < or > .

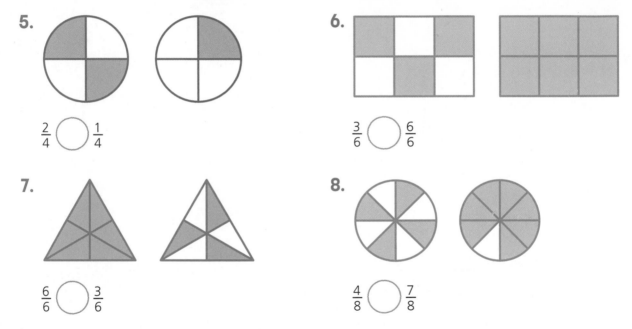

5. $\frac{2}{4}$ ◯ $\frac{1}{4}$

6. $\frac{3}{6}$ ◯ $\frac{6}{6}$

7. $\frac{6}{6}$ ◯ $\frac{3}{6}$

8. $\frac{4}{8}$ ◯ $\frac{7}{8}$

Find the fractions shown by each model. Then compare the fractions. Use <, >, or =.

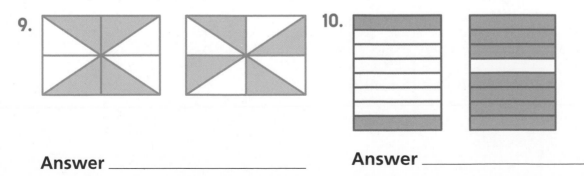

9.

Answer _____

10.

Answer _____

Independent Practice

Shade the figures to compare the fractions. Write <, >, or =.

11.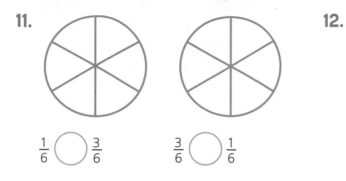

$\frac{1}{6}$ ◯ $\frac{3}{6}$ $\frac{3}{6}$ ◯ $\frac{1}{6}$

12.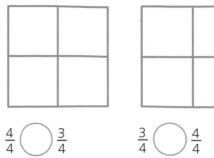

$\frac{4}{4}$ ◯ $\frac{3}{4}$ $\frac{3}{4}$ ◯ $\frac{4}{4}$

13. Which fraction is greater than $\frac{6}{8}$?

   a. $\frac{1}{8}$ **b.** $\frac{3}{8}$

   c. $\frac{5}{8}$ **d.** $\frac{9}{8}$

14. Which fraction is NOT less than $\frac{5}{6}$?

   a. $\frac{6}{6}$ **b.** $\frac{4}{6}$

   c. $\frac{2}{6}$ **d.** $\frac{1}{6}$

Compare. Write <, >, or =. Use a number line or model if needed.

15. $\frac{2}{2}$ ◯ $\frac{1}{2}$ 16. $\frac{1}{6}$ ◯ $\frac{3}{6}$

17. $\frac{2}{3}$ ◯ $\frac{3}{3}$ 18. $\frac{5}{6}$ ◯ $\frac{2}{6}$

19. $\frac{3}{8}$ ◯ $\frac{8}{8}$ 20. $\frac{4}{4}$ ◯ $\frac{3}{3}$

21. Write 3 fractions that are less than $\frac{4}{6}$.

   Answer _____

22. Write 3 fractions that are greater than $\frac{5}{8}$.

   Answer _____

Independent Practice

Solve the problems.

MP4 **23.** Before dinner, Prana finishes $\frac{4}{6}$ of her homework and Julieta finishes $\frac{5}{6}$ of her homework. There are 12 problems for homework. Who has finished more homework? Draw a model. Then compare the fractions.

Answer _____

MP2 **24.** Garrett paints his bedroom blue and white. He has $\frac{3}{8}$ gallon of white paint left and $\frac{2}{8}$ gallon of blue paint left. Draw a model to show the paint cans. Which paint can is less full? Then compare the fractions.

Answer _____

MP7 **25.** Kwame runs $\frac{5}{8}$ mile on Friday, $\frac{7}{8}$ mile on Saturday, and $\frac{4}{8}$ mile on Sunday. Draw number lines to compare the distances Kwame runs each day. On which day does Kwame run the longest distance? Then write the fractions in order from least to greatest.

Answer _____

Independent Practice

MP3 **26.** Lauren eats $\frac{1}{2}$ of a small pizza. Jared eats $\frac{1}{2}$ of a large pizza. Jared says that they both eat the same amount of pizza because $\frac{1}{2} = \frac{1}{2}$.

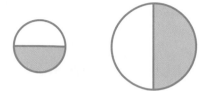

Do you agree? Explain your answer.

Answer _____

✏ **Justify your answer using words, drawings, or numbers.**

MP3 **27.** Is this fraction comparison true or false?

$$\frac{2}{8} > \frac{6}{8}$$

Use the models to help you decide.

Answer _____

✏ **Justify your answer using words, drawings, or numbers.**

Compare Fractions: Same Numerator

Guided Instruction

In this lesson you will learn to compare two fractions that have the same numerator.

Understand: Using number lines and models to compare fractions with the same numerator

> At a farm club meeting, Luke says that he collected $\frac{3}{4}$ dozen eggs that morning. Polly says that she collected $\frac{3}{2}$ dozen eggs. Who collected more eggs?

To find the answer, you can use a number line to compare $\frac{3}{4}$ and $\frac{3}{2}$.

Label the top of the number line with fractions in $\frac{1}{2}$s. Label the bottom of the number line with fractions in $\frac{1}{4}$s. When you do this, you can compare two fractions on the same number line.

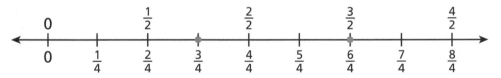

The point for $\frac{3}{2}$ is to the right of the point for $\frac{3}{4}$, so $\frac{3}{2}$ is greater than $\frac{3}{4}$.

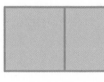 Polly collected more eggs.

You can also use models to compare $\frac{3}{4}$ and $\frac{3}{2}$.

Draw rectangles and use shading to show $\frac{3}{4}$ and $\frac{3}{2}$.

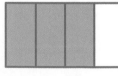

When you compare the sizes, you can see that $\frac{3}{2} > \frac{3}{4}$ and that $\frac{3}{4} < \frac{3}{2}$.

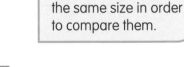 When you use models to work with fractions, how do you work with fractions that are greater than 1?

Guided Instruction

Understand: Using number strips to compare fractions with the same numerator

Haley used $\frac{3}{4}$ cup of wheat flour and $\frac{3}{6}$ cup of rye flour in a recipe. Compare the amounts of the flours that Haley used.

Step 1

Use fraction strips to represent $\frac{3}{4}$ cup and $\frac{3}{6}$ cup.

Use three $\frac{1}{4}$ fraction strips for $\frac{3}{4}$.

Use three $\frac{1}{6}$ fraction strips for $\frac{3}{6}$.

1

wheat flour

$\frac{1}{4}$	$\frac{1}{4}$	$\frac{1}{4}$

rye flour

$\frac{1}{6}$	$\frac{1}{6}$	$\frac{1}{6}$

Step 2

Compare the lengths.

The length of the fraction strips for $\frac{3}{4}$ is greater than the length of the fraction strips for $\frac{3}{6}$.

Step 3

Compare the fractions two ways. Use < and >.

$$\frac{3}{4} > \frac{3}{6} \qquad \frac{3}{6} < \frac{3}{4}$$

➡ Haley used more wheat flour than rye flour in the recipe.

✏ What does using the 1 strip help you remember?

Guided Instruction

Connect: Reasoning about fractions with the same numerator

Alex has to compare $\frac{2}{4}$ and $\frac{2}{8}$, but he wants to do it mentally. How can Alex compare the fractions?

To compare fractions with the same numerator, use what you know about the fractions.

The numerators tell you that there are the same number of parts to compare.

The denominators tell you about the size of the equal parts of the whole.

- The equal parts of a fraction with a greater denominator are smaller because the whole is divided into more parts.

This means that the fraction with the greater denominator will be the lesser fraction.

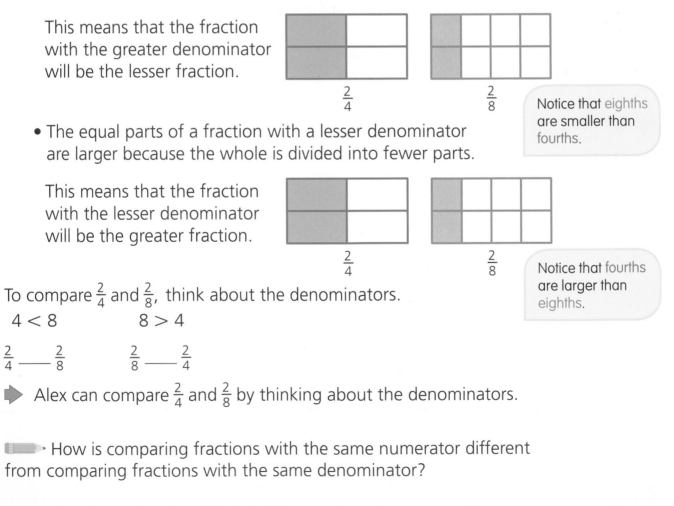

$$\frac{2}{4} \qquad \frac{2}{8}$$

Notice that eighths are smaller than fourths.

- The equal parts of a fraction with a lesser denominator are larger because the whole is divided into fewer parts.

This means that the fraction with the lesser denominator will be the greater fraction.

$$\frac{2}{4} \qquad \frac{2}{8}$$

Notice that fourths are larger than eighths.

To compare $\frac{2}{4}$ and $\frac{2}{8}$, think about the denominators.

$$4 < 8 \qquad\qquad 8 > 4$$

$$\frac{2}{4} \underline{\quad\quad} \frac{2}{8} \qquad\qquad \frac{2}{8} \underline{\quad\quad} \frac{2}{4}$$

➡ Alex can compare $\frac{2}{4}$ and $\frac{2}{8}$ by thinking about the denominators.

✏ How is comparing fractions with the same numerator different from comparing fractions with the same denominator?

Guided Practice

Use the number lines to compare the fractions. Write < or >.

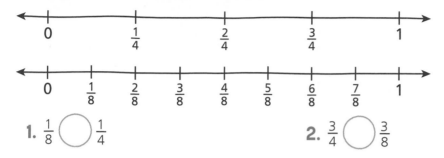

1. $\frac{1}{8}$ ◯ $\frac{1}{4}$

2. $\frac{3}{4}$ ◯ $\frac{3}{8}$

Use the models to compare the fractions. Write < or >.

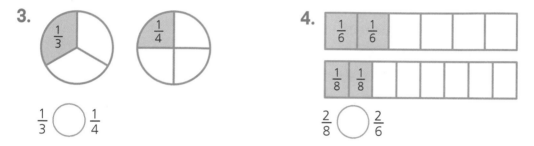

3. $\frac{1}{3}$ ◯ $\frac{1}{4}$

4. $\frac{2}{8}$ ◯ $\frac{2}{6}$

Solve the problem.

5. Zach walks $\frac{6}{2}$ blocks to the library. Lily walks $\frac{6}{3}$ blocks to the gym. Compare the distances they walk. Use a model to represent the problem.

Answer _____

⋎⋏ Think•Pair•Share

MP4 6. Arrange fraction strips of $\frac{1}{2}$, $\frac{1}{3}$, $\frac{1}{4}$, $\frac{1}{6}$, and $\frac{1}{8}$ on a desk. Place the longest strip at the top and the shortest strip at the bottom.

- What do you notice about the numerators?

- What do you notice about the denominators?

- How do the denominators relate to the size of the fraction strips?

Independent Practice

Use the number lines to compare the fractions. Write < or >.

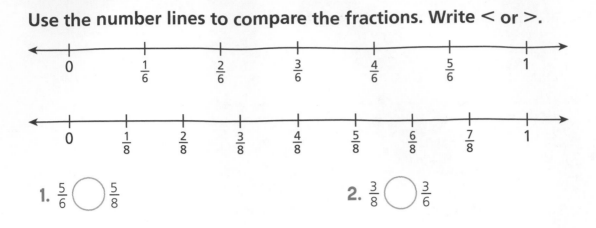

1. $\frac{5}{6}$ ◯ $\frac{5}{8}$

2. $\frac{3}{8}$ ◯ $\frac{3}{6}$

Use the models to compare the fractions. Write < or >.

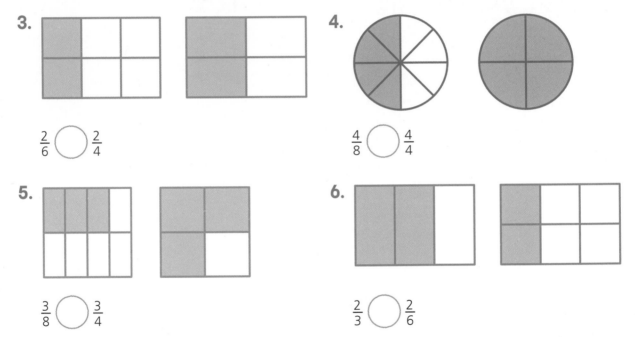

3. $\frac{2}{6}$ ◯ $\frac{2}{4}$

4. $\frac{4}{8}$ ◯ $\frac{4}{4}$

5. $\frac{3}{8}$ ◯ $\frac{3}{4}$

6. $\frac{2}{3}$ ◯ $\frac{2}{6}$

Write the fractions shown by each model. Then compare the fractions two ways. Use < and >.

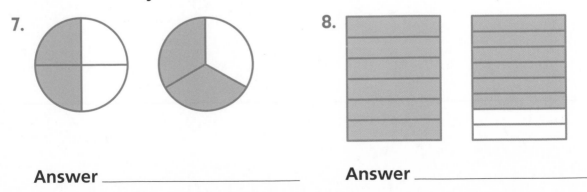

7.

Answer _____

8.

Answer _____

Independent Practice

Shade the figures to compare the fractions. Write < or >.

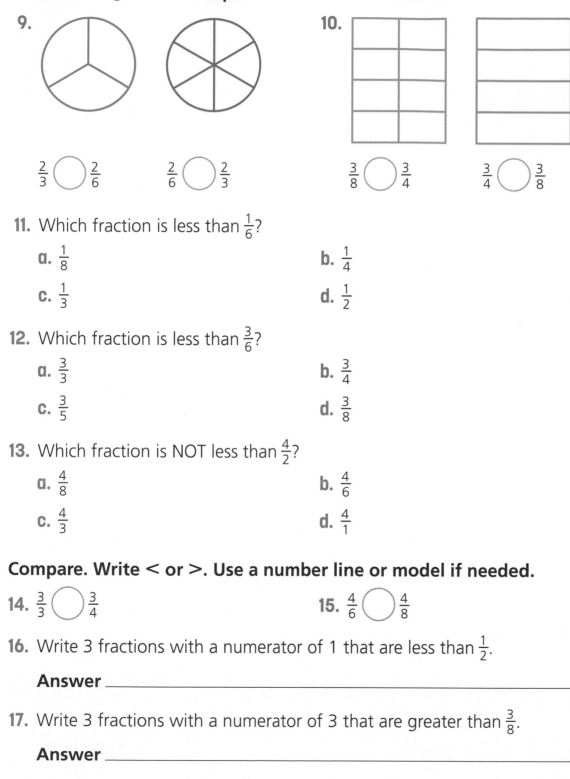

9.

$\frac{2}{3} \bigcirc \frac{2}{6}$ $\frac{2}{6} \bigcirc \frac{2}{3}$

10.

$\frac{3}{8} \bigcirc \frac{3}{4}$ $\frac{3}{4} \bigcirc \frac{3}{8}$

11. Which fraction is less than $\frac{1}{6}$?

a. $\frac{1}{8}$ b. $\frac{1}{4}$

c. $\frac{1}{3}$ d. $\frac{1}{2}$

12. Which fraction is less than $\frac{3}{6}$?

a. $\frac{3}{3}$ b. $\frac{3}{4}$

c. $\frac{3}{5}$ d. $\frac{3}{8}$

13. Which fraction is NOT less than $\frac{4}{2}$?

a. $\frac{4}{8}$ b. $\frac{4}{6}$

c. $\frac{4}{3}$ d. $\frac{4}{1}$

Compare. Write < or >. Use a number line or model if needed.

14. $\frac{3}{3} \bigcirc \frac{3}{4}$ **15.** $\frac{4}{6} \bigcirc \frac{4}{8}$

16. Write 3 fractions with a numerator of 1 that are less than $\frac{1}{2}$.

Answer _____

17. Write 3 fractions with a numerator of 3 that are greater than $\frac{3}{8}$.

Answer _____

Independent Practice

Solve the problems. Draw models to represent the problems.

MP4 **18.** Will runs $\frac{3}{6}$ mile around a track. Olivia runs $\frac{3}{4}$ mile around the track. Who runs farther? Compare the fractions.

Answer _____

MP7 **19.** Ben makes a punch. He uses $\frac{2}{3}$ quart of pineapple juice and $\frac{2}{8}$ quart of orange juice in the punch. Which juice does Ben use less of? Compare the fractions.

Answer _____

MP1 **20.** Melody buys three pieces of ribbon to make hair bows. She buys $\frac{4}{8}$ foot of blue ribbon, $\frac{4}{4}$ foot of yellow ribbon, and $\frac{4}{6}$ foot of red ribbon. Compare the lengths of the ribbons. Write the fractions in order from least to greatest.

Answer _____

Solve the problems.

MP7 **21.** Tawana drinks $\frac{5}{8}$ cup of milk. Jarrett drinks $\frac{5}{4}$ cup of milk. Who drinks more milk?

Answer _____

✏️ **Justify your answer using words, drawings, or numbers.**

MP3 **22.** Anna says that she has more pizza with peppers than Kai has.

Anna's Pizza   Kai's Pizza

Do you agree? Explain your answer.

Answer _____

✏️ **Justify your answer using words, drawings, or numbers.**

MP6 **23.** Depak says that $\frac{2}{4} < \frac{2}{8}$ because $4 < 8$. Do you agree? Use the rectangles to show $\frac{2}{4}$ and $\frac{2}{8}$.

Answer _____

✏️ **Justify your answer using words, drawings, or numbers.**

For exercises 1 and 2, use these figures.

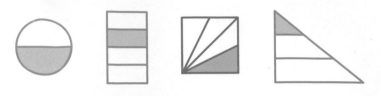

1. Circle each figure with a shaded part that can be named by a unit fraction.

2. Describe one figure that does NOT show a unit fraction. Explain.

Read the fraction. Partition the number line into equal parts. Locate the fraction on the number line and draw a point. Label the point.

3. $\frac{1}{4}$

4. $\frac{1}{2}$

Locate the fraction on the number line and draw a point. Label the point.

5. $\frac{3}{8}$

6. $\frac{2}{3}$

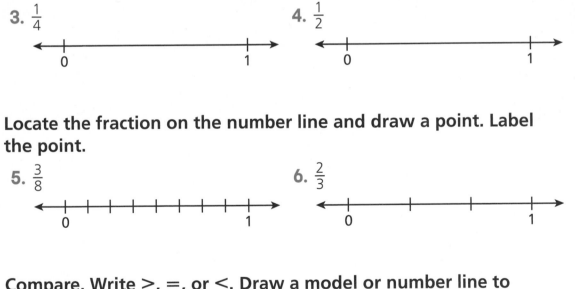

Compare. Write >, =, or <. Draw a model or number line to support your answer.

7. $\frac{5}{6}$ ◯ $\frac{3}{6}$

8. $\frac{3}{8}$ ◯ $\frac{3}{4}$

9. Which fraction is equivalent to 1?

a. $\frac{5}{4}$ b. $\frac{4}{4}$

c. $\frac{3}{4}$ d. $\frac{1}{4}$

10. Which fraction is equivalent to $\frac{1}{2}$?

a. $\frac{2}{8}$ b. $\frac{1}{3}$

c. $\frac{2}{4}$ d. $\frac{5}{6}$

For exercises 11 and 12, locate the fractions on the number line. Draw a point for each fraction. Label the points.

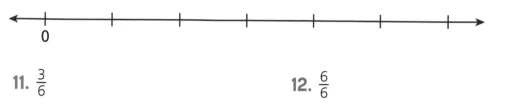

0

11. $\frac{3}{6}$ **12.** $\frac{6}{6}$

For exercises 13–16, use this problem.

Miguel and a friend order a pizza. The pizza has 8 equal slices. They eat $\frac{5}{8}$ of the pizza and take the rest home.

13. How many slices of pizza do Miguel and his friend eat?

_____

14. Use two colors. Show how much of the pizza the two friends eat. Show how much they take home.

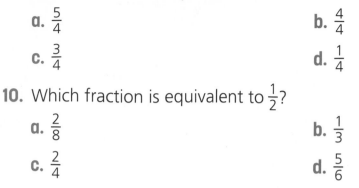

15. Write a fraction that shows the part of the pizza that Miguel and his friend take home. ____

16. Write a fraction that represents the whole pizza. ____

Solve the problems.

17. Eva makes a flag for her soccer team. She uses three different fabrics.

$\frac{1}{4}$ of the flag is striped; $\frac{1}{8}$ of the flag is red; $\frac{5}{8}$ of the flag is blue.

Make a drawing to show a possible flag that Eva made.

MP4 **18.** Kwame eats $\frac{4}{4}$ cup of soup. Jasmine eats $\frac{4}{8}$ cup of soup. Who eats more soup?

Answer _____

✏️ **Justify your answer using words, drawings, or numbers.**

MP3 **19.** Skylar cuts a submarine sandwich into 6 equal slices. He gives 2 slices each to Lily and Ben. Skylar also takes 2 slices for himself. "We each get $\frac{1}{6}$ of the sandwich," he says. What is Skylar's error?

✏️ **Show your work.**

MP5 **20.** Angela has a ribbon that is 4 feet long. She uses 3 feet of the ribbon for a craft project. What fraction of the ribbon is left?

Answer _____

✏️ **Justify your answer using words, drawings, or numbers.**

Performance Tasks

Performance Tasks show your understanding of the Math that you have learned. You will be doing various Performance Tasks as you complete your work in this text.

Beginning This Task

The next five pages provide you with the beginning of a Performance Task. You will be given 5 items to complete, and each item will have two or more parts. As you complete these items you will:

I Demonstrate that you have mastered mathematical skills and concepts

II Reason through a problem to a solution, and explain your reasoning

III Use models and apply them to real-world situations.

Extending This Task

Your teacher may extend this Performance Task with additional items provided in our online resources at sadlierconnect.com.

Scoring This Task

Your response to each item will be assessed against a rubric, or scoring guide. Some items will be worth 1 or 2 points, and others will be worth more. In each item you will show your work or explain your reasoning.

Performance Task 1

Rows of Radishes

1. Ms. Galindo counts 24 tiny radish plants. The radish plants are in rows. Each row has the same number of plants.

   a. Draw two different arrays to show how the radish plants might be growing.

   b. Write a multiplication fact for each array.

   c. Explain how each of your arrays relates to the multiplication fact.

Planting a Corn Patch

2. Tony and Marco want to plant sweet corn in their corn patch. The corn patch is partitioned into 6 equal parts.

    a. Draw a diagram to show what the corn patch might look like.

    b. Tony and Marco plant sweet corn in 1 of the parts of the corn patch.

       Write a fraction that represents the part of the corn patch that they use.

    c. Explain how the fraction you wrote represents 1 part of the corn patch.

    d. Shade in the diagram in item 2.a. to model the fraction that represents the part of the corn patch that Tony and Marco use.

Performance Task 1

A Twist in the Garden Hose

3. Mr. Chan uses a garden hose to water his garden. There is a twist in the garden hose. The number line below represents the garden hose.

   a. The twist in the garden hose is located at $\frac{1}{4}$ the distance from the faucet to the nozzle of the garden hose.

   Write the fraction $\frac{1}{4}$ in the correct location on the number line.

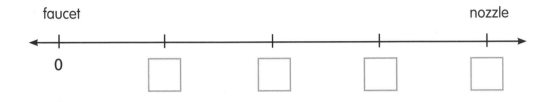

   b. Explain how you decided where to locate the fraction on the number line.

   c. How far from the nozzle is the twist located? Use a fraction to name the distance.

   d. Mr. Chan says that the twist is closer to the faucet than to the nozzle. Is Mr. Chan correct?

   Explain your reasoning.

Boxing Up the Tomatoes

4. Tina and Stewart pick tomatoes. They put all of the tomatoes in boxes. Tina puts 6 tomatoes in each of 8 boxes. Stewart puts 4 tomatoes in each of 11 boxes.

a. Write an equation to find the number of tomatoes Tina and Stewart put in boxes.

b. Use words to tell about the equation you wrote.

c. How many tomatoes do Tina and Stewart put in boxes? Solve the equation.

d. Use estimation to check if your answer is reasonable. Justify your reasoning.

Performance Task 1

Picking and Piling Peppers

5. Cynthia and Bill pick peppers. They put all of the peppers in piles of 40 peppers each.

   a. Cynthia and Bill make 9 piles. Then Cynthia picks 23 more peppers.

     Write an equation to find the number of peppers Cynthia and Bill pick altogether.

   b. How many peppers do Cynthia and Bill pick altogether?

     Solve the equation.

   c. Cynthia uses the 23 more peppers she picks to make another pile. She says that now they have 10 equal piles of peppers. Why might Bill disagree? Explain your reasoning.

Progress Check

UNIT 4

Look at how the math concepts and skills you have learned and will learn connect.

It is very important for you to understand the math concepts and skills from the prior grade level so that you will be able to develop an understanding of measurement and data in this unit and be prepared for next year. To practice your skills, go to sadlierconnect.com.

GRADE 2		GRADE 3		GRADE 4
I Can...	**Before Unit 4**	**Can I ?**	**After Unit 4**	**I Will...**
Tell and write time to the nearest five minutes	☐	Tell and write time to the nearest minute	☐	
	☐	Solve word problems by adding and subtracting time intervals in minutes	☐	
Use appropriate tools to measure length	☐	Measure and estimate liquid volumes and masses	☐	Solve word problems involving distance, time, liquid volumes, masses, and money
Solve problems involving lengths	☐	Solve one-step problems involving masses or volumes	☐	
Draw a picture graph and a bar graph for the same data set	☐	Draw a scaled picture graph or a scaled bar graph to represent a data set	☐	
Solve problems using data shown in a bar graph	☐	Solve "how many more" and "how many less" problems using information in scaled bar graphs	☐	
Show length measurements on a line plot	☐	Show length measurements in inches, half inches, and quarter inches on a line plot	☐	Display a set of measurements in fractions of a unit on a line plot
				Solve problems involving addition and subtraction of fractions by using information presented in line plots

HOME◆CONNECT...

I n this unit your child will continue to develop problem-solving skills using measurements and estimations as well as representing and interpreting data.

Scientists and mathematicians use measurements and data in their world. But families use them every day too. Support your child using the following Math vocabulary of units of measurement you use each day: **minute**, **hour**, **inch**, foot, centimeter, mile, meter, **gram**, **kilogram**, ounce, pound, quart, **liter**, and many more. When taking measurements, whether measuring **elapsed time**, **liquid volume**, **mass**, or length, you are collecting data. **Data** is information.

Once the data is collected, it can be represented in various ways. Children are already familiar with **line plots**, **picture graphs**, and **bar graphs**. Now they are given the opportunity to review and expand their knowledge of graphs as well as collect data and represent it in various formats.

On the Go: Make a plan to determine how much time a daily activity takes up in one week. Choose a daily activity such as watching TV or reading independently. Together, determine the elapsed time spent on the activity each day during the week and record the data. Then make a graph of the data and talk about what it shows.

In this unit your child will:

- Tell and write time to the nearest minute.

- Solve word problems by adding and subtracting time intervals in minutes.

- Measure and estimate liquid volumes and masses.

- Solve one-step problems involving liquid volumes and masses.

- Draw a scaled picture graph or a scaled bar graph to represent a data set.

- Solve "how many more" and "how many less" problems using information in scaled bar graphs.

- Show length measurements in inches, half inches, and quarter inches on a line plot.

Ways to Help Your Child

Is it better for your child to begin homework before after-school activities, or after dinner? Does your child need some play time or down time? Talk with your child in order to set up some ground rules for managing time after school. Make the most of whatever time of day works best.

ONLINE

For more Home Connect activities, continue online at sadlierconnect.com

Focus on Measurement and Data

UNIT 4

Essential Question:
How can data be used to solve problems?

Essential Question:
How can you solve problems involving time?

Words to Know:
time
minute
elapsed time
time interval
hour

Guided Instruction

In this lesson you will learn how to tell and write time and measure intervals of time.

Understand: How to tell and write time

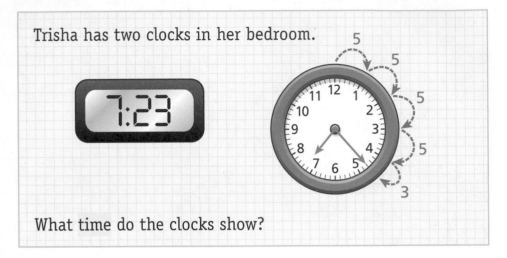

Trisha has two clocks in her bedroom.

What time do the clocks show?

Read the digital clock. 7:23

You can say, "Seven twenty-three." or "Twenty-three minutes after seven."

Read the clock with hands.
Each mark shows 1 minute.

Look at the hour hand.
The hour hand points at a little past 7.

Look at the minute hand.
5 + 5 + 5 + 5 = 20
20 + 3 = 23
The minute hand points at 23 minutes past the hour.
The clock shows 7:23.

Remember!
The hour hand moves from one number to the next in 60 minutes. The minute hand moves from one number to the next in 5 minutes.

➧ Both clocks show 7:23.

✏ Why is it important to be able to read both kinds of clocks?

Understand: How to measure intervals of time

Aaron swam from 8:45 A.M. to 9:35 A.M.
How long did Aaron swim?

You need to find the amount of time Aaron swam.
The difference from one time to another time is
called elapsed time.

To find the elapsed time, look at the minute hand for 8:45.
Count time intervals of 10 minutes to 9:35.
$10 + 10 + 10 + 10 + 10 = 50$

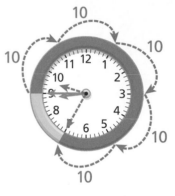

➡ Aaron swam for 50 minutes.

A soccer team practiced from 3:00 P.M. to 4:30 P.M.
How long did the team practice?

Use a number line.

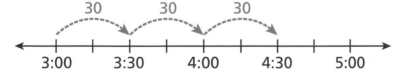

Count time intervals of 30 minutes.

30   +   30   +   30   = 90

1 hour   +   30   = 1 hour 30 minutes

Remember!
60 minutes is 1 hour.

➡ The team practiced for 90 minutes, or 1 hour 30 minutes.

✏ What other time intervals could you count to find how long the
team practiced?

Guided Instruction

Connect: Problem solving and elapsed time

Lunch starts at 12:05 P.M. and lasts for 50 minutes.
When does lunch end?

Step 1

Start at 12:05.
Decide what time interval you will count.
Try 10 minutes.

Step 2

You can add time intervals by counting on.
Count ahead by time intervals of 10 minutes.
After 50 minutes, the minute hand points to 11.

▶ Lunch ends at 12:55.

A movie ends at 8 P.M. The movie lasts 2 hours 15 minutes.
When does the movie start?

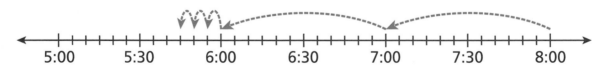

Step 1

You can subtract time intervals by counting back.
Start at 8:00.
Count back 2 hours. 8:00 ⟶ 7:00 ⟶ 6:00

Step 2

Count back 15 more minutes.
Count back by intervals of 5 minutes. 6:00 ⟶ 5:55 ⟶ 5:50 ⟶ 5:45

▶ The movie started at _____ P.M.

Guided Practice

Write the time shown by each clock.

1. 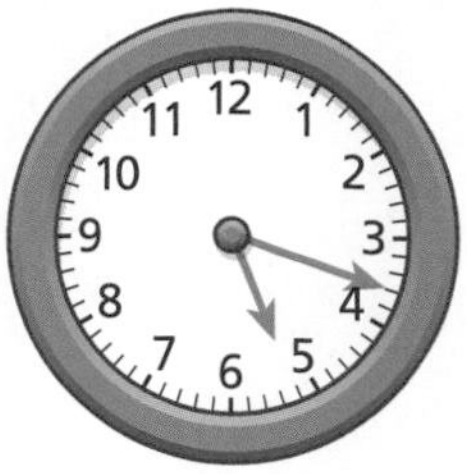

____

2. 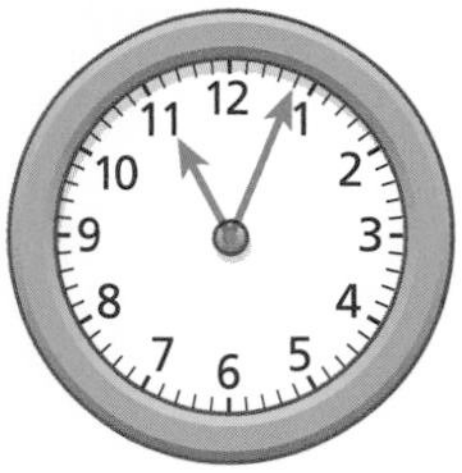

____

3. 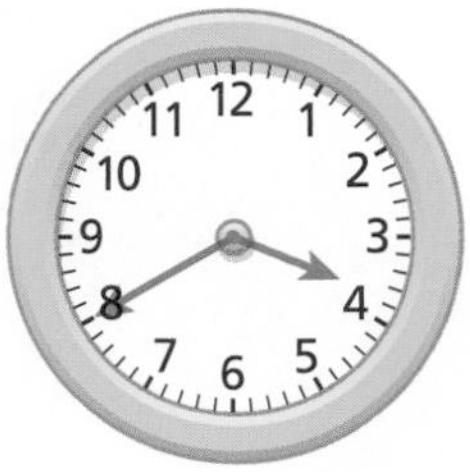

____

Solve the problems.

4. Maria leaves for school at 7:25 A.M. She arrives at school at 7:50 A.M. How long does it take her to get to school?

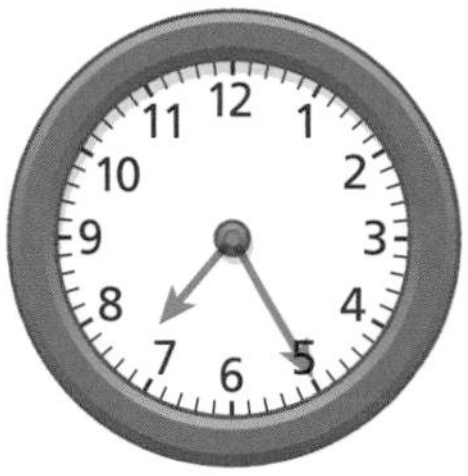

____ minutes

5. Mr. Landon put a loaf of oatmeal bread in the oven at 2:30 P.M. He takes the bread out at 3:20 P.M. How long is the bread in the oven?

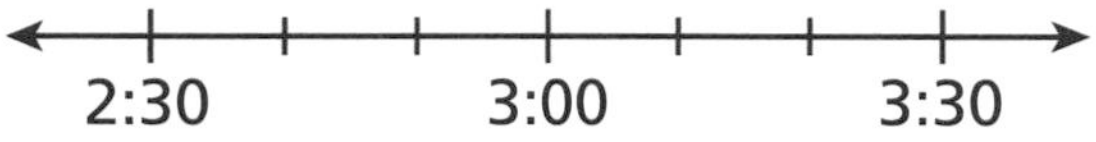

____ minutes

6. Henry works on a project for 40 minutes. If he started at 4:45 P.M., when did he finish?

________ P.M.

7. A cat wakes at 10:10 A.M. It slept for 1 hour 20 minutes. When did it go to sleep?

________ A.M.

Think•Pair•Share

MP4 8. A dinosaur movie starts at 12:30 P.M. The movie lasts 1 hour 30 minutes. Luis counts by intervals of 30 minutes to find when the movie ends. Sara counts by intervals of 10 minutes. Do Luis and Sara find the same answer to the problem? Explain your thinking.

Independent Practice

Write the time shown by each clock.

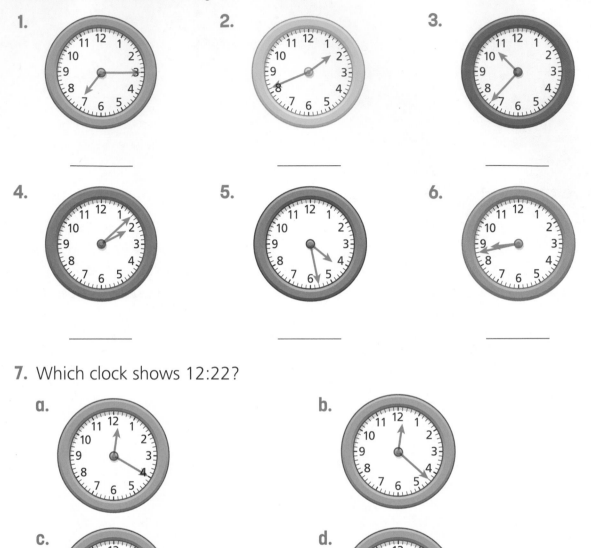

1.

_____

2.

_____

3.

_____

4.

_____

5.

_____

6.

_____

7. Which clock shows 12:22?

a.

b.

c.

d.

8. The clocks show when Nelson starts and finishes washing his mother's car. How long does it take Nelson to wash the car?

Starts   Finishes

Answer _____

_____

Independent Practice

Solve the problems.

MP2 **9.** Anna rides her bike to the library. The clocks show the time she leaves for the library and the time she arrives there. How long is Anna's ride.

Time Anna Leaves

Time Anna Arrives

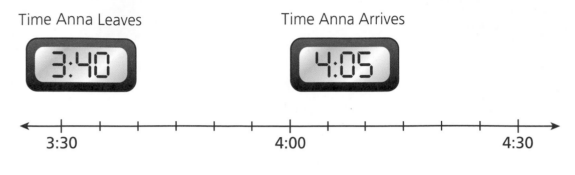

3:30   4:00   4:30

_____

MP1 **10.** Mr. Cruz drives to the grocery store. He returns at 7:20 P.M. after being gone for 45 minutes. What time did Mr. Cruz leave for the store?

Time Mr. Cruz Leaves

Time Mr. Cruz Returns

Answer _____

MP7 **11.** Jenna starts reading a story book at 6:10 P.M. She reads for 50 minutes. Then her mother tells her to set the dinner table. When does Jenna stop reading?

Answer _____

MP4 **12.** Ray and his dad go fishing. They leave the house at 5:45 A.M. They are gone for 7 hours 30 minutes. When do they come home?

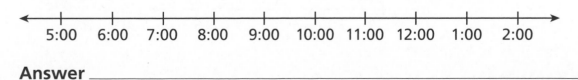

5:00 6:00 7:00 8:00 9:00 10:00 11:00 12:00 1:00 2:00

Answer _____

Independent Practice

MP8 **13.** Basketball practice starts at 3:15 P.M. and lasts 1 hour 30 minutes. Explain how to find when basketball practice will end.

MP7 **14.** Dan leaves the dentist office at 2:20 P.M. He was at the office for 50 minutes. How can Dan figure out when he arrived at the office?

MP2 **15.** Sue practices her violin each day for 45 minutes. Today she starts practicing at 4:55 P.M. When does she finish?

➡ **Show your work.**

Answer _____

MP1 **16.** A plane arrives at an airport at 7:10 A.M. The flight lasted 2 hours 20 minutes. When did the plane take off?

➡ **Show your work.**

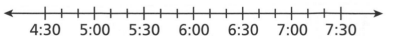

Answer _____

Independent Practice

MP5 **17.** Lucy walks to the bus stop, waits for the bus, and then takes the bus to school. She walks 10 minutes. She waits 5 minutes. And the bus trip lasts 25 minutes. If Lucy leaves her home at 7:15 A.M., when does she arrive at school?

✏️▸ **Show your work.**

Answer _____

MP4 **18.** At Culver Elementary, the school day lasts 6 hours 30 minutes. The first bell rings at 8:00 A.M. When does the last bell ring?

Answer _____

✏️▸ **Justify your answer using words, drawings, or numbers.**

```
←─┼┼┼┼┼┼┼┼┼┼┼┼┼┼┼┼┼┼┼┼┼┼┼┼┼┼┼┼┼┼┼┼┼┼┼→
  8:00    9:00    10:00   11:00   12:00   1:00    2:00    3:00
     8:30    9:30    10:30   11:30   12:30   1:30    2:30
```

MP2 **19.** Marcy's mother takes a roast out of the oven at 7:35 P.M. The roast was in the oven for 1 hour 45 minutes. When did Marcy's mother put the roast in the oven?

Answer _____

✏️▸ **Justify your answer using words, drawings, or numbers.**

Problem Solving: Liquid Volumes and Masses

Essential Question:
How can you solve problems involving liquid volume and mass?

Words to Know:
 liquid volume
 liter (L)
 mass
 gram (g)
 kilogram (kg)

Guided Instruction

In this lesson you will learn about liquid volume and mass.

Understand: How to estimate liquid volume

Liquid volume is the amount of liquid a container can hold.

Fred filled a pitcher with juice.

Which is the best estimate of the liquid volume of the pitcher?

1 L

less than 1 liter   **1 liter**   **more than 1 liter**

Use a benchmark to get an idea of how much 1 liter is. A tall water bottle has a liquid volume of 1 liter. Compare the amount of juice in the pitcher with the amount of water that would fill a 1-liter bottle.

⮕   The liquid volume of the pitcher is more than 1 liter.

Understand: How to solve problems involving liquid volume

Teresa has a fish tank that holds 25 liters of water.
She takes out 9 liters of water to clean the tank.
How many liters of water are still in the tank?

Write a subtraction equation for the problem.
$25 - 9 = w$

Solve the subtraction equation.
$25 - 9 = 16$

⮕   16 liters of water are still in the tank.

✏️ Write an addition equation you could use to solve the problem.

Guided Instruction

Understand: How to estimate mass

Mass is the amount of matter an object contains.

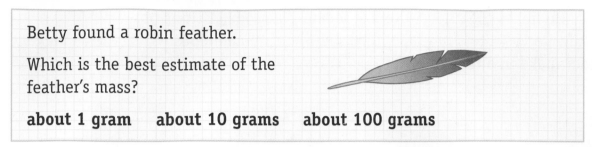

Betty found a robin feather.

Which is the best estimate of the feather's mass?

about 1 gram   about 10 grams   about 100 grams

Use a benchmark. Look at the chart. Which of the benchmark objects has about the same mass as a feather? A pencil is too heavy, so use a paper clip. A paper clip has a mass of about 1 gram.

➡ The feather has a mass of about 1 gram.

Benchmarks	
Object	Mass
Paper clip	1 gram
Pencil	10 grams
Cell phone	100 grams
1-liter bottle of water	1000 grams

Understand: How to solve problems involving mass

At the aquarium, Henry filled 6 small paper bags with fish food flakes. He made this drawing of his balance to show how he measured the mass of 1 filled bag.

What is the mass of the fish flakes Henry used to fill the 6 small bags?

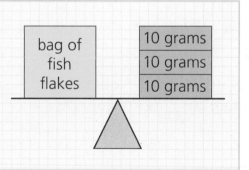

Start by using the drawing to find the mass of 1 bag.

The drawing shows that the mass of 1 bag of fish flakes is about 30 grams.

Hint: A bag has very little mass, so do not worry about including the mass of a bag.

Then use this information to write an equation.

$f = 6 \times 30$
$f = 180$

➡ Six bags of fish flakes have a mass of about 180 grams.

Guided Instruction

Connect: Solving problems involving liquid volumes and masses

> The Fielder family is having a party. Mr. Fielder makes a large batch of punch. He mixes together 5 liters of lemon-lime soda, 2 liters of orange juice, and 4 liters of grape juice. How much punch does Mr. Fielder make in all?

Step 1

Use a drawing to write an equation.

$5 + 2 + 4 = p$

liters of punch in all		
5 liters	2 liters	4 liters

Step 2

Solve the equation.

$5 + 2 + 4 = 11$

➡ Mr. Fielder makes 11 liters of punch in all.

A kilogram is a unit used to measure mass. 1 kg = 1000 g

> Tina has a softball bat. Help Tina find the best estimate of the mass of the bat.
>
> **about 1 kilogram**   **about 3 kilograms**   **about 5 kilograms**

Step 1

Use a benchmark.
Look at the chart.
Which of the benchmark objects has about the same mass as a bat?
A brick is too heavy, so it is a math book.

Benchmarks	
Object	Mass
Math book	1 kilogram
Brick	3 kilograms
Medium size cat	5 kilograms

Step 2

A math book has a mass of about 1 kilogram.

MATH

➡ The bat has a mass of about ____ kilogram.

Circle the best estimate of the liquid volume.

1.

1 liter   10 liters   50 liters

2.

1 liter   10 liters   20 liters

Circle the best estimate of the mass.

3.

1 kilogram   10 kilograms   100 kilograms

4.

1 gram   25 grams   50 grams

Solve each problem.

5. Ms. Lewis makes 6 mini bran muffins. Each muffin has a mass of 20 grams. What is the total mass of the bran muffins?

_____ grams

6. Jerry's two fish tanks have liquid volumes of 90 liters and 38 liters. How many fewer liters of water does the smaller tank hold than the larger tank?

_____ liters

Think•Pair•Share

MP1   7. Abu wants to estimate the mass of two nickels. He knows that the mass of a pencil is about 10 grams and the mass of a cell phone is about 100 grams. He estimates that the two nickels have a mass of about 100 grams. What mistake did Abu make? Explain.

Independent Practice

Draw a line connecting each object with the best estimate of its liquid volume.

1.   6 liters

2.   1 liter

3.   500 liters

4.   20 liters

Circle the best estimate of the mass of each object.

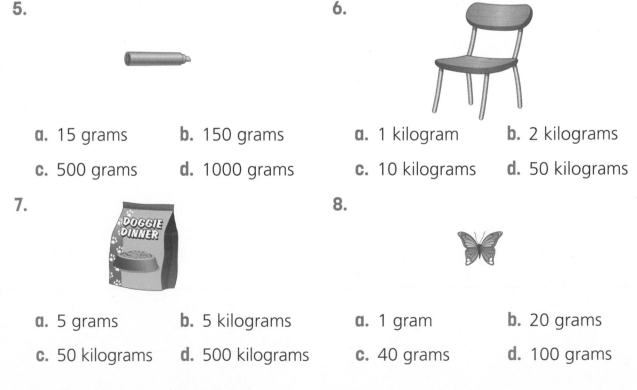

5.

a. 15 grams   **b.** 150 grams

c. 500 grams   **d.** 1000 grams

6.

a. 1 kilogram   **b.** 2 kilograms

c. 10 kilograms   **d.** 50 kilograms

7.

a. 5 grams   **b.** 5 kilograms

c. 50 kilograms   **d.** 500 kilograms

8.

a. 1 gram   **b.** 20 grams

c. 40 grams   **d.** 100 grams

Independent Practice

Solve the problems.

9. In science class, Ms. Franklin wants to combine two liquids. How big of a container does she need?

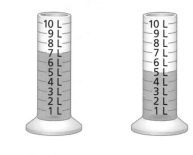

_____-liter container

10. Ed takes 9 packages to the post office. Each package has the same mass. What is the mass of the packages?

3 kg	3 kg	3 kg
3 kg	3 kg	3 kg
3 kg	3 kg	3 kg

_____ kilograms

11. BriAnna has a bag of pebbles. She puts an equal amount of pebbles into each of 5 flowerpots. If she uses all the pebbles, how much does she put in each pot?

PEBBLES
450 g

_____ grams of pebbles

12. Steve fills a bucket with water. He pours 12 liters of the water into a trough for his horse. How much water is left in the bucket?

18 L

_____ liters of water

Circle the correct answer.

13. Mr. Neil buys a piece of cheese that has a mass of 1000 grams. After he slices off some cheese, the piece has a mass of 680 grams. How much cheese does he slice off?

a. 320 grams   **b.** 480 grams

c. 620 grams   **d.** 1680 grams

14. Samantha has 8 tomato plants. She waters them with a can that holds 4 liters. If she gives each plant a full can of water, how much water does she use?

a. 15 liters   **b.** 24 liters

c. 32 liters   **d.** 36 liters

Independent Practice

Solve the problems.

MP4 **15.** Trent made a drawing to show how
he measured the mass of 1 plum.

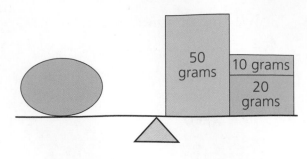

a. About what is the mass of 1 plum?

_____

b. About what would the mass of 6 plums be?

_____

MP2 **16.** Ms. Rivera has two goldfish ponds. The first pond holds 190 liters
of water. The second pond holds 28 fewer liters than the first
pond. How can she find the liquid volume of the second pond?

MP1 **17.** Helen buys a fish tank. She puts in 65 liters of water on Monday.
She adds 42 liters of water on Tuesday and 83 liters of water on
Wednesday to fill the tank. What is the liquid volume of the tank?

✏️➤ **Show your work.**

Answer _____

MP2 **18.** Dave has a sack of concrete. The mass of the concrete is
24 kilograms. When he pours equal amounts of concrete into
some buckets, he empties the sack. Each bucket has 3 kilograms
of concrete. How many buckets does he use?

✏️➤ **Show your work.**

Answer _____

Independent Practice

MP6 **19.** A box contains 80 crackers. Each cracker has a mass of 5 grams. What is the total mass of the crackers?

    Show your work.

    Answer _____

MP1 **20.** Ms. Thomson puts 480 liters of water in a wading pool. Her children and their friends play in the pool. Now the pool has 393 liters of water. How much water do the children and their friends splash out?

    Answer _____

    Justify your answer using words, drawings, or numbers.

MP2 **21.** Sam makes a regular veggie burger and a super veggie burger. He uses mustard from a 250-gram jar in the veggie burgers. The regular veggie burger has a mass of 140 grams. The super veggie burger has a mass of 235 grams. What is the total mass of the veggie burgers?

    Answer _____

    Justify your answer using words, drawings, or numbers.

Draw Graphs to Represent Categorical Data

Essential Question:
How can I draw graphs to show data?

Words to Know:
picture graph
data
key
bar graph
scale

Guided Instruction

In this lesson you will learn about picture graphs and bar graphs.

Understand: How to draw picture graphs

A picture graph shows data, or information.

The data in the tally chart to the right show the favorite fruits of students in a third-grade class. How many students chose peaches as their favorite fruit?

Favorite Fruit	
Peaches	̶H̶H̶T̶ ̶H̶H̶T̶
Strawberries	̶H̶H̶T̶ I
Bananas	IIII
Oranges	̶H̶H̶T̶ III

➡ Ten students chose peaches as their favorite fruit.

You can use the data from the tally chart to make a picture graph. Each picture or symbol represents a number of data.

Look at the row for Peaches in the tally chart.
Ten students chose peaches as their favorite fruit.

Look at the row for Peaches in the picture graph.
There are 5 🗑 symbols. Look at the key.
The key tells what each symbol represents.
Each 🗑 symbol represents 2 students.
    $5 \times 2 = 10$

Favorite Fruit	
Peaches	🗑 🗑 🗑 🗑 🗑
Strawberries	🗑 🗑 🗑
Bananas	🗑 🗑
Oranges	🗑 🗑 🗑 🗑

Key: 🗑 = 2 students

✏ Explain why the picture graph shows the data for oranges correctly.

Guided Instruction

Understand: **How to draw bar graphs**

A bar graph is another way to represent data.

The tally chart shows how students in a third-grade class get to school. How many students ride their bikes to school?	Ways to Get to School	
	Bus	ЖЖ ЖЖ ‖
	Car	‖
	Bike	ЖЖ ‖‖‖
	Walk	ЖЖ ‖

➡ Eight students ride their bikes to school.

You can use the data from the tally chart to make a bar graph.

Each bar represents a row of data from the tally chart. The length of the bar shows the number of students.

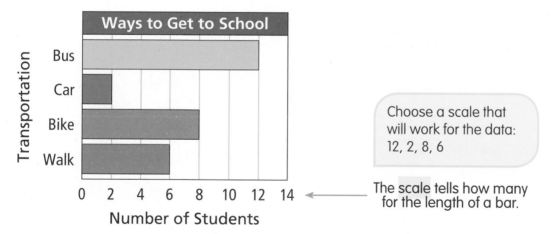

Choose a scale that will work for the data: 12, 2, 8, 6

The scale tells how many for the length of a bar.

Look at the bike data in the tally chart.
Eight students ride their bikes to school.

Look at the bike bar in the bar graph.
Read the scale below the end of the bar.
The end of the bar is at 8.

✏ How can you tell whether the car data in the bar graph is the same as the car data in the tally chart?

Guided Instruction

Connect: What you know about graphs to solve problems

The bar graph shows the kinds of sandwiches Lana ate for lunch last month.

How many more egg salad sandwiches did Lana eat than cheese sandwiches?

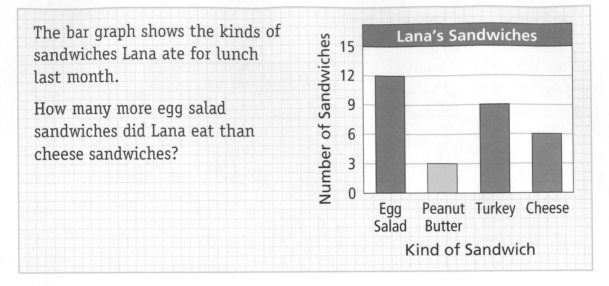

Step 1

Find the number of egg salad sandwiches.
Read the scale on the left side of the graph.
The end of the egg salad bar is at 12.
Lana ate 12 egg salad sandwiches.

Step 2

Find the number of cheese sandwiches.
Read the scale to find the number Lisa ate.
The end of the cheese bar is at 6.
Lana ate 6 cheese sandwiches.

Step 3

Write and solve a subtraction equation.
$12 - 6 = n$

$12 - 6 =$ _____

➡ Lana ate 6 more egg salad sandwiches than cheese sandwiches.

✏ Write an addition equation you can use to solve the problem.

Use data from the tally chart.

Plants in Will's Garden	
Melon	IIII
Tomato	ⵜⵜ III
Squash	ⵜⵜ ⵜⵜ
Carrot	ⵜⵜ ⵜⵜ II

Plants in Will's Garden	
Melon	● ●
Tomato	
Squash	● ● ● ● ●
Carrot	
Key: ● = 2 plants	

1. Draw ● symbols in the picture graph to represent Will's tomato plants.

2. Draw ● symbols in the picture graph to represent Will's carrot plants.

Use the bar graph to answer exercises 3–5.

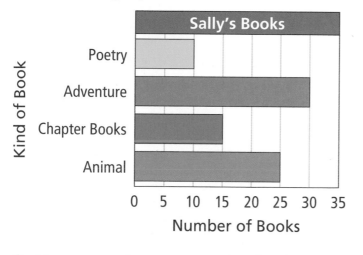

3. How many fewer poetry books does Sally have than animal books?

_____

4. How many more adventure books does Sally have than animal books?

_____

✦ Think•Pair•Share

MP2 5. Sally gets 10 more Chapter Books. Explain how she should change the bar graph.

Independent Practice

Use the tally chart and picture graph.

Students' Favorite Colors	
Green	卌 IIII
Red	卌 卌 II
Blue	卌 I
Orange	III

Students' Favorite Colors	
Green	
Red	▲ ▲ ▲ ▲
Blue	▲ ▲
Orange	
Key: ▲ = 3 students	

1. How many students are represented by each ▲ symbol in the picture graph?

   _____ students

2. Draw ▲ symbols in the picture graph to represent students whose favorite color is green.

3. Draw ▲ symbols in the picture graph to represent students whose favorite color is orange.

Use the tally chart and bar graph.

Baseball Hits	
Mindy	卌 卌 卌 卌 IIII
Ed	卌 卌 卌 卌
Tom	卌 III
Lisa	卌 卌 卌 I

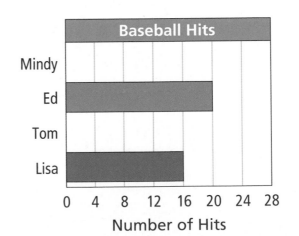

4. What does each distance between two vertical lines in the bar graph represent?

   _____

5. Draw the bar for Mindy.

6. Draw the bar for Tom.

Independent Practice

Use the bar graph to answer exercises 7–12.

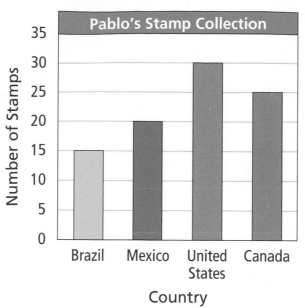

Circle the correct answer.

7. How many more stamps from Canada does Pablo have than stamps from Brazil?

a. 2 stamps   b. 5 stamps

c. 10 stamps   d. 12 stamps

8. How many fewer stamps from Brazil does Pablo have than stamps from the United States?

a. 15 stamps   b. 10 stamps

c. 5 stamps   d. 3 stamps

9. How many more stamps from Brazil and Mexico does Pablo have than stamps from the United States?

a. 4 stamps   b. 5 stamps

c. 10 stamps   d. 15 stamps

10. How many fewer stamps from Mexico does Pablo have than stamps from the United States and Canada?

a. 15 stamps   b. 20 stamps

c. 35 stamps   d. 40 stamps

11. How many more stamps from Mexico and Canada does Pablo have than stamps from the United States?

a. 30 stamps   b. 25 stamps

c. 20 stamps   d. 15 stamps

12. How many fewer stamps from Canada does Pablo have than stamps from Mexico and Brazil?

a. 0 stamps   b. 5 stamps

c. 10 stamps   d. 20 stamps

Independent Practice

Use the picture graph to answer exercises 13–16.

✏️ **Show your work.**

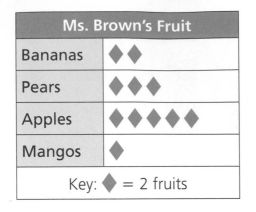

Ms. Brown's Fruit	
Bananas	◆ ◆
Pears	◆ ◆ ◆
Apples	◆ ◆ ◆ ◆
Mangos	◆
Key: ◆ = 2 fruits	

MP4 **13.** How many more bananas than mangos does Ms. Brown have?

Answer _____

MP2 **14.** How many fewer bananas than apples does Ms. Brown have?

Answer _____

MP1 **15.** Ms. Brown gives 4 pears to her neighbor. How many pears does Ms. Brown have left?

Answer _____

MP6 **16.** Ms. Brown has 3 children. She gives each child an apple each day. How many apples does she have after 3 days?

Answer _____

Independent Practice

Use the bar graph to answer exercises 17–19.

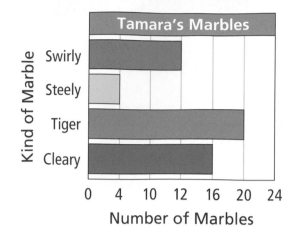

MP2 **17.** How many fewer swirly and steely marbles does Tamara have than tiger and cleary marbles?

✏️ **Show your work.**

Answer _____

MP7 **18.** Does Tamara have more than 40 marbles in all?

Answer _____

✏️ **Justify your answer using words, drawings, or numbers.**

MP3 **19.** Tamara wants to change the scale on her bar graph. She decides to make the distance between vertical lines represent 3 marbles. Is that a good choice?

Answer _____

✏️ **Justify your answer using words, drawings, or numbers.**

Generate and Graph Measurement Data

Essential Question:
How can I draw line plots to show measurement data?

Words to Know:
line plot
half-inch
quarter-inch

Guided Instruction

In this lesson you will learn about line plots.

Understand: How to draw line plots

Anya gathers data by pulling some carrots from her garden. She measures the length of each carrot. She records the data in a tally chart.

For homework she has to use the tally chart to make a line plot of the data. Then she has to write a question about her data.

What question can she write?

Lengths of Carrots (in.)	
Length (in.)	Tally
6	II
$6\frac{1}{2}$	I
7	III
$7\frac{1}{2}$	IIII
8	I

To make a line plot, she draws a number line that includes all her data. She uses half-inch intervals on the scale.

She draws an X for each carrot length above that number.

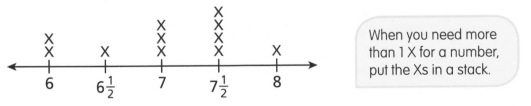

Carrot Lengths (in.) ←——— A line plot needs a title.

When you need more than 1 X for a number, put the Xs in a stack.

Anya decides to ask a question about carrots that are less than $7\frac{1}{2}$ inches long.

➡ She can write this question: How many carrots are less than $7\frac{1}{2}$ inches long?

To answer, use the line plot to count the Xs to the left of $7\frac{1}{2}$ inches. There are 6 carrots less than $7\frac{1}{2}$ inches long.

✏ What are some other questions Anya could write?

Guided Instruction

Connect: Drawing line plots to show measurement data

Dan measures the lengths of his toy cars. He records the data in a chart.

Use the chart to make a line plot of the measurement data.

Find how many toy cars are 3 inches or longer.

Lengths of Toy Cars (in.)		
$2\frac{1}{4}$	3	$2\frac{1}{2}$
$2\frac{3}{4}$	$3\frac{1}{4}$	3
$2\frac{1}{2}$	$2\frac{1}{2}$	3
$2\frac{3}{4}$	$3\frac{1}{2}$	$2\frac{1}{2}$

Step 1

Draw a number line. Show inches, half-inches, and quarter-inches on the scale.

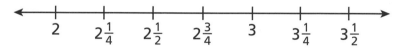

Step 2

Draw an X for each toy car above its length.
Write a title for the line plot.

Lengths of Toy Cars (in.)

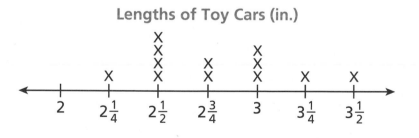

To find how many toy cars are 3 inches or longer, look at the line plot.

Count the Xs above 3 inches.   _____ Xs

Count the Xs to the right of 3 inches.   _____ Xs

3 + 2 = _____

➡ There are 5 toy cars that are 3 inches or longer.

Guided Practice

Use the chart to complete the line plot of the measurement data.

Earthworm Lengths (in.)

5	4	$4\frac{1}{2}$
$5\frac{1}{2}$	3	4
$3\frac{1}{2}$	$5\frac{1}{2}$	$5\frac{1}{2}$
4	5	$3\frac{1}{2}$

1. Complete the scale of the number line.

2. Draw an X for each earthworm that is 4 inches long.

3. Draw an X for each earthworm that is $4\frac{1}{2}$ inches long.

4. Draw an X for each earthworm that is 5 inches long.

5. Draw an X for each earthworm that is $5\frac{1}{2}$ inches long.

6. Write a title for the line plot.

7. How many earthworms are less than 5 inches long?

    ____ earthworms

8. How many earthworms are more than 5 inches long?

    ____ earthworms

Guided Practice

9. Measure each line segment. Record each length in the chart.

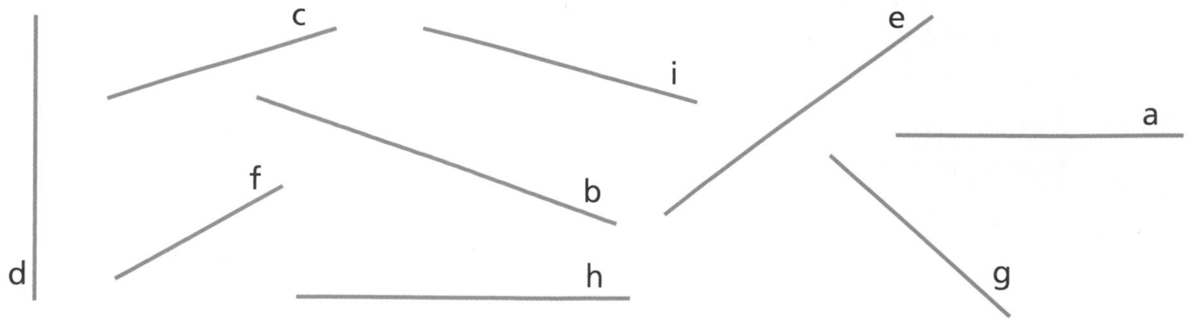

Line Segment Lengths (in.)

a:	b:	c:
d:	e:	f:
g:	h:	i:

Use your chart to make a line plot of your measurement data.

10. Complete the scale of the number line.

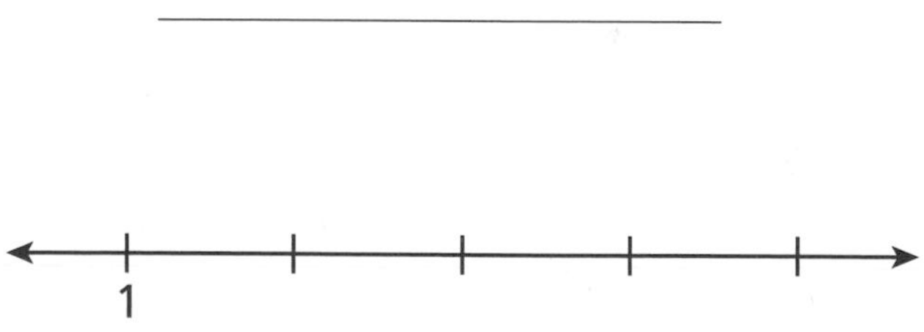

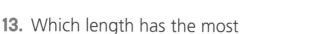

11. Draw an X for each line segment above its measurement.

12. Write a title for your line plot.

13. Which length has the most line segments? ________

Think•Pair•Share

MP4 **14.** Why is it not necessary to make a tally chart first when you make a line plot?

Independent Practice

Ines and Marco find a frog in the garden. They measure the lengths of its hops. They record the data in a chart.

Use the chart to make a line plot of the measurement data.

Frog Hops (in.)		
8	7	$8\frac{1}{2}$
$8\frac{1}{2}$	9	7
8	$9\frac{1}{2}$	$8\frac{1}{2}$
$9\frac{1}{2}$	$8\frac{1}{2}$	8

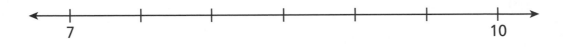

7   10

1. Complete the scale of the number line.

2. Draw an X for each hop above its measurement.

3. Write a title for the line plot.

Circle the correct answer.

4. How many of the frog's hops are longer than 9 inches?

   a. 1 hop   **b.** 2 hops

   c. 3 hops   **d.** 4 hops

5. How many of the frog's hops are 8 inches or shorter?

   a. 2 hops   **b.** 4 hops

   c. 5 hops   **d.** 10 hops

6. Which frog hop length occurs most often?

   a. $7\frac{1}{2}$ inches   **b.** $8\frac{1}{2}$ inches

   c. $9\frac{1}{2}$ inches   **d.** 10 inches

7. Which lengths, in inches, had no frog hops?

   a. 7 and $7\frac{1}{2}$ **b.** 8 and 9

   c. 9 and $9\frac{1}{2}$ **d.** $7\frac{1}{2}$ and 10

Independent Practice

8. Heidi cut some little boards to make a model barn. Measure each board. Record each length in the chart.

Board Lengths (in.)

a:	b:	c:
d:	e:	f:

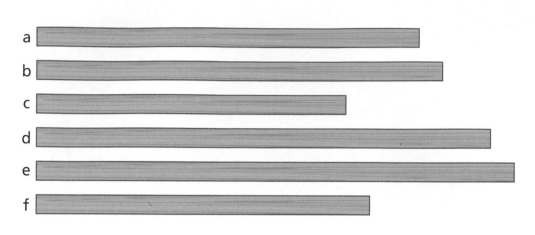

Use your chart to make a line plot of the measurement data.

9. Write a scale for the number line.

10. Draw an X for each board above its measurement.

11. Write a title for your line plot.

Circle the correct answer.

12. How many boards are $4\frac{1}{2}$ inches long?

   a. 0 boards   **b.** 1 board

   c. 2 boards   **d.** 3 boards

13. How many boards are at least $4\frac{1}{4}$ inches long?

   a. 2 boards   **b.** 3 boards

   c. 4 boards   **d.** 5 boards

Lesson 27 Generate and Graph Measurement Data

Independent Practice

MP3 **14.** Stan measures 9 pieces of celery. He records his data in a chart. He wants to make a line plot of the data. What scale should he use? Explain.

Celery Lengths (in.)

$7\frac{1}{2}$	$7\frac{1}{2}$	6
$6\frac{1}{2}$	8	$6\frac{1}{2}$
8	7	$6\frac{1}{2}$

MP1 **15.** Stan measures 3 more pieces of celery. The lengths are $7\frac{3}{4}$ inches, $6\frac{1}{4}$ inches, and 7 inches. How should he change his scale to show the new celery pieces?

Use the line plot to answer exercises 16 and 17.

Lengths of Chicken Footsteps (in.)

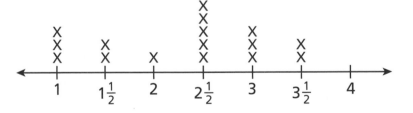

MP6 **16.** How many chicken footsteps are $1\frac{1}{2}$ inches or shorter?

➡ **Show your work.**

Answer _____

MP7 **17.** How many chicken footsteps are measured in all?

➡ **Show your work.**

Answer _____

Independent Practice

MP4 **18.** Nancy measures the widths of her favorite books. She records her data in a chart. How many of the books are wider than $5\frac{1}{2}$ inches?

✏️ **Show your work.**

Book Widths (in.)

$4\frac{1}{2}$	6	$5\frac{1}{2}$
4	7	$5\frac{1}{2}$
$4\frac{1}{2}$	$5\frac{1}{2}$	6

Answer _____

Use the chart of measurement data to answer questions 19 and 20.

MP3 **19.** Edgar wants to make a line plot of the guppy lengths. "There are 12 measurements," he says. "I should make the scale go from 1 to 12." Is he right?

Guppy Lengths (in.)

$2\frac{1}{4}$	2	$1\frac{1}{2}$
2	$1\frac{1}{4}$	$2\frac{1}{2}$
1	$1\frac{1}{4}$	2
$1\frac{1}{4}$	$1\frac{1}{2}$	$2\frac{1}{4}$

Answer _____

✏️ **Justify your answer using words, drawings, or numbers.**

MP5 **20.** How many of the guppies are less than 2 inches long?

Answer _____

✏️ **Justify your answer using words, drawings, or numbers.**

Write the time shown by each clock.

1.

_____

2.

_____

3.

_____

Dionne surveyed 70 students about their favorite color. The pictograph shows her data. Use the pictograph for exercises 4–8.

4. In Dionne's survey, 10 students chose green as their favorite color. Complete the pictograph.

5. Which color was chosen by 15 students?

_____

6. How many more students chose red than purple? _____

Favorite Colors	
Color	Number of Students
Blue	■ ■ ■ ■
Green	
Purple	■ ■ ■
Red	■ ■ ■ ■
Yellow	■
Key: ■ = 5 students	

Circle the best estimate of the liquid volume.

7.

Milk

1 liter   4 liters   16 liters

8.

2 liters   20 liters   200 liters

Circle the best estimate of the mass.

9.

15 kilograms   150 kilograms   1500 kilograms

10.

1 gram   10 grams   100 grams

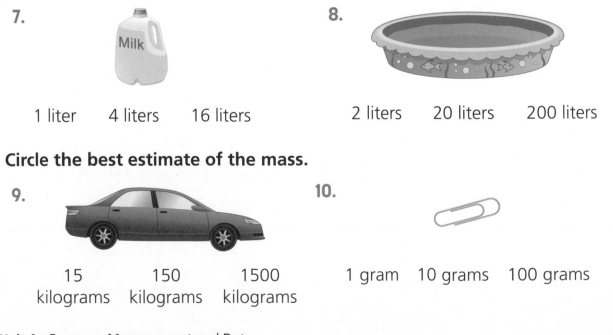

For exercises 11–16, use the table of Leaf Lengths.

Leaf Lengths (in.)

$3\frac{3}{4}$	$4\frac{1}{2}$	$3\frac{1}{4}$	$3\frac{3}{4}$
$3\frac{1}{4}$	$3\frac{3}{4}$	$4\frac{1}{2}$	5
$3\frac{3}{4}$	3	$3\frac{1}{4}$	$3\frac{3}{4}$

MP6 **11.** Jill collected 12 leaves for a science project. She measured the length of each leaf to the nearest $\frac{1}{4}$ inch and recorded the lengths in the chart. Jill will use the chart to make a line plot of the measurement data. What scale should Jill use for the line plot? Explain.

_____

12. Record the scale on the number line below.

13. Draw an X for each leaf above its measurement on the number line.

14. Write a title for the line plot.

$\longleftrightarrow$

15. How many leaves have a length longer than 3 inches and shorter than 4 inches? _____ leaves

16. Jacob measured the same 12 leaves to the nearest inch. What scale should Jacob use for his line plot?

For exercises 17 and 18, use the line plot above. Circle the correct answer.

17. Which leaf length occurs most often?

   a. 3 in.   **b.** $3\frac{1}{4}$ in.

   c. $3\frac{3}{4}$ in.   **d.** $4\frac{1}{2}$ in.

18. How many leaves are longer than 4 inches?

   a. 12   **b.** 8

   c. 5   **d.** 3

Solve the problems.

MP5 **19.** Ian needs to leave for school at 7:35 each morning It takes him 5 minutes to get dressed, 20 minutes to eat, and 15 minutes to walk his dog. What time should Ian wake up?

Answer _____

➤ **Justify your answer using words, drawings or numbers.**

MP3 **20.** Kimora surveyed her classmates to find their favorite lunches. She made the bar graph to show her data.

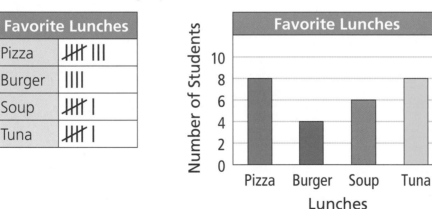

Favorite Lunches	
Pizza	卌 |||
Burger	||||
Soup	卌	
Tuna	卌	

Compare the tally chart and the bar graph. What error did Kimora make on the bar graph? How can she correct it?

Answer _____

_____

_____

Progress Check

Look at how the math concepts and skills you have learned and will learn connect.

It is very important for you to understand the math concepts and skills from the prior grade level so that you will be able to develop an understanding of measurement and data / geometry in this unit and be prepared for next year. To practice your skills, go to sadlierconnect.com.

GRADE 2 — I Can...	Before Unit 5	GRADE 3 — Can I?	After Unit 5	GRADE 4 — I Will...
Partition a rectangle into same-size squares and count to find the total number	☐	Understand area and area measurement	☐	
Partition a rectangle into same-size squares and count to find the total number	☐	Measure area by counting unit squares	☐	
	☐	Find the area of a rectangle by multiplying side lengths	☐	Solve real-world and mathematical problems using the area and perimeter formulas for rectangles
	☐	Use area models to represent the distributive property	☐	
	☐	Find areas of figures composed of rectangles	☐	
	☐	Solve real-world and mathematical problems involving perimeter	☐	Solve real-world and mathematical problems using the area and perimeter formulas for rectangles
Identify and draw shapes with given attributes	☐	Explain that shapes in different categories may share attributes	☐	Classify shapes by properties of their lines and angles
Identify triangles, quadrilaterals, pentagons, hexagons, and cubes	☐	Classify quadrilaterals by their attributes	☐	Recognize right triangles as a category
Partition shapes into two, three, or four equal shares and describe as halves, thirds, or fourths	☐	Partition a whole into parts with equal areas	☐	
Describe a whole as two halves, three thirds, or four fourths	☐	Describe the area of an equal part of a whole as a unit fraction	☐	

In this unit your child will:

- Find areas of rectangles using tiling, multiplication, and decomposition.

- Find perimeters of polygons.

- Compare perimeters and areas.

- Recognize and name quadrilaterals according to their attributes.

- Partition shapes into parts with equal areas.

Shapes are all around us. Some shapes, or **polygons**, are named by the number of sides and the number of **vertices** they have. A **vertex** is where two sides of a **plane**, or flat, figure meet. Working with geometric figures, your child will learn practical skills used to measure these figures. Support your child by using the following Math vocabulary:

- A **quadrilateral** is a polygon with four sides and include squares and rectangles. **Rhombuses** are quadrilaterals with all four sides the same length.

- The **area** of a figure is the number of **square units** needed to cover the figure without gaps or overlaps.

- Some of the units used to find areas are **square inch**, **square foot**, **square centimeter**, and **square meter**.

- Your child will use various strategies to find areas include **tiling**, covering the figure with square units; multiplying measurements of the figure; and **decomposing**, or breaking the figure into smaller parts and adding the areas of the parts.

- The **perimeter** of a figure is the sum of the lengths of the figure's sides.

Ways to Help Your Child

A great way to experience math with your child is to play games! Many old-fashioned card games and board games use mathematics and will help your child practice the math skills learned all year. Digital games are also readily available and can be fun to play as a family, too.

Activity: Bring a measuring tape or yardstick with you when you are out running errands. Ask your child to take measurements to find the perimeter and area of items in the world around them, for example, items in the grocery store; the table in a restaurant; a waiting room.

ONLINE

For more Home Connect activities, continue online at sadlierconnect.com

Focus on Measurement and Data / Geometry

Essential Question:
How can you find the area and perimeter of geometric shapes?

Lesson 28

Understand Concepts of Area Measurement

Essential Question:
How can you measure the area of plane figures?

Words to Know:
plane figure
unit square
area
square inch
square foot
square centimeter
square meter

Guided Instruction

In this lesson you will learn about area.

Understand: The meaning of area

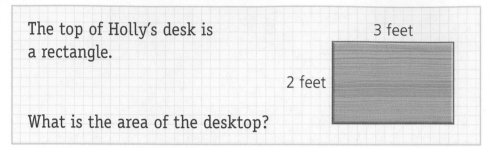

The top of Holly's desk is a rectangle.

3 feet

2 feet

What is the area of the desktop?

A plane figure is flat. A rectangle is a plane figure. A unit square is a square with sides that are 1 unit long.

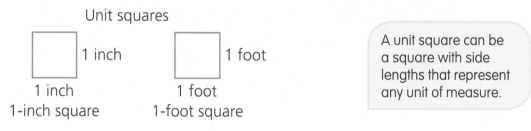

Unit squares

1 inch

1 inch
1-inch square

1 foot

1 foot
1-foot square

A unit square can be a square with side lengths that represent any unit of measure.

The area of a plane figure is the number of unit squares needed to cover the figure without gaps or overlaps.

The 1-inch square has an area of 1 square inch, which can be written as *square in*. The 1-foot square has an area of 1 square foot, which can be written as *square ft*.

Look at Holly's desktop. You can use unit squares that measure 1 square foot each to cover the desktop.
Count the number of unit squares that cover the desktop.

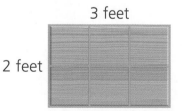

3 feet

2 feet

6 unit squares cover the desktop.

➡ The area of the desktop is 6 square feet.

Guided Instruction

Connect: Measuring the area of figures

Ted drew a figure on grid paper.

What is the area of the figure?

Step 1

Determine the unit square.

Each square in the grid has sides that are 1 centimeter long.

Each centimeter square in the grid has an area of 1 square centimeter, which can be written as *square cm*.

1 centimeter

1 centimeter

Step 2

Count the centimeter squares that cover Ted's figure.

____ centimeter squares cover the figure.

➡ The area of the figure is 5 square centimeters.

✏ Draw two different figures, each with an area of 5 square centimeters.

Guided Practice

Find the area of each figure. Use a ruler.

1.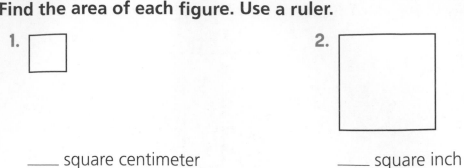

___ square centimeter

2.

___ square inch

Find the area of each figure. Use the key.

3. Key: 1 square = 1 square cm

___ square cm

4. Key: 1 square = 1 square inch

___ square in.

5. Key: 1 square = 1 square meter

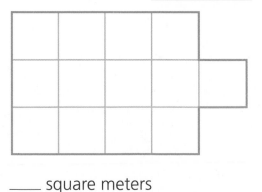

___ square meters

6. Key: 1 square = 1 square foot

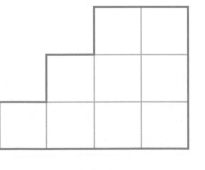

___ square feet

Guided Practice

Cut out centimeter squares. Use them to find the area of each figure.

7.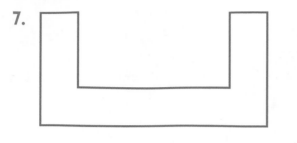

_____

8.

_____

Cut out inch squares. Use them to find the area of each figure.

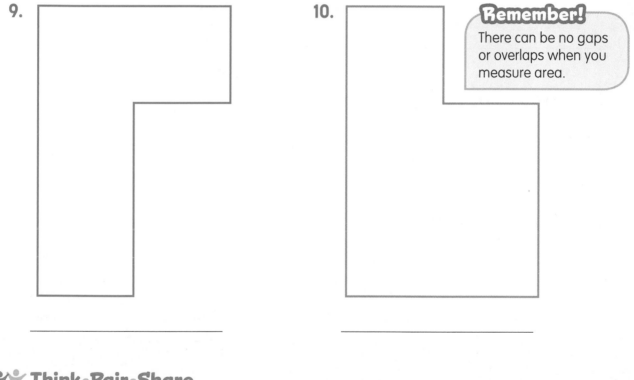

9.

_____

10.

Remember!

There can be no gaps or overlaps when you measure area.

_____

☆ Think•Pair•Share

MP3 11. Uma says the area of the square is 1 square unit.
Peter says the area of the square is 4 square units.
Can both students be right? Explain your reasoning.

Independent Practice

Find the area of each figure. Determine the unit square. Use a ruler.

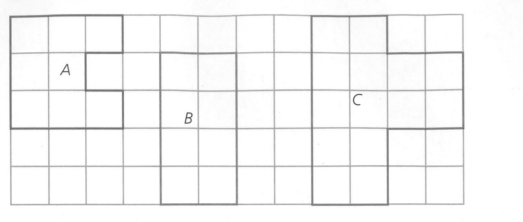

1. Figure A

_____

2. Figure B

_____

3. Figure C

_____

Find the area of each figure. Use the key.

4. Key: 1 square = 1 square foot

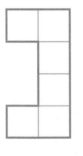

_____

5. Key: 1 square = 1 square inch

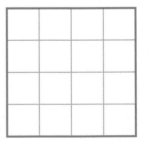

_____

6. Key: 1 square = 1 square meter

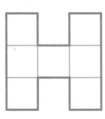

_____

7. Key: 1 square = 1 square centimeter

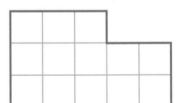

_____

Independent Practice

Cut out centimeter squares. Use them to find the area of each figure.

8.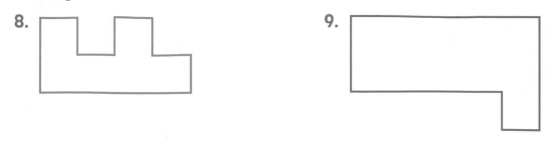

_____

9.

_____

Cut out inch squares. Use them to find the area of each figure.

10.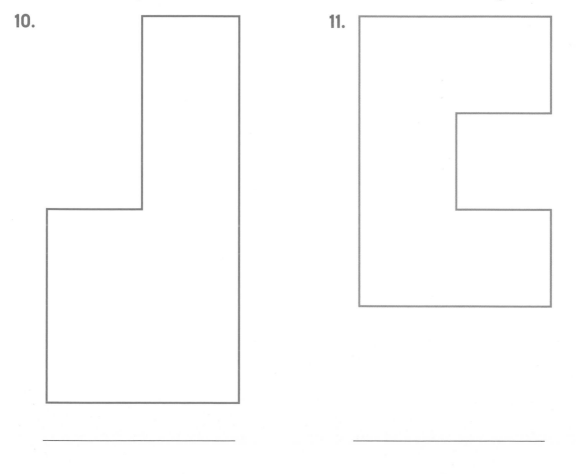

_____

11.

_____

Independent Practice

MP7 **12.** Draw two types of unit squares. How are they alike? How are they different?

MP6 **13.** Roberta wants to find the area of her bedroom window. She asks you for help. What would you tell her?

MP4 **14.** Mike is building a tree house. The floor will have an area of 18 square feet. Draw an outline of a floor Mike could use.

Key: 1 square = 1 square foot

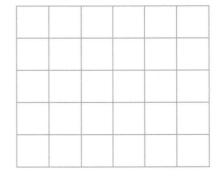

MP5 **15.** Gina is making a poster for a school fair. She wants to draw a figure with an area of 13 square inches. Draw a figure that Gina could use.

Key: 1 square = 1 square inch

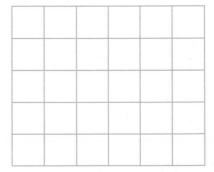

Independent Practice

MP4 **16.** Mr. Davis is planning his summer garden. He decides to make a pumpkin patch with an area of 14 square meters. Draw an outline of a pumpkin patch Mr. Davis could make.

Key: 1 square = 1 square meter

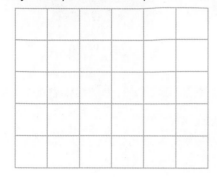

MP4 **17.** Amanda uses chalk to draw a picture on a sidewalk. She draws a square with sides that are each 3 feet long. What is the area of the square?

Answer _____

✏️ **Justify your answer using words, drawings, or numbers.**

Key: 1 square = 1 square foot

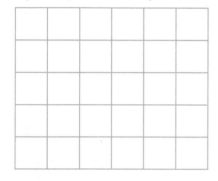

MP6 **18.** Richard measures the top of his desk. The desktop is a rectangle with side lengths 4 feet and 2 feet. "My desktop has an area of 6 square feet," he says. Is Richard right?

Answer _____

✏️ **Justify your answer using words, drawings, or numbers.**

Key: 1 square = 1 square foot

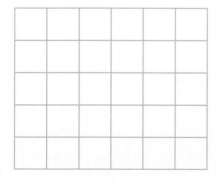

Find Areas of Rectangles: Tile and Multiply

Essential Question:
How can you use tiling and multiplication to find the area of a rectangle?

Words to Know:
  tiling

Guided Instruction

In this lesson you will learn about the areas of rectangles.

Understand: Finding the area of a rectangle

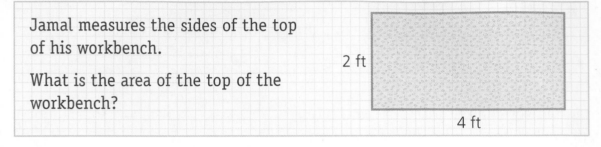

Jamal measures the sides of the top of his workbench.

What is the area of the top of the workbench?

2 ft

4 ft

Method 1 Tiling

Tile the top of the workbench. To tile, cover the area with unit squares that represent 1-foot squares.
Count the unit squares that cover the top of the workbench.

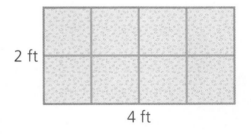

2 ft

4 ft

Eight unit squares cover the top of the workbench.
The sides are measured in feet, so the area will be in square feet.

▶ The area of the top of the workbench is 8 square feet.

Method 2 Multiplying

Each unit square has an area of 1 square foot. There are 2 rows of unit squares. Each row has an area of 4 square feet.

Multiply the side lengths of the top of the workbench.
$2 \times 4 = 8$

▶ The area of the top of the workbench is 8 square feet.

Tiling and multiplying give the same answer.
You can use either method to find the area of a rectangle.

Guided Instruction

Connect: Solving problems about the area of rectangles.

Ms. Walker has a picture of her dog.

What is the area of the picture?

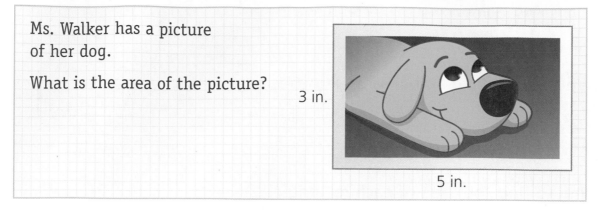

3 in.

5 in.

Method 1 Tiling

Tile with unit squares to find the area.
Count the unit squares that will cover the picture.

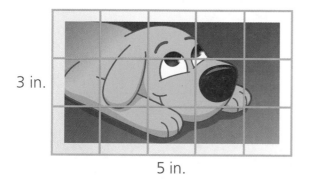

3 in.

5 in.

15 unit squares cover the picture.
The sides are measured in inches, so the area will be in square inches.
Each square represents an area of 1 square inch.

➡ The area of the picture is 15 square inches.

Method 2 Multiplying

Multiply the side lengths of the picture to find the area.

$3 \times 5 = $ _____

➡ The area of the picture is 15 square inches.

Multiplying and tiling give the same answer.

✏ Write another multiplication sentence you could use to find the

area of the picture. _____

Guided Practice

1. Use tiling to find the area of the rectangle.

   ____ meter squares cover the rectangle.

   Area: ____ square meters

2. Use multiplication to find the area of the rectangle.

   ____ × ____ = ____

   Area: ____ square meters

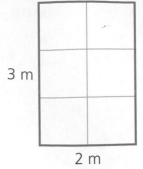

3 m

2 m

Use tiling to find the area of each rectangle.
Then use multiplication to check your answer.

3.

1 cm

4 cm

____ centimeter squares cover
the rectangle.

____ × ____ = ____

Area: ____ square centimeters

4.

3 ft

3 ft

____ foot squares cover
the rectangle.

____ × ____ = ____

Area: ____ square feet

5.

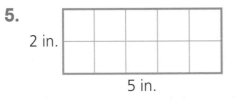

2 in.

5 in.

____ inch squares cover
the rectangle.

____ × ____ = ____

Area: ____ square inches

6.

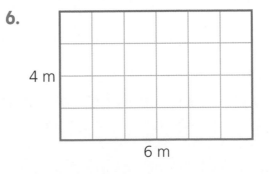

4 m

6 m

____ meter squares cover
the rectangle.

____ × ____ = ____

Area: ____ square meters

Guided Practice

Multiply to solve each problem.

7. Tina measures one of her animal stickers. What is the area of the sticker?

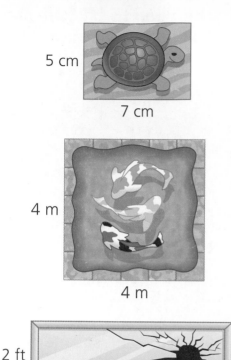

5 cm

7 cm

_____

8. Mr. Smith's class makes a square wall mural of a fish pond. What is the area of the mural?

4 m

4 m

_____

9. Waldron hits a baseball. The ball breaks his bedroom window. What is the area of the original window?

2 ft

6 ft

_____

10. The Berners are getting a new kitchen floor. The floor is a rectangle. One side length is 6 feet. The other side length is 10 feet. What is the area of the floor?

_____

11. Charles has a music box. The top of the box is a rectangle. One side measures 7 inches. The other side measures 8 inches. What is the area of the music box top?

_____

☆ Think•Pair•Share

MP3 12. Maria draws two rectangles with different side lengths. She says that both rectangles have the same area: 20 square centimeters. Can she be right? Explain your reasoning.

Independent Practice

**Use tiling to find the area of each rectangle.
Then use multiplication to check your answer.**

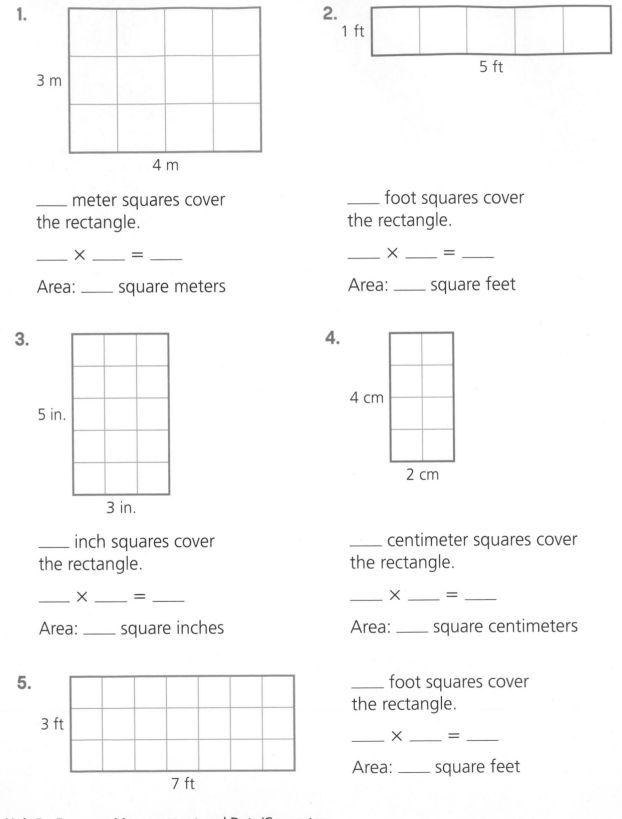

1.

3 m

4 m

_____ meter squares cover
the rectangle.

_____ × _____ = _____

Area: _____ square meters

2.

1 ft

5 ft

_____ foot squares cover
the rectangle.

_____ × _____ = _____

Area: _____ square feet

3.

5 in.

3 in.

_____ inch squares cover
the rectangle.

_____ × _____ = _____

Area: _____ square inches

4.

4 cm

2 cm

_____ centimeter squares cover
the rectangle.

_____ × _____ = _____

Area: _____ square centimeters

5.

3 ft

7 ft

_____ foot squares cover
the rectangle.

_____ × _____ = _____

Area: _____ square feet

Independent Practice

Multiply to solve each problem.

6. Sarah buys a rug for her cat. What is the area of the rug?

_____

6 ft

6 ft

7. Gilberto measures a cookie sheet. What is the area of the cookie sheet?

_____

8 in.

10 in.

Circle the letter with the correct answer for exercises 8–11.

8. Andrea makes a birthday card for her dad. The card is a rectangle. One side length is 8 inches. The other side length is 6 inches. What is the area of the card?

   a. 14 square in.   b. 24 square in.

   c. 28 square in.   d. 48 square in.

9. Stanley is making a table. The table's top is a rectangle. One side measures 3 feet. The other side measures 8 feet. What is the area of the top of the table?

   a. 11 square ft   b. 22 square ft

   c. 24 square ft   d. 36 square ft

10. Ellen measures her family's driveway. The driveway is a rectangle. One side is 10 meters long. The other side is 5 meters long. What is the area of the driveway?

    a. 30 square m   b. 50 square m

    c. 60 square m   d. 65 square m

11. José puts together a dinosaur picture puzzle. The puzzle is a rectangle. One side measures 9 centimeters. The other side measures 8 centimeters. What is the area of the puzzle?

    a. 17 square cm   b. 34 square cm

    c. 72 square cm   d. 81 square cm

Independent Practice

MP7 **12.** Paula uses tiling to find the area of a rectangle. Zoe multiplies to find the area of the same rectangle. Which method is better?

MP6 **13.** Steve wants to find the area of a poster board that is 3 feet long. He asks you for help. What would you tell him?

Solve the problems.

MP4 **14.** Mr. Baker paints a picture. The picture is a rectangle. One side of the picture is 7 inches long. The other side is 4 inches long. What is the area of the picture?

➡ **Show your work.**

Answer _____

MP1 **15.** Jen has a postcard that shows her town one hundred years ago. The card is a rectangle. One side measures 6 centimeters. The other side measures 9 centimeters. What is the area of the card?

➡ **Show your work.**

Answer _____

Independent Practice

MP2 **16.** The floor of a school hallway is a rectangle. One side length is 4 meters. The other side length is 20 meters. What is the area of the hallway floor?

    ▰▰▰▶ **Show your work.**

    Answer _____

MP7 **17.** Eric's favorite rug is a rectangle. The area of the rug is 60 square feet. If one side of the rug measures 10 feet, what is the length of the other side?

    Answer _____

    ▰▰▰▶ **Justify your answer using words, drawings, or numbers.**

MP1 **18.** Mark's closet floor is a rectangle. One side length is 3 feet. The other side length is 6 feet. His sister's closet is bigger. One side is the same length as a side of Mark's closet floor. The other side is 3 feet longer than a side of Mark's closet floor. What is the area of the floor in Mark's sister's closet?

    Answer _____

    ▰▰▰▶ **Justify your answer using words, drawings, or numbers.**

Find Areas of Rectangles: Use the Distributive Property

Guided Instruction

In this lesson you will learn to use area models to show the Distributive Property.

Understand: Using tiling to show the Distributive Property

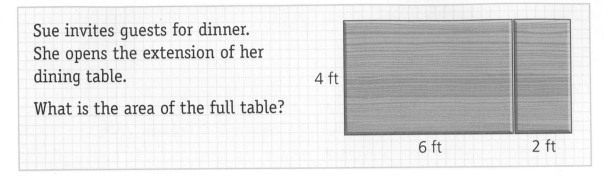

Sue invites guests for dinner. She opens the extension of her dining table.

What is the area of the full table?

4 ft

6 ft   2 ft

Method 1

Tile the table with unit squares. Find one side length of the full table. Find the other side length of the full table. Multiply to find the area.

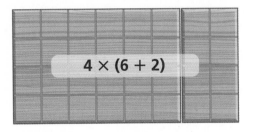

$4 \times (6 + 2)$

One side length of the table is 4. The other side length of the table is $6 + 2$.

$$4 \times (6 + 2)$$
$$= 4 \times \quad 8 = 32$$

➡ The area of the full table is 32 square feet.

Method 2

Tile the table with unit squares. Find the area of the original table. Find the area of the extension. Add the two areas.

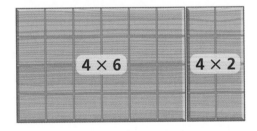

4×6 4×2

The area of the original table is 4×6.
The area of the extension is 4×2.

$$(4 \times 6) + (4 \times 2)$$
$$= \quad 24 \quad + \quad 8 = 32$$

➡ The area of the full table is 32 square feet.

The two methods show the Distributive Property.
$4 \times (6 + 2) = (4 \times 6) + (4 \times 2)$

Guided Instruction

Understand: Using area models to represent the Distributive Property

Lenny wants to solve the multiplication problem 4 × 9. Mary says, "You can use the Distributive Property. Since 9 = 5 + 4, multiply 4 × 5 and 4 × 4 and then add the products."

Use an area model to show why Mary's method works.

Draw an area model.
One side length is 4.
The other side length is 9.

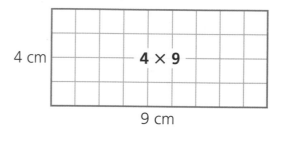

You can use any unit of length for your area model.

Since 9 = 5 + 4, you can break the rectangle into these two rectangles.

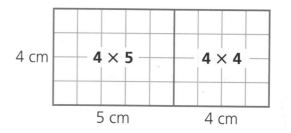

Find the area of the first rectangle.
Find the area of the second rectangle.
Add the two areas.

$4 \times 9 = 4 \times (5 + 4)$
$= (4 \times 5) + (4 \times 4)$
$= 20 + 16$
$= 36$

So, $4 \times 9 = 36$

➡ The area models above show that the Distributive Property works, since $4 \times 9 = (4 \times 5) + (4 \times 4)$.

Guided Instruction

Connect: Solving area problems using the Distributive Property

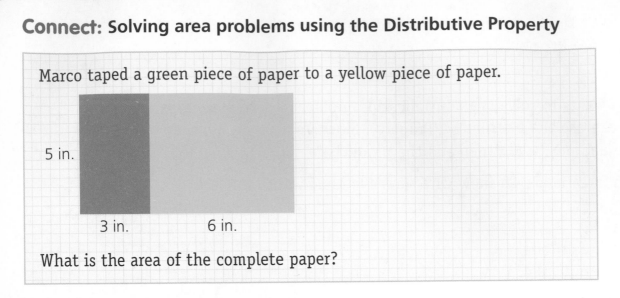

Marco taped a green piece of paper to a yellow piece of paper.

5 in.

3 in.   6 in.

What is the area of the complete paper?

Use the Distributive Property to find the area.

Step 1

Tile the figure with unit squares.
Find the area of the green paper.
Find the area of the yellow paper.

The area of the green paper is 5×3.
The area of the yellow paper is 5×6.

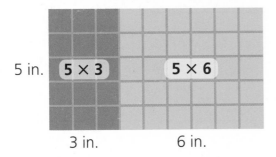

5 in.   **5 × 3**   **5 × 6**

3 in.   6 in.

Step 2

Add the two areas.

$$5 \times (3 + 6) = (5 \times 3) + (5 \times 6)$$
$$= \quad 15 \quad + \quad 30$$
$$= \underline{\quad\quad}$$

➤ The area of the complete paper is 45 square inches.

Guided Practice

The rectangles are tiled with unit squares.
Use the Distributive Property to find the total area.

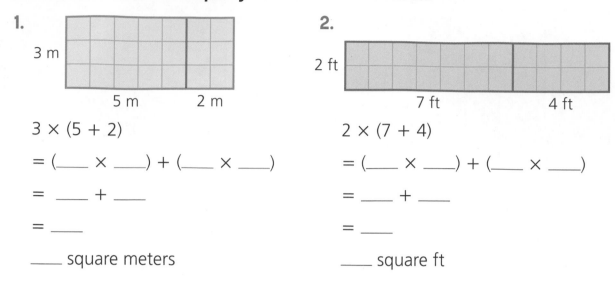

1.

3 m

5 m   2 m

$3 \times (5 + 2)$

$= (\underline{} \times \underline{}) + (\underline{} \times \underline{})$

$= \underline{} + \underline{}$

$= \underline{}$

___ square meters

2.

2 ft

7 ft   4 ft

$2 \times (7 + 4)$

$= (\underline{} \times \underline{}) + (\underline{} \times \underline{})$

$= \underline{} + \underline{}$

$= \underline{}$

___ square ft

Draw an area model to represent each problem.
Use your area model to solve the problem.

3. $5 \times (2 + 6)$

4. $6 \times (4 + 3)$

$5 \times (2 + 6) = \underline{}$

$6 \times (4 + 3) = \underline{}$

Think•Pair•Share

MP7 **5.** Bob and Rick are trying to find the
area of the rectangle.
Bob writes $3 \times (6 + 3)$.
Rick writes $3 \times (4 + 5)$.
Explain why both students are right.

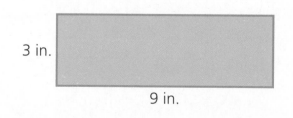

3 in.

9 in.

Independent Practice

The rectangles are tiled with unit squares.
Use the Distributive Property to find the total area.

1.

7 ft

2 ft   5 ft

$7 \times (2 + 5)$

$= (\underline{} \times \underline{}) + (\underline{} \times \underline{})$

$= \underline{} + \underline{} = \underline{}$

$\underline{}$ square feet

2.

6 cm

4 cm   4 cm

$6 \times (4 + 4)$

$= (\underline{} \times \underline{}) + (\underline{} \times \underline{})$

$= \underline{} + \underline{} = \underline{}$

$\underline{}$ square centimeters

3.

3 in.

3 in.   5 in.

$3 \times (3 + 5)$

$= (\underline{} \times \underline{}) + (\underline{} \times \underline{})$

$= \underline{} + \underline{} = \underline{}$

$\underline{}$ square inches

4.

4 cm

6 cm   4 cm

$4 \times (6 + 4)$

$= (\underline{} \times \underline{}) + (\underline{} \times \underline{})$

$= \underline{} + \underline{} = \underline{}$

$\underline{}$ square meters

5. Which answer represents the area model?

3 ft

4 ft   8 ft

a. $(3 + 4) \times (3 + 8)$

b. $(3 \times 4) + (3 \times 8)$

c. $3 + 4 \times 8$

d. $(3 \times 4) \times (3 \times 8)$

Independent Practice

**Draw an area model to represent each problem.
Use your area model to solve the problem.**

6. 3 × (2 + 6)

7. 4 × (5 + 7)

_____

_____

8. 6 × (5 + 2)

9. 7 × (3 + 3)

_____

_____

10. Which area model represents 3 × (4 + 3)?

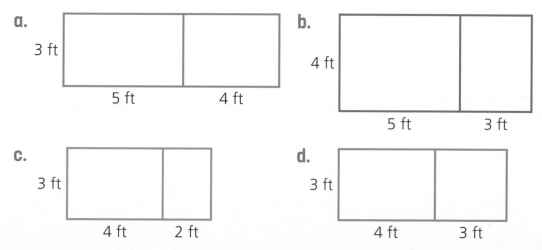

a.
3 ft
5 ft   4 ft

b.
4 ft
5 ft   3 ft

c.
3 ft
4 ft   2 ft

d.
3 ft
4 ft   3 ft

Independent Practice

MP1 **11.** Compare the two area models.
How are they alike?
How are they different?

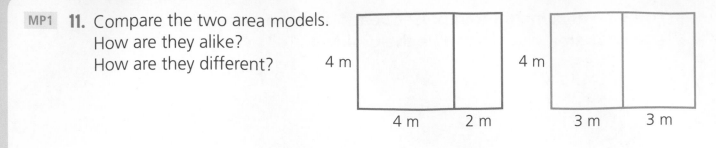

MP6 **12.** Heather wants to use the Distributive Property to find 8 × 12.
She draws an area model. One side length is 8 inches. What could
Heather use for the other side length? Explain.

Solve the problems.

MP7 **13.** Andy grows red roses and white roses in
his garden. Use the Distributive Property
to find the total area of Andy's rose garden.

⬛➤ **Show your work.**

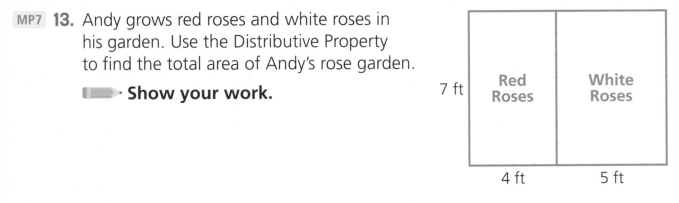

Answer _____

MP4 **14.** Ines wants to find the area of her backyard. The yard is a rectangle.
She measures the yard in meters. Then she writes 6 × (8 + 4).
Draw an area model for the backyard. Use your model to find the
area of the yard.

⬛➤ **Show your work.**

Answer _____

Independent Practice

MP4 15. The Wilsons' porch floor is a rectangle.
Part is brick, and part is concrete.
Use the Distributive Property to find
the total area of the porch floor.

→ **Show your work.**

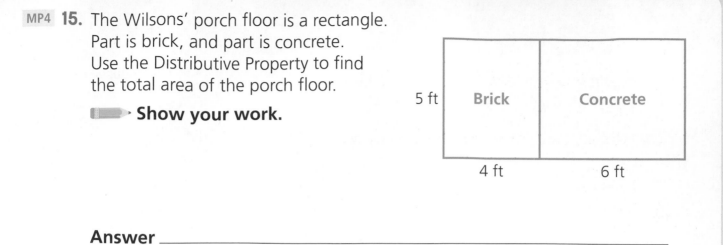

Answer _____

MP8 16. Kendra tapes red, blue, and yellow paper strips together to make a
flag. Each strip has one side 8 inches long. The red strip has a side
3 inches long, the blue strip has a side 4 inches long, and the
yellow strip has a side 5 inches long. What is the area of the flag
that Kendra makes?

Answer _____

→ **Justify your answer using words, drawings, or numbers.**

MP3 17. Jed wants to know the product
for 4×11. He decides to
use the Distributive Property.
He draws this area model.
"The product is 48," says Jed.
Is Jed right?

Answer _____

→ **Justify your answer using words, drawings, or numbers.**

31 Find Areas: Decompose Figures into Rectangles

Essential Question:
How can you find the area of a figure by decomposing it into rectangles?

Words to Know:
decompose

Guided Instruction

In this lesson you will learn to decompose a figure into rectangles so that you can find the area.

Understand: Decomposing figures into rectangles to find their areas

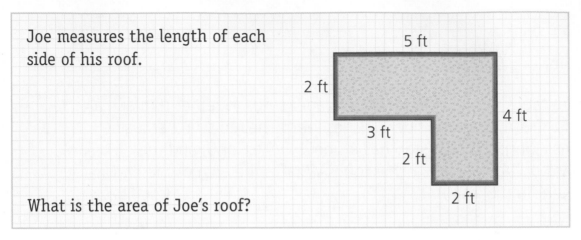

Joe measures the length of each side of his roof.

What is the area of Joe's roof?

Decompose, or break down, Joe's desktop into two rectangles that do not overlap.

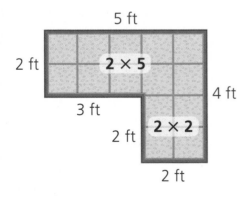

Remember!
To find the area of a rectangle, you can count unit squares, or you can multiply side lengths.

Find the area of one rectangle. ⟶ 2 × 5 = 10 square feet
Find the area of the other rectangle. ⟶ 2 × 2 = 4 square feet
Add the two areas. ⟶ 10 + 4 = 14 square feet

➡ The area of Joe's roof is 14 square feet.

✏ Show another way to decompose the figure into two rectangles.

Guided Instruction

Connect: **What you know about area and decomposing figures**

Sherry planted her garden with beans and carrots.

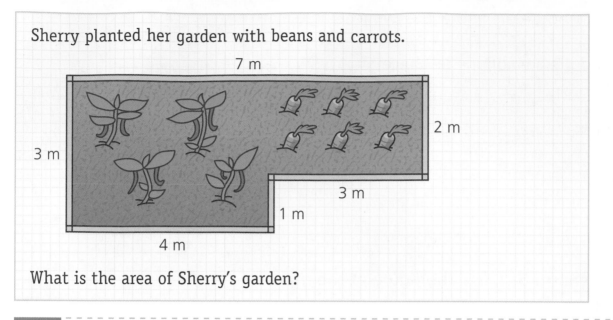

7 m

2 m

3 m

3 m

1 m

4 m

What is the area of Sherry's garden?

Step 1

Decompose the figure into two rectangles.

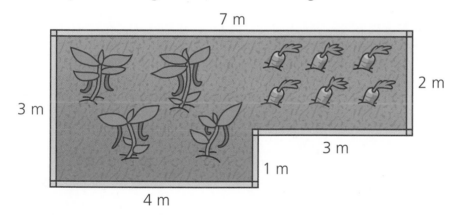

7 m

2 m

3 m

3 m

1 m

4 m

Step 2

Find the area of the bean rectangle. ⟶ $3 \times 4 = 12$ square meters
Find the area of the carrot rectangle. ⟶ $2 \times 3 = 6$ square meters

Step 3

Add the two areas.

$12 + 6 = $ _____ square meters

The area of Sherry's garden is 18 square meters.

Guided Practice

For exercises 1–4, use the figure at the right.

1. Decompose the figure into two rectangles.

2. Find the area of one rectangle.

   ___ × ___ = ___ square in.

3. Find the area of the other rectangle.

   ___ × ___ = ___ square in.

4. What is the area of the figure?

   ___ + ___ = ___ square in.

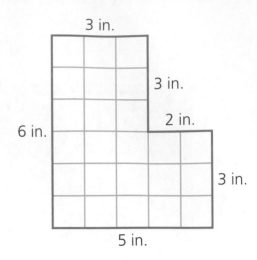

3 in.

3 in.

2 in.

6 in.

3 in.

5 in.

For exercises 5–8, use the figure at the right.

5. Decompose the figure into two rectangles.

6. Find the area of one rectangle.

   ___ square cm

7. Find the area of the other rectangle.

   ___ square cm

8. What is the area of the figure?

   ___ square cm

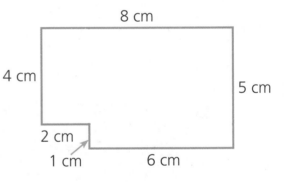

8 cm

4 cm

5 cm

2 cm

1 cm

6 cm

For exercises 9–11, use the figure at the right.

9. Decompose the figure into rectangles.

10. Find the area of each rectangle.

11. What is the area of the figure?

   ___ square cm

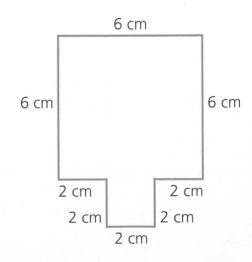

6 cm

6 cm

6 cm

2 cm

2 cm

2 cm

2 cm

2 cm

Guided Practice

12. Larry measures the floor of his kitchen. What is the area of the kitchen floor?

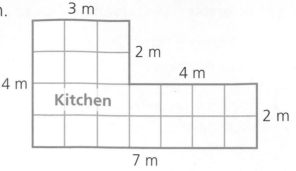

_____

13. Ms. Kim has a front porch. What is the area of the floor of the porch?

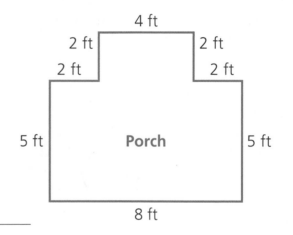

_____

☝☝ Think•Pair•Share

MP7 14. Brian wants to find the area of the figure. He cannot decide which way to decompose it. Does it matter? Explain your reasoning.

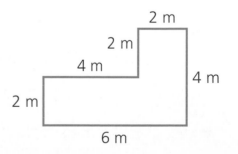

Independent Practice

For exercises 1–4, use the figure at the right.

1. Decompose the figure into two rectangles.

2. Find the area of one rectangle.

   ___ × ___ = ___ square in.

3. Find the area of the other rectangle.

   ___ × ___ = ___ square in.

4. What is the area of the figure?

   ___ + ___ = ___ square in.

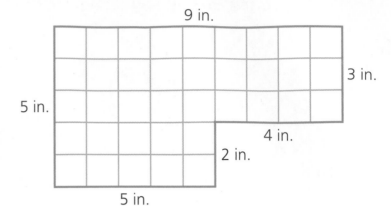

For exercises 5–8, use the figure at the right

Show your work.

5. Decompose the figure into two rectangles.

6. Find the area of one rectangle.

   _____ square cm

7. Find the area of the other rectangle.

   _____ square cm

8. What is the area of the figure?

   _____ square cm

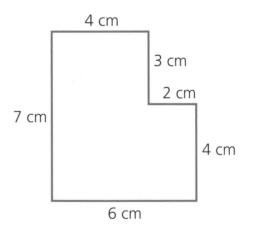

Independent Practice

9. Zach built a tree fort in his backyard. He measures the floor of his fort. What is the area of the fort's floor?

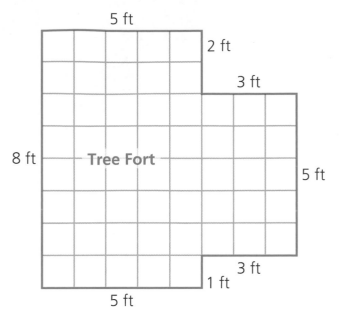

Circle the letter of the correct answer.

10. Dawn measures the floor of her bedroom and closet. What is the total area of the bedroom and closet floor?

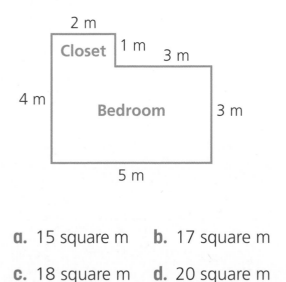

a. 15 square m   **b.** 17 square m

c. 18 square m   **d.** 20 square m

11. Bill digs a vegetable garden. What is the area of the garden?

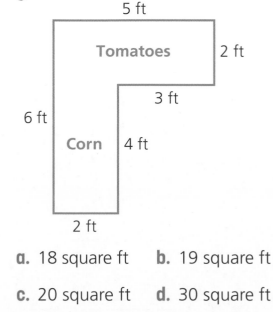

a. 18 square ft   **b.** 19 square ft

c. 20 square ft   **d.** 30 square ft

Independent Practice

MP2 12. Samantha wants to find the area of the hallway floor but she does not want to multiply 3 × 14. How could she use decomposition to find the area?

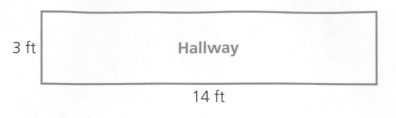

3 ft

Hallway

14 ft

MP3 13. Daniel decomposed the figure to find its area. He wrote 3 × 3 for the area of one rectangle. He wrote 1 × 5 for the area of the other rectangle. Daniel says the area of the figure is 14 square centimeters. What mistake did he make? Explain.

5 cm

1 cm

2 cm

2 cm

3 cm

3 cm

Solve the problems.

MP4 14. Sean measures the floor of his hamster's house. What is the area of the floor?

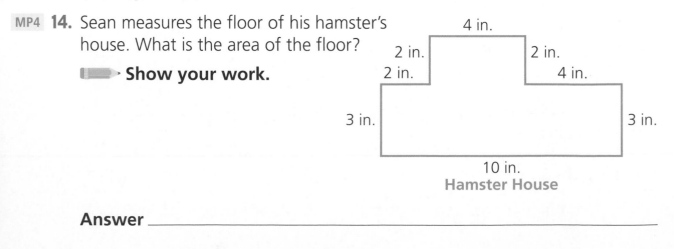

▬▬▶ **Show your work.**

4 in.

2 in.   2 in.
2 in.   4 in.

3 in.   3 in.

10 in.
Hamster House

Answer _____

Independent Practice

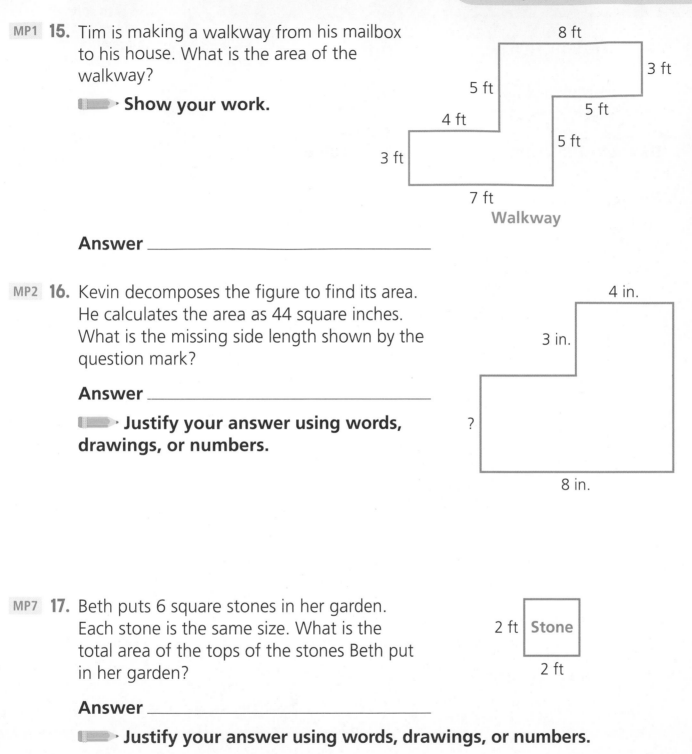

MP1 15. Tim is making a walkway from his mailbox to his house. What is the area of the walkway?

✏️ **Show your work.**

8 ft

3 ft

5 ft

5 ft

4 ft

5 ft

3 ft

7 ft

Walkway

Answer _____

MP2 16. Kevin decomposes the figure to find its area. He calculates the area as 44 square inches. What is the missing side length shown by the question mark?

Answer _____

✏️ **Justify your answer using words, drawings, or numbers.**

4 in.

3 in.

?

8 in.

MP7 17. Beth puts 6 square stones in her garden. Each stone is the same size. What is the total area of the tops of the stones Beth put in her garden?

2 ft | Stone

2 ft

Answer _____

✏️ **Justify your answer using words, drawings, or numbers.**

Essential Question:
How can you make
drawings to solve
problems with
measurements?

Guided Instruction

In this lesson you will learn to make drawings to solve
problems about measurement.

Understand: Using a drawing to help solve a problem

> Sharon has a square piece of cloth 8 feet long on each side. From the
> corner of the cloth, Sharon cuts out a square 4 feet long on each side.
> Sharon gives the small square piece to her sister.
> What is the area of the piece Sharon has left?

Draw a picture to show the
information in the problem.

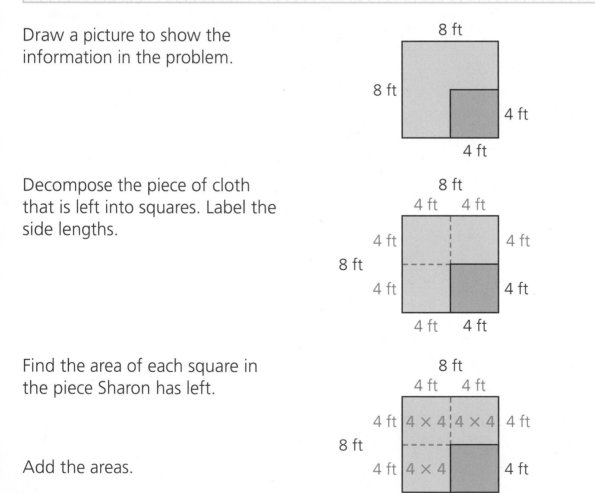

Decompose the piece of cloth
that is left into squares. Label the
side lengths.

Find the area of each square in
the piece Sharon has left.

Add the areas.

$16 + 16 + 16 = 48$

▶ The area of the piece of cloth Sharon has left is 48 square feet.

Guided Instruction

Connect: Drawing a picture to solve a problem

> Eric stacks 4 books in a pile. Each book is 6 centimeters thick.
> How high is the stack of books?

Step 1

Make a drawing.

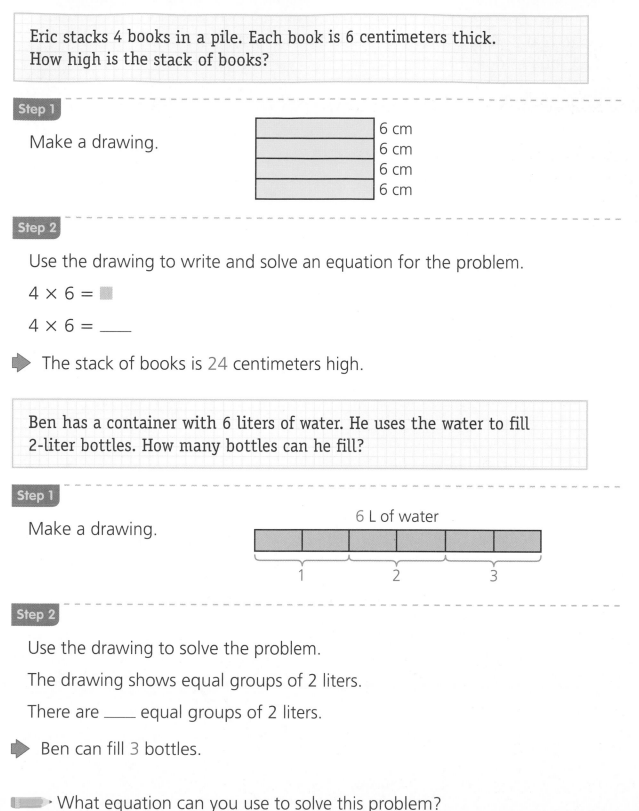

	6 cm
	6 cm
	6 cm
	6 cm

Step 2

Use the drawing to write and solve an equation for the problem.

$4 \times 6 = $ ▓

$4 \times 6 = $ ____

➡ The stack of books is 24 centimeters high.

> Ben has a container with 6 liters of water. He uses the water to fill
> 2-liter bottles. How many bottles can he fill?

Step 1

Make a drawing.

6 L of water

1   2   3

Step 2

Use the drawing to solve the problem.

The drawing shows equal groups of 2 liters.

There are ____ equal groups of 2 liters.

➡ Ben can fill 3 bottles.

✏ What equation can you use to solve this problem?

Guided Practice

Make a drawing. Solve the problem.

1. Jeff tapes together small paper squares that are 3 inches on each side to make a large square 6 inches on each side. How many small squares does he use?

   ✏ **Show your work.**

   Answer _____

2. Ginger makes 15 liters of fruit punch. She pours all of the punch into some bowls. If each bowl has 3 liters of punch, how many bowls does Ginger fill?

   ✏ **Show your work.**

   Answer _____

3. Ben uses 1 liter of water to fill 5 paper cups. How many liters of water will he use to fill 20 paper cups?

   ✏ **Show your work.**

   Answer _____

Guided Practice

4. Fluffy the cat has a mass of 8 kilograms. This is 2 kilograms more than the mass of Frisky the cat. What is the mass of Frisky the cat?

➡ **Show your work.**

Answer _____

5. Henry buys a sack of gravel. The mass is 900 grams. Henry pours 524 grams of the gravel into his turtle's tank. How much gravel is left in the sack?

➡ **Show your work.**

Answer _____

👥 **Think•Pair•Share**

MP3 **6.** Ann says that sometimes you can find the answer to a word problem by just using a drawing, but sometimes the drawing just helps you decide how to solve the problem. Do you agree? Explain your reasoning.

Independent Practice

Make a drawing for each problem. Solve the problem.

MP7 **1.** Sam has a rectangular sheet of cardboard with side lengths
11 inches and 9 inches. He cuts off a piece with side lengths
2 inches and 9 inches and uses that piece to make a bookmark.
What is the area of the piece of cardboard left over?

▶ **Show your work.**

Answer _____

MP4 **2.** How many 2-liter bottles can Glen fill from a container holding
18 liters of water?

▶ **Show your work.**

Answer _____

MP5 **3.** How many books each 3 centimeters thick do you need to make a
stack 9 centimeters high?

▶ **Show your work.**

Answer _____

Independent Practice

MP4 **4.** Thomas cuts a 32-inch piece of rope into 4 equal length pieces. What is the length of each piece?

 **Show your work.**

Answer _____

MP1 **5.** Five potatoes have a mass of 1 kilogram. What is the mass of 30 potatoes of the same size?

Show your work.

Answer _____

MP4 **6.** Adam's packed suitcase has a mass of 10 kilograms. This is 2 kilograms more than the mass of his sister's packed suitcase. What is the mass of his sister's packed suitcase?

Show your work.

Answer _____

Independent Practice

MP1 **7.** A nickel has a mass of 5 grams. Ben and Sarah want to know the mass of 3 nickels. Ben says the way to find out is by making a drawing. Sarah says you can just write and solve an equation. Who is right?

MP7 **8.** The two drawings below both show a ribbon 12 feet long cut into 3 equal pieces.

Drawing A: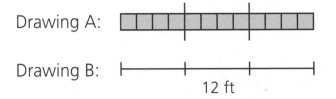

Drawing B:

12 ft

How are the drawings different? How can you use each drawing to find the length of one of the pieces of ribbon?

Solve the problems.

MP2 **9.** Latisha's fish tank holds 65 liters of water. Pam's fish tank holds 48 liters of water. How much more water does Latisha's tank hold than Pam's tank?

➡ **Show your work.**

Answer _____

MP5 **10.** An egg has a mass of 50 grams. What is the mass of 6 eggs that are the same size?

➡ **Show your work.**

Answer _____

Independent Practice

MP6 **11.** Maria uses 2 cuts to cut a piece of yarn 18 feet long into pieces with equal lengths. How long is each piece?

➡ **Show your work.**

Answer _____

MP1 **12.** Ginger makes a craft project. She starts with a rectangular mirror with side lengths 6 inches and 4 inches. She glues 1-inch square tiles on the mirror along the edge to make a frame. What is the area of the mirror that is not covered with tiles?

Answer _____

➡ **Justify your answer using words, drawings, or numbers.**

MP7 **13.** Look back at exercise 12. Ginger does the project again using a larger mirror and the same 1-inch tiles. This mirror has side lengths 12 inches and 10 inches. What is the area of the mirror that is not covered with tiles?

Answer _____

➡ **Justify your answer using words, drawings, or numbers.**

Problem Solving:
Perimeter

Essential Question:
How can you solve problems about the perimeters of polygons?

Words to Know:
closed figure
polygon
perimeter
quadrilateral

Guided Instruction

In this lesson you will learn about the perimeter of a polygon.

Understand: The meaning of perimeter

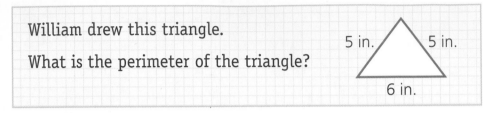

William drew this triangle.

What is the perimeter of the triangle?

5 in.   5 in.

6 in.

A closed figure has no breaks in its sides.
A polygon is a plane closed figure with straight sides.
The perimeter of a polygon is the sum of the lengths of its sides.

Add the side lengths to find the perimeter of the triangle.

$$5 + 5 + 6 = P$$
$$10 + 6 = 16$$

➡ The perimeter of the triangle is 16 inches.

Understand: Finding an unknown side length of a polygon

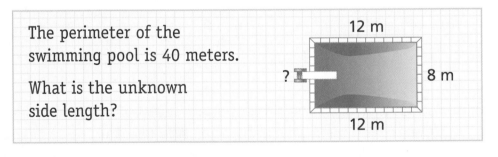

The perimeter of the swimming pool is 40 meters.

What is the unknown side length?

12 m

?

8 m

12 m

Find the sum of the known side lengths.

$$12 + 8 + 12 = \blacksquare$$
$$20 + 12 = 32$$

Subtract the sum of the known side lengths from the perimeter.

$$40 - 32 = 8$$

➡ The unknown side length is 8 meters.

Guided Instruction

Connect: What you know about side lengths and perimeter

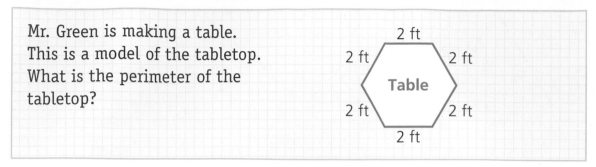

Mr. Green is making a table.
This is a model of the tabletop.
What is the perimeter of the
tabletop?

Write and solve an addition equation.

$2 + 2 + 2 + 2 + 2 + 2 = P$

$2 + 2 + 2 + 2 + 2 + 2 = 12$

Or, since all side lengths are the same length, you can multiply to find the perimeter.

$6 \times 2 = 12$

The perimeter of the tabletop is 12 feet.

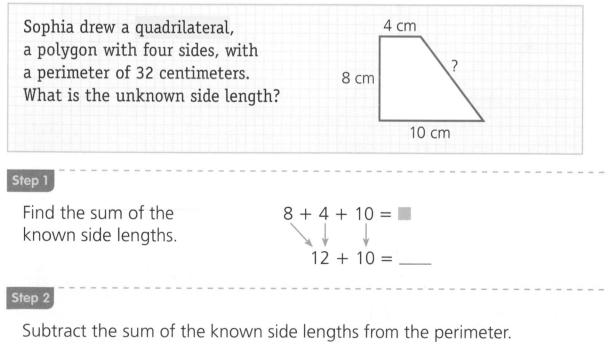

Sophia drew a quadrilateral,
a polygon with four sides, with
a perimeter of 32 centimeters.
What is the unknown side length?

Step 1

Find the sum of the
known side lengths.

$8 + 4 + 10 = \blacksquare$

$12 + 10 = \underline{\quad}$

Step 2

Subtract the sum of the known side lengths from the perimeter.

$32 - 22 = \underline{\quad}$

The missing side length is ____ centimeters.

Guided Practice

Find the perimeter of each figure.

1.

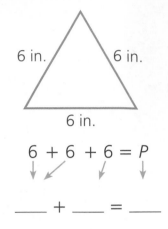

6 in.   6 in.

6 in.

$6 + 6 + 6 = P$

___ + ___ = ___

Perimeter: ___ inches

2.

3 ft   5 ft

7 ft

$3 + 5 + 7 = P$

___ + ___ = ___

Perimeter: ___ feet

Solve the problems.

3. The model shows the shape of Mason's front lawn. Mason measures the side lengths of his front lawn. What is the perimeter?

   The perimeter is ___ meters.

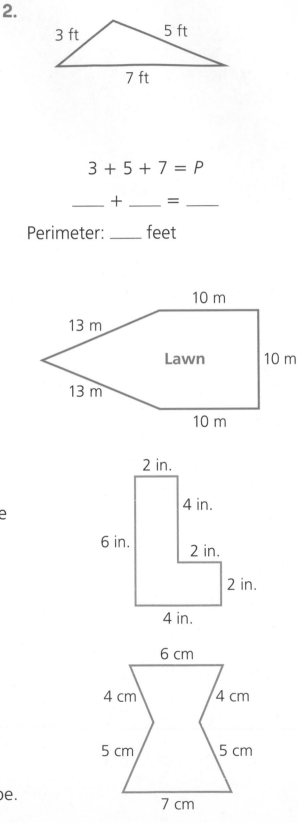

10 m

13 m

Lawn   10 m

13 m

10 m

4. Linda draws this "L." She wants to glue gold ribbon on the outline of the letter. How much gold ribbon does Linda need? How do you know?

   Linda needs ___ inches of ribbon.

2 in.

4 in.

6 in.   2 in.

2 in.

4 in.

5. Stanley is painting a design on his wall that looks like an hourglass. He wants to outline the figure with tape before he paints. How much tape will he need?

   Stanley needs ___ centimeters of tape.

6 cm

4 cm   4 cm

5 cm   5 cm

7 cm

Guided Practice

Find each unknown side length.

6.
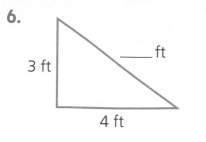

Perimeter: 12 feet

7.
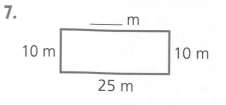

Perimeter: 70 meters

8.
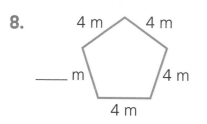

Perimeter: 20 meters

9.
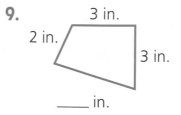

Perimeter: 12 inches

Solve the problem.

10. Lisa measures a wall of her doll house. The perimeter of the wall is 60 centimeters. What is the unknown side length?

The unknown side length is ___ centimeters.

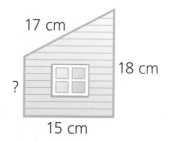

☆☆ Think•Pair•Share

MP3 **11.** Paul uses addition to find the perimeter of the square. Barbara uses multiplication to find the perimeter. Explain why both methods work.

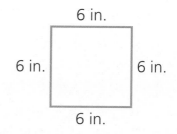

Independent Practice

Find the perimeter of each figure.

1.

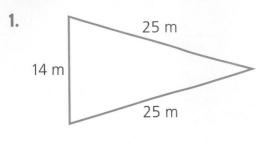

25 m

14 m

25 m

Perimeter: ____ meters

2.

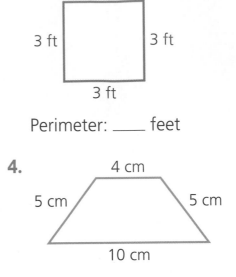

3 ft

3 ft   3 ft

3 ft

Perimeter: ____ feet

3.

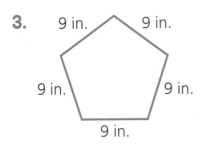

9 in.   9 in.

9 in.   9 in.

9 in.

Perimeter: ____ inches

4.

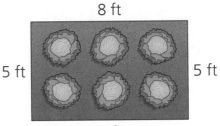

4 cm

5 cm   5 cm

10 cm

Perimeter: ____ centimeters

Solve the problems.

MP1 **5.** Rabbits are eating Mrs. Gianni's lettuce. She decides to put a fence around her lettuce patch. How much fencing should she buy?

Mrs. Gianni should buy ____ feet of fencing.

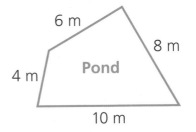

8 ft

5 ft   5 ft

8 ft

MP6 **6.** Michael builds a frog pond. What is the perimeter of the pond?

The perimeter of the pond is ____ meters.

6 m

8 m

4 m   **Pond**

10 m

MP2 **7.** Emily is helping to build a platform for the school play. It is in the shape of a square with one side equal to 5 feet. The students plan to put a piece of fabric around the sides of the square. What length of fabric will they need?

The students will need a length of fabric ____ feet long.

Independent Practice

Find each unknown side length.

8.

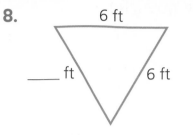

6 ft

____ ft

6 ft

Perimeter: 18 feet

9.

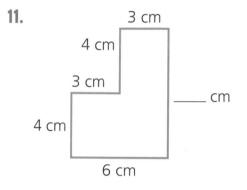

7 in.

3 in.

3 in.

____ in.

Perimeter: 20 inches

10.

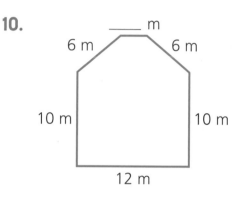

____ m

6 m   6 m

10 m   10 m

12 m

Perimeter: 47 meters

11.

3 cm

4 cm

3 cm

____ cm

4 cm

6 cm

Perimeter: 28 centimeters

Solve the problems.

MP1 **12.** This is the shape of the kite that Stan makes. The perimeter of the kite is 10 feet. What is the unknown side length?

The length of the unknown side is ____ feet.

2 ft

2 ft   3 ft

?

MP6 **13.** This is the shape of Mr. Dean's deck. He measured the deck and found that the perimeter is 22 meters. What is the unknown side length?

The unknown side length is ____ meters.

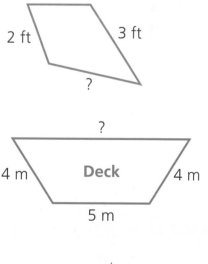

?

4 m   Deck   4 m

5 m

MP4 **14.** Jasman is cutting out stars for a science poster. The perimeter of each star is 30 centimeters and all the sides are equal. What is the length of each side?

The length of each side is ____ centimeters.

Independent Practice

MP6 **15.** Mr. Peters wants to put weather stripping around a door. Explain how Mr. Peters can find out how much weather stripping he needs.

MP3 **16.** Sharon knows the perimeter of a quadrilateral. She also knows three side lengths of the quadrilateral. Sharon says that she can find the unknown side length just by subtracting. Is she right?

Answer _____

▶ **Justify your answer using words, drawings, or numbers.**

Solve the problems.

MP4 **17.** Ave drew this model of a soccer field. The perimeter of the real soccer field is 190 meters. What is the unknown side length?

▶ **Show your work.**

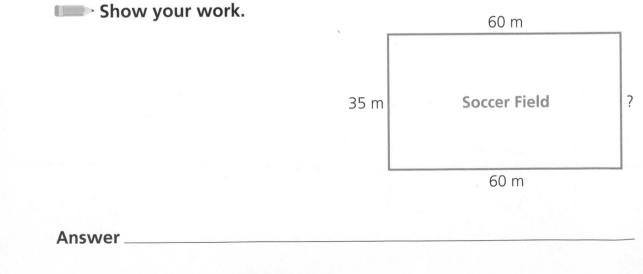

Answer _____

Independent Practice

Solve the problems.

MP5 **18.** Compare the perimeter of Rectangle A with the perimeter of Rectangle B. Write <, >, or =.

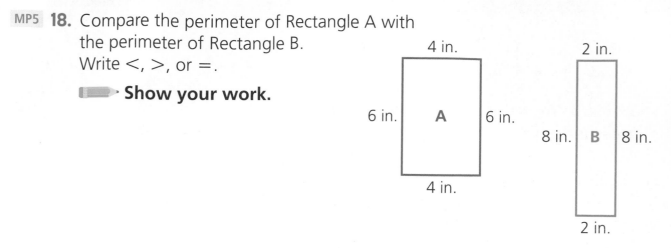

➡ **Show your work.**

The perimeter of Rectangle A _____ the perimeter of Rectangle B.

MP7 **19.** Jill has two windows in her bedroom. The height of each window is 3 feet. The left window is 4 feet wide. The right window is 5 feet wide. How much greater is the perimeter of the right window than the perimeter of the left window?

Answer _____

➡ **Justify your answer using words, drawings, or numbers.**

MP4 **20.** Jack bought 30 feet of fencing. He uses all of the fencing to make a pen for his goat. The pen is shaped like a triangle. Each of two sides is 9 feet long. What is the length of the third side?

Answer _____

➡ **Justify your answer using words, drawings, or numbers.**

Problem Solving: **Compare** Perimeter and Area

Guided Instruction

In this lesson you will learn more about using perimeter and area to solve problems.

Understand: Areas of different rectangles with the same perimeter

Angela has 14 feet of fencing. She wants to make a pen for her guinea pigs. She draws two models of rectangles that have a perimeter of 14 feet.

	6 ft			5 ft	
1 ft	**Pen A**	1 ft	2 ft	**Pen B**	2 ft
	6 ft			5 ft	

Which pen will have the greater area?

Find the area of Pen A.

$$1 \times 6 = 6$$

The area of Pen A is 6 square feet.

Find the area of Pen B.

$$2 \times 5 = 10$$

The area of Pen B is 10 square feet.

Compare the areas of the two pens.

6 square feet < 10 square feet

➡ Pen B will have the greater area.

Remember!
To find the area of a rectangle, you can multiply side lengths, or count unit squares.

✏ Draw a rectangle with a perimeter of 14 feet that has an area greater than Pen B's area.

Guided Instruction

Understand: Perimeters of different rectangles with the same area

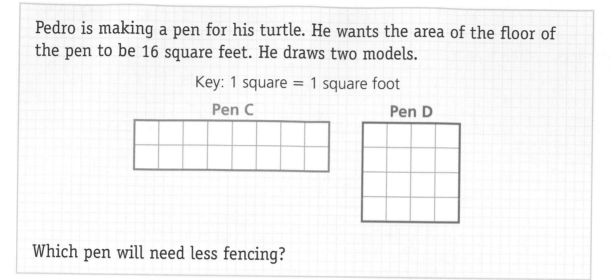

Pedro is making a pen for his turtle. He wants the area of the floor of the pen to be 16 square feet. He draws two models.

Key: 1 square = 1 square foot

Pen C

Pen D

Which pen will need less fencing?

Find the perimeter of Pen C.

$$2 + 8 + 2 + 8 = ?$$
$$10 \ + \ 10 \ = 20$$

Remember!

To find the perimeter of a polygon, add the side lengths.

The perimeter of Pen C is 20 feet.

Find the perimeter of Pen D.

$$4 + 4 + 4 + 4 = 16$$

The perimeter of Pen D is 16 feet.

Compare the perimeters of the two pens.

20 feet > 16 feet

➡ Pen D will need less fencing.

✏ Can you draw a rectangle with an area of 16 square feet that would use less fencing than Pen D?

Guided Instruction

Connect: What you know about perimeter and area to solve problems

Ms. Gonzalez has 12 inches of wood to make a picture frame. She draws three models. Which frame has the least area?

5 in.

1 in. | Frame A | 1 in.

5 in.

4 in.

2 in. | Frame B | 2 in.

4 in.

3 in.

3 in. | Frame C | 3 in.

3 in.

Step 1

Find the area of each frame.

Frame A
$1 \times 5 = 5$

The area of Frame A is 5 square inches.

Frame B
$2 \times 4 = 8$

The area of Frame B is 8 square inches.

Frame C
$3 \times 3 = 9$

The area of Frame C is 9 square inches.

Step 2

Compare the areas of the frames.

5 square inches ____ 8 square inches ____ 9 square inches

➡ Frame A has the least area.

▱ Compare the perimeters of the frames.

	Frame A	Frame B	Frame C
Perimeter:	____ in.	____ in.	____ in.
Compare perimeters:	Frame A ____	Frame B ____	Frame C

306 Unit 5 ▪ Focus on Measurement and Data/Geometry

Guided Practice

In exercises 1 and 2, draw a different rectangle with the same perimeter. Then find the area of each rectangle.

1. Perimeter: 10 centimeters

   Key: 1 square = 1 square centimeter

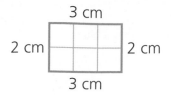

3 cm
2 cm   2 cm
3 cm

   Area: _____ square cm

   Area: _____ square cm

2. Perimeter: 16 inches

   Key: 1 square = 1 square inch

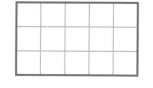

   Area: _____ square in.

   Area: _____ square in.

Draw a different rectangle with the same area. Then find the perimeter of each rectangle.

3. Area = 12 square meters

   Key: 1 square = 1 square meter

   Perimeter: _____ meters

   Perimeter: _____ meters

☫ Think•Pair•Share

MP2 4. Manuel says that if two rectangles have the same area, they must have the same perimeter. Is he right? Explain your reasoning.

Independent Practice

In exercises 1 and 2, draw a different rectangle with the same perimeter. Then find the area of each rectangle.

1. Perimeter = 8 feet

   Key: 1 square = 1 square foot

   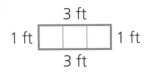
   3 ft
   1 ft [   ] 1 ft
   3 ft

   Area: ____ square feet

   Area: ____ square feet

2. Perimeter: 18 inches

   Key: 1 square = 1 square inch

   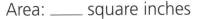

   Area: ____ square inches

   Area: ____ square inches

3. Fatima wants to grow strawberries. She has 20 feet of fencing to protect the plants. She draws four models of gardens with a perimeter of 20 feet. Choose the model for the garden that will let Fatima grow the most strawberries.

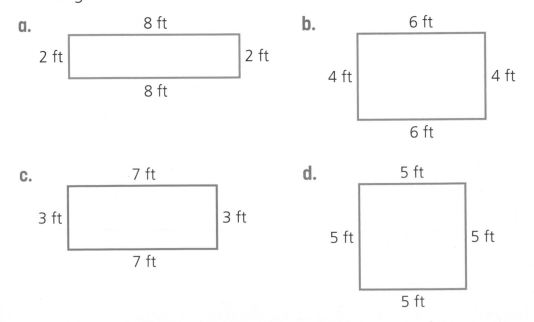

a.
8 ft
2 ft [   ] 2 ft
8 ft

b.
6 ft
4 ft [   ] 4 ft
6 ft

c.
7 ft
3 ft [   ] 3 ft
7 ft

d.
5 ft
5 ft [   ] 5 ft
5 ft

Independent Practice

In exercises 4 and 5, draw a different rectangle with the same area. Then find the perimeter of each rectangle.

4. Area: 10 square centimeters   Key: 1 square = 1 square centimeter

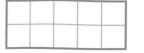

Perimeter: _____ centimeters   Perimeter: _____ centimeters

5. Area: 18 square inches   Key: 1 square = 1 square inch

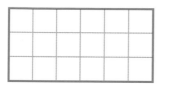

Perimeter: _____ inches   Perimeter: _____ inches

Solve the problems.

MP4 6. Harry wants to make a corral for his toy dinosaur with an area of 24 square inches. He draws the model shown below. Draw another model of a corral that has a smaller perimeter. Then find the perimeter of each corral.

Harry's Dinosaur Corral

Perimeter: _____   Perimeter: _____

MP5 7. Draw a model for the coral floor from exercise 6 that will have a greater perimeter than Harry's model. Then find the perimeter of your model.

Perimeter: _____

Independent Practice

MP7 **8.** Compare the dinosaur corrals in exercise 6. How are they alike? How are they different?

MP4 **9.** Andrew draws a rectangle with side lengths of 1 inch and 5 inches. How can Andrew draw a different rectangle with the same perimeter?

MP6 **10.** Cheryl has 24 inches of ribbon. She wants to paste the ribbon around a birthday card for her mother. Cheryl draws two models of the card. Which card has the lesser area?

Show your work.

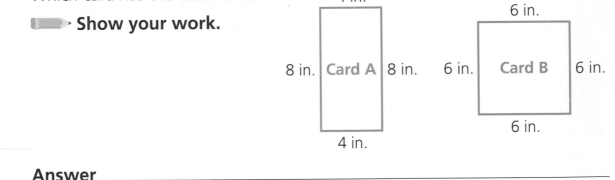

Answer _____

MP1 **11.** Ms. Hansen is making a pen for her ducks. She wants the area of the floor of the pen to be 40 square meters. Ms. Hansen draws two models. Which model will need less fencing? How much less fencing will it need?

Show your work.

Key: 1 square = 1 square meter

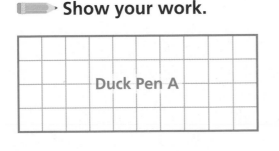

Answer _____

Independent Practice

MP4 **12.** Cindy reads that the mouse family home is very dark with just one window. Draw a window with the same perimeter that will let in more light. How much greater is the area of your window than the area of the old window?

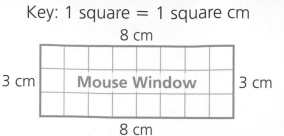

Key: 1 square = 1 square cm

➡ **Show your work.**

Answer _____

MP2 **13.** Abel has two desks in his attic. Each desktop is a different rectangle shape with an area of 6 square feet. If Abel puts glow-in-the-dark tape around the edges of both desktops, how much tape will he need?

Answer _____

➡ **Justify your answer using words, drawings, or numbers.**

MP7 **14.** Vicky has 20 inches of wire. She uses all the wire to make a rectangle. What is the least possible area of the rectangle? What is the greatest possible area?

Answer _____

➡ **Justify your answer using words, drawings, or numbers.**

Understand Shapes and Attributes

Essential Question:
How do you use attributes to identify shapes?

Words to Know:
vertex (vertices)
angle
right angle
rhombus

Guided Instruction

In this lesson you will learn how to use attributes to identify shapes.

Understand: Using number of sides and number of vertices to identify polygons

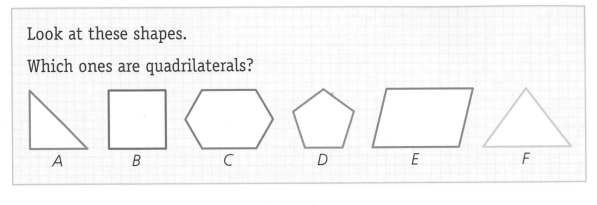

Look at these shapes.

Which ones are quadrilaterals?

A   B   C   D   E   F

Two sides of a polygon meet at a vertex and form an angle.
You can identify a polygon by counting its sides and its vertices.

A quadrilateral is a polygon that has 4 straight sides and 4 vertices.
Count the number of sides and vertices of each shape above.
Shapes *B* and *E* each have 4 sides and 4 vertices.
They are quadrilaterals.

▷ Shapes *B* and *E* are quadrilaterals.

▬▶ Name each shape if you can. Tell how many sides and vertices each has.

Guided Instruction

Understand: Using lengths of sides and right angles to identify special quadrilaterals

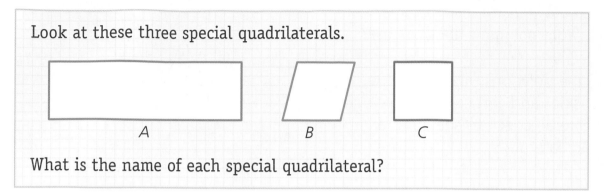

Look at these three special quadrilaterals.

A   B   C

What is the name of each special quadrilateral?

Look at the sides and the angles.

Quadrilateral *A* has opposite sides that are the same length. It has 4 angles that are square corners. Each of these angles is called a right angle.

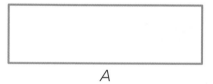

A

Quadrilateral *A* is a rectangle.

All 4 sides of Quadrilateral *B* are the same length.

B

Quadrilateral *B* is a rhombus.

All 4 sides of Quadrilateral C are the same length. It has 4 right angles.

C

Since Quadrilateral *C* has the attributes of both a rhombus and a rectangle, Quadrilateral *C* is a square.

▶ Quadrilateral *A* is a rectangle; Quadrilateral *B* is a rhombus; Quadrilateral *C* is a square.

✏ Draw a quadrilateral that is NOT a rectangle, a rhombus, or a square.

Guided Instruction

Connect: **What you know about attributes of polygons**

Clara used polygons to make this drawing. What polygons did Clara use?

To identify the polygons, first count the number of sides and vertices. If the polygon is a quadrilateral, check to see if it is a special quadrilateral.

Step 1

The head has 4 sides and 4 vertices. The head is a quadrilateral. Check to see if the quadrilateral is a special quadrilateral. The head has 4 equal sides and 4 right angles.

The head is a _____.

Step 2

Each ear has 6 sides and 6 vertices.

Each ear is a _____.

> **Remember!**
> A polygon with 6 sides and 6 vertices is a hexagon.

Step 3

The body has 3 sides and 3 vertices.

The body is a _____

Step 4

Each leg has 4 sides and 4 vertices. Each leg is a quadrilateral. Each leg has opposite sides that are equal and 4 right angles.

> **Remember!**
> Check if the quadrilateral is a special quadrilateral.

Each leg is a _____.

➡ To make the drawing, Clara used _____, _____, _____, and _____.

For each polygon, write the number of sides and the number of vertices. Write triangle, quadrilateral, pentagon, or hexagon to name each figure.

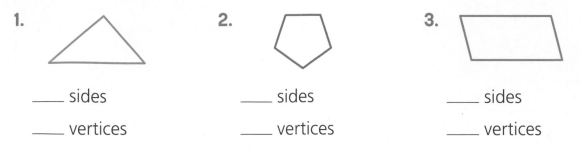

1.

____ sides

____ vertices

_____

2.

____ sides

____ vertices

_____

3.

____ sides

____ vertices

_____

Use the quadrilateral at the right for exercises 4–7.

4. Are the opposite sides the same length? _____

5. Are all 4 sides the same length? _____

6. Does the quadrilateral have 4 right angles? _____

7. Is the quadrilateral a rectangle, rhombus, or square? _____

Solve the problem.

8. Orlando has a garden in the shape of a quadrilateral. Each side of the garden is 6 feet long. The garden has four right angles. Draw and label a picture to show Orlando's garden. What is the best name for the shape of the garden?

⚜ **Think•Pair•Share**

MP3 9. Irene says that a rectangle is always a quadrilateral. Jamie says that a rectangle is sometimes a square. Are both students correct? Explain your reasoning.

Independent Practice

Write the name for the figure. Choose triangle, quadrilateral, rectangle, rhombus, square, pentagon, or hexagon.

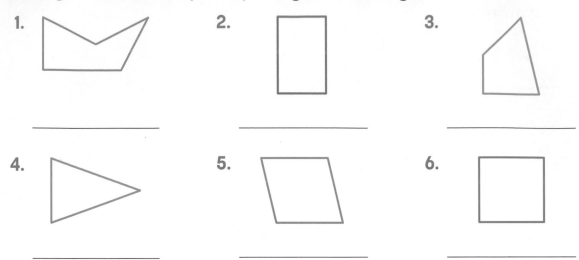

1. _____

2. _____

3. _____

4. _____

5. _____

6. _____

7. Are any of the quadrilaterals in exercises 1–6 special quadrilaterals? If so, write the problem number and the special name.

Draw each figure.

8. rectangle

9. rhombus

10. square

11. quadrilateral that is not a rectangle, a rhombus, or a square

Independent Practice

12. Which figure is a rectangle?

a.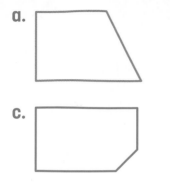

b.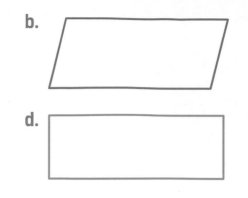

c.

d.

13. Which figure is a rhombus?

a.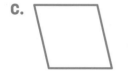

b.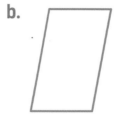

c.

d.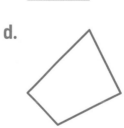

14. Which figure is NOT a quadrilateral?

a.

b.

c.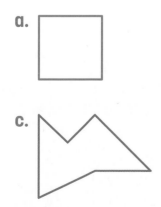

d.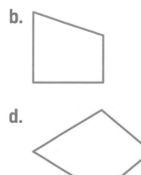

Independent Practice

MP7 **15.** Draw two different quadrilaterals.

How are the quadrilaterals you drew alike? How are they different?

MP6 **16.** A window has 6 panes of glass.

What is the shape of the window?
What is the shape of each pane of glass?
How did you identify the shapes?

MP4 **17.** Lance made this drawing of his kite.

What is the shape of the kite?
How do you know?

Independent Practice

MP6 **18.** Christine thinks that both of these figures are quadrilaterals.

Is she correct?

Answer _____

🖊 **Justify your answer using words, drawings, or numbers.**

MP3 **19.** Juan says that any square is also a rhombus. Clay says that any rhombus is also a square. Who is correct?

Answer _____

🖊 **Justify your answer using words, drawings, or numbers.**

MP6 **20.** Victoria says that a quadrilateral can have more than one name. Is she correct?

Answer _____

🖊 **Justify your answer using words, drawings, or numbers.**

Lesson 36

Partition Shapes to Make Equal Areas

Essential Question:
How do you partition shapes to make equal areas?

Guided Instruction

In this lesson you will learn how to partition shapes to make equal areas.

Understand: Partitioning a circle into 4 parts with equal area

Amos has a pizza that he wants to cut into 4 slices. He wants each slice to have the same area. How can Amos cut the pizza? What fraction or part of the pizza does each slice represent?

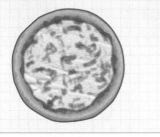

You can draw lines to partition a whole into 4 equal parts.
Use a horizontal line and a vertical line. Or use two diagonal lines.

Remember!
Write a unit fraction to identify one equal part of the whole. The whole has 4 equal parts. One equal part is $\frac{1}{4}$ of the whole.

The pizza is now cut into four equal parts.
Each part of the pizza has the same area.
The area of each part is $\frac{1}{4}$ of the area of the whole pizza.

▶ Amos can cut the pizza into fourths as shown above.
Each slice of the pizza is $\frac{1}{4}$ the area of the whole pizza.

✏️ Draw a rectangle. Partition the whole rectangle into 4 equal parts. What fraction is each part of the whole rectangle?

Guided Instruction

Understand: Partitioning a rectangle into 8 parts with equal area

Rachel has a rectangular garden. She wants to partition the garden into 8 equal parts. She will plant different vegetables in each part, including carrots.

How can Rachel partition her garden? What fraction represents the area of each part of the garden? What part of the garden will Rachel plant with carrots?

Partition a rectangle into 8 equal parts.

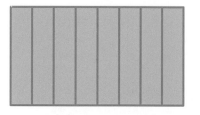

Partition a rectangle into 8 equal parts in another way.

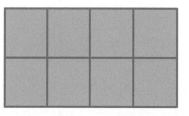

There are 8 equal parts. Each section of the garden is 1 equal part of the garden. The area of each part of the garden is $\frac{1}{8}$ of the whole garden.

Remember!
Write a unit fraction to show one equal part of the whole.

➡ Rachel can partition her garden into 8 equal parts as shown above. The area of each part of the garden is $\frac{1}{8}$ the area of the whole garden. She will plant $\frac{1}{8}$ of the garden with carrots.

✏ Show another way that Rachel could partition her garden into 8 equal parts.

Guided Instruction

Connect: What you know about partitioning shapes to make equal areas

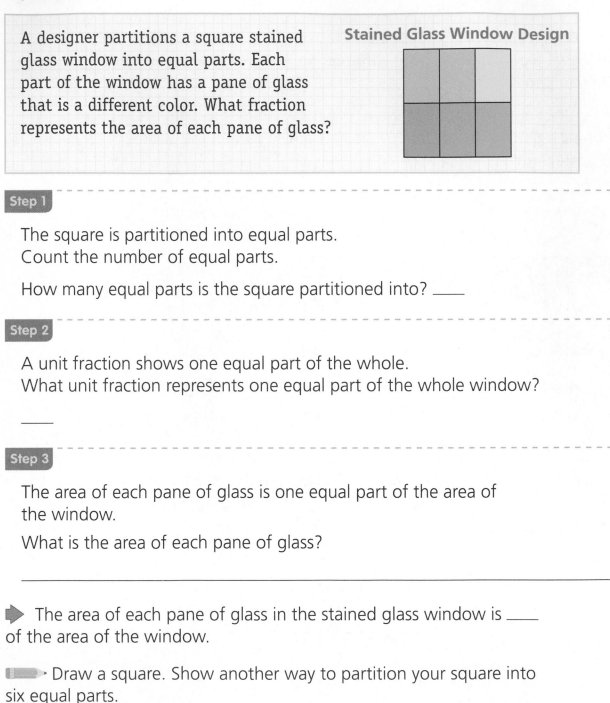

A designer partitions a square stained glass window into equal parts. Each part of the window has a pane of glass that is a different color. What fraction represents the area of each pane of glass?

Stained Glass Window Design

Step 1

The square is partitioned into equal parts.
Count the number of equal parts.

How many equal parts is the square partitioned into? ____

Step 2

A unit fraction shows one equal part of the whole.
What unit fraction represents one equal part of the whole window?

____

Step 3

The area of each pane of glass is one equal part of the area of the window.

What is the area of each pane of glass?

_____

➡️ The area of each pane of glass in the stained glass window is ____ of the area of the window.

✏️ Draw a square. Show another way to partition your square into six equal parts.

In exercises 1–3, each shape is partitioned into parts with equal areas. Express the area of one equal part of each as a unit fraction of the whole area.

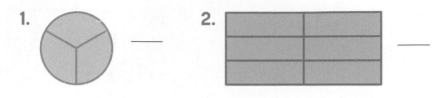

1. ____   2. ____   3. ____

Use the circles below for exercises 4–8.

Circle A   Circle B

4. Partition each circle into two equal parts in different ways.

5. Look at Circle A. What unit fraction represents each equal part of the circle? ____

6. Look at Circle B. What unit fraction represents each equal part of the circle? ____

7. What is the area of each part of Circle A?

   _____

8. What is the area of each part of Circle B?

   _____

Think·Pair·Share

MP7 9. Both of these squares are partitioned into equal parts. Are the areas of each part of these squares the same? Explain your reasoning.

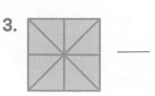

Independent Practice

In exercises 1–3, each shape is partitioned into parts with equal areas. Express the area of each part as a unit fraction of the whole area.

1.

2.

3.

_____   _____   _____

4. Which rectangle is partitioned into 6 parts with equal areas?

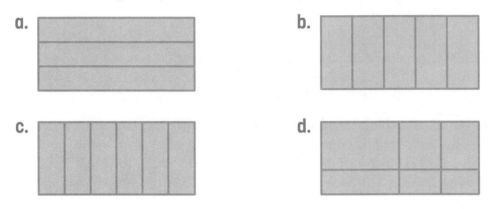

a.

b.

c.

d.

5. What unit fraction represents each equal area of the circle?

a. $\frac{1}{8}$ b. 1

c. $\frac{8}{8}$ d. 8

6. Look at the rectangles in exercises 4 a, b, and c. The rectangles are all the same size and area. Find the unit fraction for one part of each of the rectangles. Write the unit fraction next to the rectangle. Compare the unit fractions here.

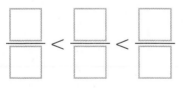

Independent Practice

In exercises 7–9, show two different ways to partition each figure into the given number of equal parts. Then write the fraction that represents each equal part of the whole area.

7. 4 equal parts

Answer _____   **Answer** _____

8. 6 equal parts

Answer _____   **Answer** _____

9. 8 equal parts

Answer _____   **Answer** _____

10. Draw two matching rectangles. Show two different ways to partition the rectangle into thirds.

Independent Practice

MP7   **11.** Look back at your drawings for exercise 9. Compare your drawings with those of a partner. What can you say about the area of each part in your drawings and in your partner's drawings?

Solve the problems.

MP4   **12.** Zach has a piece of carpet. He plans to cut the carpet into 3 equal size pieces. What unit fraction represents each equal size piece of the carpet? What fraction represents the area of each piece of the carpet?

   ✏️ **Make a drawing.**

Answer _____

MP4   **13.** Jessica has a tablecloth. She folds it into 8 equal parts. What fraction represents each of the folded parts of the tablecloth? What fraction represents the area of each of the folded parts?

   ✏️ **Make a drawing.**

Answer _____

MP4   **14.** Carl has a large piece of cotton fabric. He wants to cut it into 6 equal, smaller pieces. What fraction represents each smaller piece of the fabric? What fraction represents the area of each of the smaller pieces?

   ✏️ **Make a drawing.**

Answer _____

Independent Practice

Solve the problems.

MP7 **15.** Ron has a large poster board for a report he is doing. He partitions the poster board into parts with equal-size areas. The area of each part is $\frac{1}{6}$ of the area of the whole poster board. Ron will put a picture of a different animal in each part. How many animals can Ron put on his poster?

Answer _____

✏️ **Justify your answer using words, drawings, or numbers.**

MP3 **16.** Mr. Drake cut construction paper into 8 triangles for his students to make flags. Each triangle has an equal area. The area of each triangle is $\frac{1}{4}$ of the area of the whole sheet of construction paper. How many pieces of construction paper did Mr. Drake cut? How many triangles did he make from each piece of construction paper?

Answer _____

✏️ **Justify your answer using words, drawings, or numbers.**

MP6 **17.** Delia has a sheet of plastic shaped like a hexagon. She needs to cut the plastic into pieces with equal areas. She says that she can use both of these patterns to cut the plastic. Do you agree? Explain your reasoning.

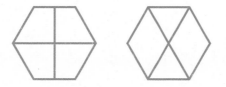

Answer _____

✏️ **Justify your answer using words, drawings, or numbers.**

For exercises 1 and 2, draw an example of the shape.

1. rhombus

2. quadrilateral that is not a rectangle or rhombus

For exercises 3–5, use the figure at the right.

3. What is the area of the shaded figure?

_____ square units

4. What is the area of the part of the figure that is not shaded? _____ square units

5. What is the perimeter of the shaded figure?

_____ units

For exercises 6–9, use the rectangle at the right.

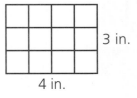

3 in.

4 in.

6. Shade one unit square in the rectangle. What is the area of the square you shaded? _____

7. How many 1-inch square tiles would you need to cover the rectangle completely? _____

8. What is the perimeter of the rectangle? _____

9. What is the area of the rectangle? _____

Circle the correct answers.

10. A rectangle has side lengths of 6 meters and 14 meters. Wei-Yin wants to use the Distributive Property to find the area of the rectangle. Which equations could Wei-Yin use?

a. $(6 \times 4) + (6 \times 10)$

b. $(6 \times 4) \times (6 \times 10)$

c. $6 \times (4 + 10)$

d. $(2 \times 14) + (4 \times 14)$

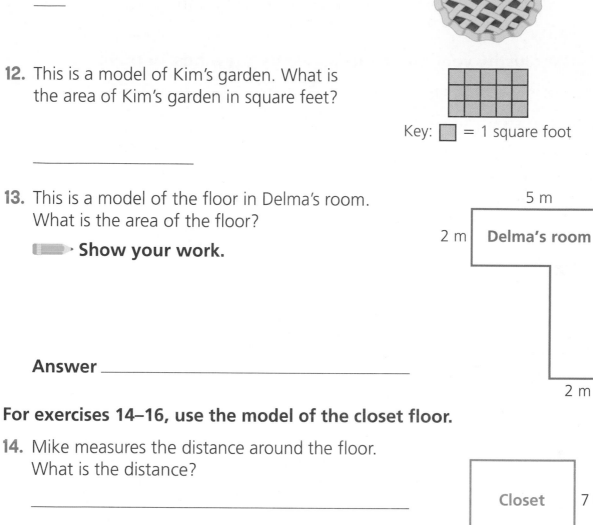

11. Partition the pie into eight equal slices.

Write the fraction that represents one slice.

____

12. This is a model of Kim's garden. What is the area of Kim's garden in square feet?

Key: ☐ = 1 square foot

_____

13. This is a model of the floor in Delma's room. What is the area of the floor?

✏️ **Show your work.**

5 m

2 m Delma's room

6 m

2 m

Answer _____

For exercises 14–16, use the model of the closet floor.

14. Mike measures the distance around the floor. What is the distance?

_____

15. What is the area of the floor?

_____

Closet 7 ft

9 ft

16. A carpet tile is 1-foot square. Each box contains 10 tiles. How many boxes of tiles should Mike buy to cover the floor with tiles?

✏️ **Show your work.**

Answer _____

Solve the problems.

MP3 **17.** Ciro says that a rectangle is always a square. Rewrite his statement to make it correct.

Answer _____

✏️ **Justify your answer using words, drawings, or numbers.**

MP4 **18.** Krissa has 24 feet of fencing. She wants to make a pen in the shape of a rectangle for her turtles. What is the least possible area of a rectangle Krissa can make? What is the greatest possible area?

Answer _____

✏️ **Justify your answer using words, drawings, or numbers.**

MP8 **19.** The tray on Mr. Garth's desk is shaped like a rectangle. The tray has two sections. Mr. Garth measures the tray in inches. He wants to find the area of the tray and writes $9 \times (3 + 5)$. What is the area of the tray?

Answer _____

✏️ **Justify your answer using words, drawings, or numbers.**

Performance Tasks

Performance Tasks show your understanding of the Math that you have learned. You will be doing various Performance Tasks as you complete your work in this text.

Beginning This Task

The next five pages provide you with the beginning of a Performance Task. You will be given 5 items to complete, and each item will have two or more parts. As you complete these items you will:

  I Demonstrate that you have mastered mathematical skills and concepts

  II Reason through a problem to a solution, and explain your reasoning

  III Use models and apply them to real-world situations.

Extending This Task

Your teacher may extend this Performance Task with additional items provided in our online resources at sadlierconnect.com.

Scoring This Task

Your response to each item will be assessed against a rubric, or scoring guide. Some items will be worth 1 or 2 points, and others will be worth more. In each item you will show your work or explain your reasoning.

Performance Task 2

Planning a Mural

1. The students at Foster Park School are planning to paint a
   wall mural. The principal explains the project at a 50-minute
   all-school meeting.

   a. The meeting starts at 1:20 P.M. Draw a point on the number line
      to show 1:20 P.M.

   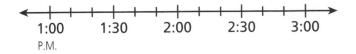

   b. Explain how you decided where to place the point on the
      number line.

   c. The all-school meeting lasts 50 minutes. Use the number line
      above to find when the meeting ends. What time does the
      meeting end?

   d. Isabella says that the meeting ends at 1:70 P.M. What mistake did
      Isabella make?

Gathering Paintbrushes

2. Teresa and Joel gather paintbrushes from the supply closet. They measure the lengths of the paintbrushes and record the measurements in the chart below.

Paintbrush Lengths (in.)

11	$10\frac{1}{4}$	11
$10\frac{1}{2}$	$10\frac{3}{4}$	$11\frac{1}{4}$
10	11	$10\frac{1}{4}$
$10\frac{3}{4}$	$11\frac{1}{4}$	$10\frac{3}{4}$

a. Use the data in the chart to make a line plot of the paintbrush lengths.

Title: _____

b. How did you know where to place the point for $10\frac{1}{2}$ inches on the number line?

c. What is the length of the shortest paintbrush? What is the length of the longest paintbrush?

d. How will the line plot change if Teresa and Joel find a long brush that is $11\frac{3}{4}$ inches long?

Drawing Rectangles

3. Sonia, Steven, and Sam draw rectangles for a large wall mural at their school.

a. Sonia draws this rectangle. Use tiling to find the area.

b. Steven draws this rectangle. Use multiplication to find the area.

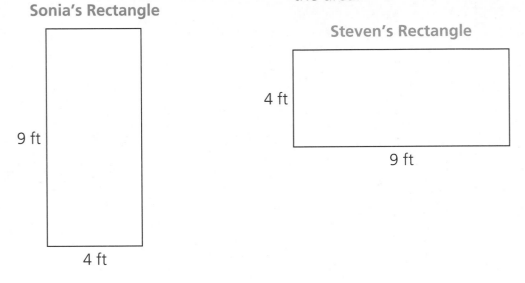

c. Compare the areas of Sonia's and Steven's rectangles. Explain why the areas are the same or different.

d. Sam draws a rectangle that has the same area as Steven's rectangle but Sam's rectangle has a different perimeter. Draw a rectangle that could be Sam's.

The Class Painting

4. The students in Pedro's class paint a picture of a mountain range. The diagram below shows the shape and size of the painting.

   a. What is the best name for the shape of the painting? Explain.

   b. What is the area of the painting?

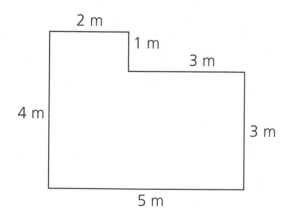

   c. Explain how you found the area of the painting.

   d. Paint costs 8¢ for each square meter of the picture. What is the total cost of the paint?

Performance Task 2

Heidi's Hexagon

5. A hexagon is Heidi's favorite polygon. She draws a hexagon to hang in her room and paints it.

a. Before Heidi paints the hexagon, she outlines the border with masking tape. Use addition to show how much tape Heidi uses.

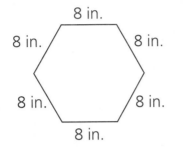

b. Use multiplication to find how much tape Heidi uses. Compare adding and multiplying to find how much tape Heidi uses.

c. To find the amount of tape Heidi needs, did you find the perimeter or the area of Heidi's hexagon? Explain.

d. Heidi will use three different colors to paint the inside of her hexagon. She outlines the areas that she will paint as shown below. Is each part $\frac{1}{3}$ of the area of the shape? Explain.

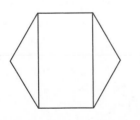

336 Performance Task 2

A review of prerequisite mathematics needed to understand the concepts and skills of Grade 3.

A. Understand: Using an array to find how many in all

When you arrange things in equal rows, you make an array.

Row 1 ⟶ ●●●●   There are 4 counters in Row 1.
Row 2 ⟶ ●●●●   There are 4 counters in Row 2.
Row 3 ⟶ ●●●●   There are 4 counters in Row 3.

Write an equation to find how many counters in all.

You can add to find how many in all. $4 + 4 + 4 = 12$

There are 12 counters in all.

B. Understand: Using related addition and subtraction equations to solve subtraction problems

There were some apples on a tray.
Steve takes 20 apples.
Then 18 apples are left.
How many apples were on the tray at the start?

Make a drawing to show the problem.

```
|———————————————— ▧ apples on the tray at start ————————————|
| 20 apples that Steve takes | 18 apples left |
```

Use the drawing to write an equation.

$$\blacksquare \quad - \quad 20 \quad = \quad 18$$

   ↑   ↑   ↑
apples on   apples that   apples left
tray at start   Steve takes

Write a related addition equation.
    $18 + 20 = \blacksquare$ Add: $18 + 20 = 38$

There were 38 apples on the tray at the start.

C. **Understand: Models can show that 10 tens is the same as 1 hundred**

Each model has 10 ones.
Each model is 1 ten.

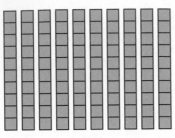

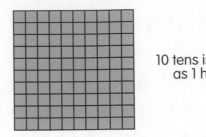

10 tens is the same as 1 hundred.

Put 10 tens together.

The new model has 100 ones.

You can also show 100 in a place-value chart.

hundreds	tens	ones
1	0	0

Digits are used to show numbers.
The digits are 0, 1, 2, 3, 4, 5, 6, 7, 8, 9.

D. **Understand: Adding two 2-digit numbers using place value**

Write an addition equation.

$$16 + 23 = \blacksquare$$

Use models for the tens and ones.

16 = 1 ten 6 ones   23 = 2 tens 3 ones

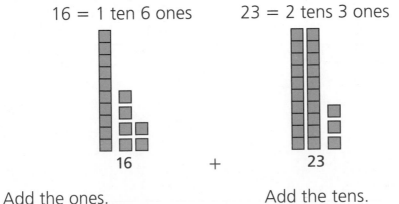

16   +   23

Add the ones.
6 ones + 3 ones = 9 ones

Add the tens.
1 ten + 2 tens = 3 tens

3 tens 9 ones = 39
16 + 23 = 39

E. Understand: Equal shares

Each of these squares is cut into equal shares.

Square A shows two equal shares.
Each share is 1 half of the whole.
There are 2 halves in the whole.

A

Square B shows two equal shares.
Each share is 1 half of the whole.
There are 2 halves in the whole.

B

Square C shows two equal shares.
Each share is 1 half of the whole.
There are 2 halves in the whole.

C

F. Understand: Using a number line to add

12 + 16 = ■

Use a number line. Start with the greater addend, 16.
Break the other addend into tens and ones.
First add the 10. Start at 16 and jump forward 10.

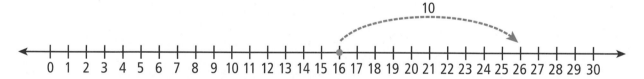

When you jump forward 10, you land on 26.
Now add the 2. Start at 26 and jump forward 2.

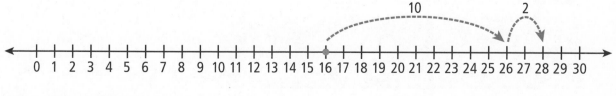

12 + 16 = 28

G. Understand: Reading time to the nearest five minutes

What time does the clock show?

The short hand is the hour hand.
The long hand is the minute hand.

The hour hand is between the 9 and the 10.
This means that the time is past 9 o'clock,
but not yet 10 o'clock.

Look at the marks around the clock face.
Each of them stands for one of the 60 minutes
that make up 1 hour.
There are 5 marks between each number and the next.

Start at 12.
Skip count by 5s until you reach the minute hand.
It is 20 minutes past 9 o'clock.

The time on the clock is 9:20.

H. Understand: Using an inch ruler to find the length of an object

How long is the pencil?

An inch is a unit of measure used to measure lengths.
You can measure the length of the pencil using inches.

Use an inch ruler. Line up one end of the pencil with the 0-mark on the ruler.

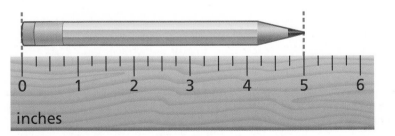

Find the number of inches that lines up with the tip of the pencil.
The pencil is 5 inches long.

I. Understand: Making a bar graph

The table shows how many flowers four children picked.

Make a bar graph to show the data.

Use the title Flowers Picked.

Make the scale on the left side of the graph go from 0 to 10.

Label the columns with the names of the children.

Make the bars show the number of flowers each child picked.

Flowers Picked	
Name	Number of Flowers
Joey	6
Zoe	8
Anna	5
Pat	9

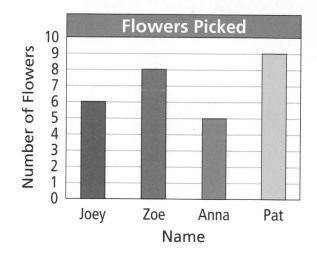

J. Understand: Making a line plot

Make a line plot of the heights of the tomato plants. Use the data in the table.

Tomato Plants	Height (inches)	5	6	7	8
	Number of Plants	3	2	4	3

Draw a number line.

Label it with the heights of the plants.

Place an X above the label for the height of each plant.

Give the line plot a title.

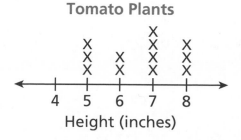

K. Understand: Using sides and angles to identify a flat shape

	Shape	Number of Sides	Number of Angles
Triangle		3	3
Quadrilateral		4	4
Pentagon		5	5
Hexagon		6	6

L. Understand: Counting to find the number of same-size squares in a rectangle

Find the number of same-size squares in the rectangle.

One way: Add the squares in the rows.

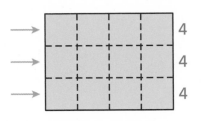

There are 4 same-size squares in each row.

There are three rows.

Use repeated addition.

Add 4 three times.

$$4 + 4 + 4 = 12$$

Another way: Add the squares in the columns.

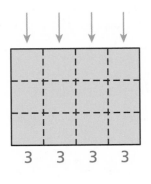

There are 3 same-size squares in each row.

There are four columns.

Use repeated addition.

Add 3 four times.

$$3 + 3 + 3 + 3 = 12$$

There are 12 same-size squares in the rectangle.

You can use this model to solve problems.

Read

Read the problem.
Focus on the facts and the questions.

- What facts do you know?
- What do you need to find out?

Plan

Outline a plan.
Plan how to solve the problem.

- What operation will you use?
- Do I need to use 1 step or 2 steps?
- Will you draw a picture?
- How have you solved similar problems?

Solve

Follow your plan to solve the problem.

- Did you answer the question?
- Did you label your answer?

Check

Test that the solution is reasonable.

- Does your answer make sense? If not, review and revise your plan.
- How can you solve the problem a different way? Is the answer the same?
- How can you estimate to check your answer?

A Number Pattern Problem

Rita made up this number pattern.
1, 5, 4, 8, 7, 11, 10, ■ , ■ , 17
What are the unknown eighth and ninth terms in Rita's pattern?

Read

Visualize the pattern on the number line.

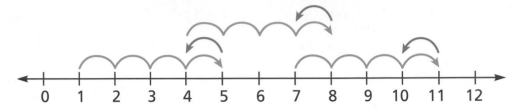

Facts: The number pattern has 10 terms.
The numbers in the pattern increase, then decrease.

Question: What are the missing eighth and ninth terms?

Plan

Look at the numbers in Rita's pattern.

Since the second number is greater and the third number is less, try adding first, subtracting next, and so on.

$$1, \quad 5, \quad 4, \quad 8, \quad 7, \quad 11, \quad 10$$
$$\underbrace{+4}\ \underbrace{-1}\ \underbrace{+4}\ \underbrace{-1}\ \underbrace{+4}\ \underbrace{-1}$$

The pattern is: Start at 1. Add 4, subtract 1.

Solve

Use the pattern.
$10 + 4 = 14$ eighth term
$14 - 1 = 13$ ninth term

▷ The missing eighth and ninth terms are 14 and 13.

Check

The tenth term in the pattern is 17.
Check your computation.
Does $13 + 4 = 17$? Yes.

344 **Problem-Solving Model**

A Spending Problem

Aiden and Max are shopping for a greeting card. Aiden has 50¢. Max has 30¢ more than Aiden. Do they have enough money altogether to buy a card that costs $1?

Read

Visualize the problem as you reread it.
Focus on the facts and the question.

Facts: Aiden—50¢
Max—30¢ more than Aiden
card—costs $1

Question: Do they have enough money to buy a card that costs $1?

Plan

To find if Aiden and Max have enough money, first add together the amounts of money they have. Then compare the total amount with the cost of the card.

Is more than one step needed? Yes.

Solve

Find the amount Max has.

Remember!
$1 = 100¢

$$
\begin{array}{r}
50¢ \\
+30¢ \\
\hline
80¢
\end{array}
\text{ Max's money}
\qquad
\begin{array}{r}
50¢ \\
+80¢ \\
\hline
130¢
\end{array}
\begin{array}{l}
\text{Aiden's money} \\
\text{Max's Money} \\
\text{altogether}
\end{array}
$$

130¢ > 100¢

➡ Aiden and Max have enough money.

Check

Does your answer make sense?
Aiden has 50¢. Since Max has more than 50¢, they have enough money.

50¢ + 50¢ = 100¢ = $1

The answer is reasonable.

Standards for Mathematical Practice

The Standards for Mathematical Practice, identified here, are an important part of learning mathematics. They are covered in every lesson in this book.

MP1 **Make sense of problems and persevere in solving them.**

- Analyze and plan a solution
- Relate to a similar problem
- Assess progress
- Use concrete objects or pictures
- Check solutions

MP2 **Reason abstractly and quantitatively.**

- Pay attention to all mathematical language
- Represent problems using symbols
- Consider units in problem solving
- Use properties of operations and objects

MP3 **Construct viable arguments and critique the reasoning of others.**

- Analyze a problem situation
- Share reasoning with others
- Explain an approach to a problem
- Construct arguments by using drawings or concrete objects

MP4 **Model with mathematics.**

- Relate mathematics to everyday problems
- Make assumptions and estimations
- Explain the relationship of quantities
- Use concrete tools to explain operations
- Interpret the solution in the context of a situation

MP5 **Use appropriate tools strategically.**

- Consider the range of available tools (e.g., place-value charts, graphs, clocks, etc.)
- Decide on appropriate tools to use for each situation
- Use tools carefully and strategically

MP6 **Attend to precision.**

- Communicate with precision
- Identify the meaning of symbols
- Use measurement units appropriately
- Calculate accurately
- Carefully formulate full explanations

MP7 **Look for and make use of structure.**

- Search for patterns or structure
- Evaluate the structure or design of a problem
- Discuss geometric shapes in terms of their similarities and differences

MP8 **Look for and express regularity in repeated reasoning.**

- Make generalizations in computation
- Obtain fluency using patterns
- Look for patterns with shapes and designs
- Use patterns to relate operations
- Evaluate reasonableness of answers

Key: MP = Mathematical Practice

Glossary

A

angle Formed when two sides extend from a common endpoint called the vertex.

area The number of unit squares needed to cover the figure without gaps or overlaps.

array An arrangement of objects or symbols in equal rows and equal columns.

Associative Property of Addition Changing the grouping of addends does not change the sum.

For example, 50 + (90 + 7) = (50 + 90) + 7

Associative Property of Multiplication Changing the grouping of factors does not change the product.

For example, 2 × 3 × 2 = (2 × 3) × 2
2 × 3 × 2 = 2 × (3 × 2)

B

bar graph A display of data, or information, that uses either vertical or horizontal bars.

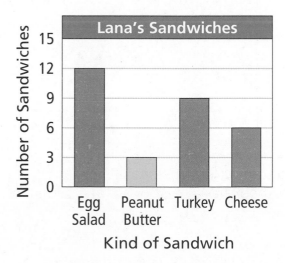

C

closed figure A two-dimensional figure that has no breaks.

Commutative Property of Addition Changing the order of addends does not change the sum.

For example, 50 + (7 + 90) + 4 = 50 + (90 + 7) + 4

Commutative Property of Multiplication Changing the order of factors does not change the product.

For example, 2 × 3 = 6
3 × 2 = 6

compatible numbers Numbers that can be easily added, subtracted, multiplied, or divided.

D

data Facts or information.

decompose Breaking apart a plane figure into simpler plane figures to find the area of the entire figure.

denominator The number of equal parts in the whole, shown below the bar in a fraction.

For example, $\frac{1}{3}$ ← denominator

Distributive Property The product of a number and the sum of two numbers is equal to the sum of the two products. Multiplication can be distributed over addition.

For example, 7 × 9 = 7 × (5 + 4)
= (7 × 5) + (7 × 4).

divide Perform a division with two numbers.

dividend The number to be divided.

Glossary 347

division An operation used when partitioning a group of objects to find either the number of equal shares or the number in each equal share.

divisor The number by which the dividend is divided.

E

elapsed time The amount of time between two given times.

equation A number sentence that includes an equal sign.

For example, $4 \times 8 = 32$

equivalent fractions Fractions that have different names but are at the same point on the number line.

For example, $\frac{1}{3} = \frac{2}{6}$

estimation A strategy used to determine an approximate answer.

even Any number that can be divided by 2 with no remainder.

F

fact family A set of equations that shows related addition and subtraction facts or related multiplication and division facts.

For example, fact family for 3, 7, and 21:

$3 \times 7 = 21$ $7 \times 3 = 21$
$21 \div 3 = 7$ $21 \div 7 = 3$

factor Each of the numbers being multiplied that will result in a product.

fraction A number that names part of a whole, an area, or a group. It can be expressed in the form $\frac{a}{b}$.

G

gram (g) A metric unit of mass. A paper clip has a mass of about 1 gram.

H

half inch A customary unit of length.

hexagon A polygon with six sides and six vertices or angles.

hour (h) A unit of time. 1 hour = 60 minutes

I

Identity Property of Multiplication The product of any number and 1 is that number.

For example, $5 \times 1 = 5$

K

key Tells what each symbol in a picture graph stands for.

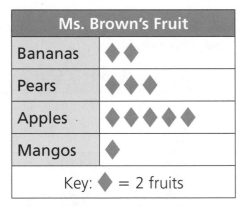

Ms. Brown's Fruit	
Bananas	◆ ◆
Pears	◆ ◆ ◆
Apples	◆ ◆ ◆ ◆ ◆
Mangos	◆
Key: ◆ = 2 fruits	

kilogram (kg) A metric unit of mass. A textbook has a mass of about 1 kilogram. 1 kilogram = 1000 grams

L

line plot A graph that uses a number line and symbols to represent data.

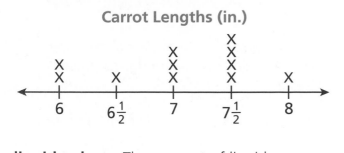

Carrot Lengths (in.)

liquid volume The amount of liquid a container can hold.

liter (L) A metric unit of liquid volume. A tall water bottle can hold about 1 liter of liquid.

M

mass The measure of the amount of matter an object contains.

minute (min) A unit of time.
60 minutes = 1 hour

multiple The product of a given whole number and another whole number.

multiplication A joining operation on two or more numbers to find a total for equal groups.

multiply Perform multiplication with two or more numbers.

N

number line A line used to show the order of numbers. The numbers are represented by points that are spaced equally.

numerator The number of equal parts being considered in a fraction, shown above the bar in a fraction.
For example, $\frac{1}{3}$ ←— numerator

O

odd Any number that when divided by 2 has a remainder of 1.

operations Mathematical processes, such as addition, subtraction, multiplication, and division.

P

parentheses ( ) Symbols used to show grouping within equations.
For example, $(2 \times 3) \times 2 =$ ▪

partition Separate into equal parts.

pattern A predictable sequence.
For example, 123123123

perimeter The sum of the lengths of the sides of a polygon.

picture graph A display of data, or information, that uses symbols or pictures.

Favorite Fruit		
Peaches	🧺 🧺 🧺 🧺 🧺
Strawberries	🧺 🧺 🧺
Bananas	🧺 🧺
Oranges	🧺 🧺 🧺 🧺
Key: 🧺 = 2 students		

plane figure A two-dimensional figure.

polygon A plane closed figure with straight sides.

product The answer in multiplication.

property A mathematical rule.

Q

quadrilateral A polygon with four sides and four vertices or angles.

quarter inch A customary unit of length.

quotient The answer in division.

R

rhombus A quadrilateral that has sides of equal length.

right angle An angle that forms a square corner.

round A method to estimate by changing numbers to the nearest 10 or 100.

rule Tells the number to start with and how to find the next number in an arithmetic pattern.

S

scale On a bar graph, it tells how many are represented by the length of a bar.

square centimeter The area of a square whose side lengths measure 1 centimeter. Can be written as *square cm*.

square foot The area of a square whose side lengths measure 1 foot. Can be written as *square ft*.

square inch The area of a square whose side lengths measure 1 inch. Can be written as *square in*.

square meter The area of a square whose side lengths measure 1 meter. Can be written as *square m*.

T

tile A method of determining area by joining unit squares along their edges to cover a figure.

time A quantity that can be measured using years, months, days, hours, minutes, and/or seconds.

time interval A segment of time.

U

unit fraction Represents the quantity, or amount, in one of the equal parts of a whole.

unit square A square with side lengths of 1 unit.

unknown A value in a mathematical problem that is not known.

V

vertex (vertices) The point at which two sides meet to form an angle.

W

whole number Any of the numbers 0, 1, 2, 3, 4, 5, and so on.

Z

Zero Property The product of any number and 0 is 0.

For example, $5 \times 0 = 0$